The Silver of the Sierra Madre

The Silver of the Sierra Madre

John Robinson, Boss Shepherd, and the People of the Canyons

JOHN MASON HART

The University of Arizona Press   Tucson

The University of Arizona Press
© 2008 The Arizona Board of Regents
All rights reserved
www.uapress.arizona.edu

Library of Congress Cataloging-in-Publication Data
Hart, John M. (John Mason), 1935–
The silver of the Sierra Madre : John Robinson,
Boss Shepherd, and the people of the canyons /
John Mason Hart.
p. cm.
Includes bibliographical references and index.
ISBN 978-0-8165-2704-5 (hardcover : alk. paper)
1. Batopilas (Mexico)—History. 2. Batopilas Mining
Company. 3. Shepherd, Alexander Robey, 1835–
1902. 4. Silver mines and mining—Mexico—Copper
Canyon. 5. Tarahumara Indians—History.
6. Robinson, John Riley. I. Title.
F1391.B37H37 2008
972'.16—dc22 2008003987

Manufactured in the United States of America on acid-free, archival-
quality paper containing a minimum of 30% post-consumer waste and
processed chlorine free.

13 12 11 10 09 08   6 5 4 3 2 1

In return for facing the multitude of dangers, the fatigue, and privations; the intrepid adventurers that enter this unexplored and mountainous country, with its hostile Indians, can be overwhelmingly compensated by the shiny precious metals, which, through their seductive and supernatural powers, provoke insatiable desires among mere mortals.

—José Sánchez Pareja

Contents

Illustrations

The Silver of the Sierra Madre

Introduction

BARELY VISIBLE IN THE PREDAWN LIGHT, the old man stood in the cold waters of the Río Batopilas alongside the ancient settlement of the same name and began his day's work. He deftly scooped a shovelful of gravel from the bottom and ran it through his sluice. It was Thursday and he had not seen that hoped-for flash of gold since Tuesday, when a nugget almost as large as the nail on his gnarled smallest finger had justified the toil.

Not far away, a younger miner crouched low in the stream, slowly sliding his pan into the gravelly bottom before lifting it out and swishing the water across the captured deposit. His practiced eye searched for the glint of gold. Even though it was only April, by noon, the sun had turned the cool, sweet air of morning into a cauldron of heat. The men worked until two, as usual, and then retired to their respective small homes, where fresh water and the afternoon meal of corn tortillas, beans, rice, and a trace of chicken or goat meat awaited them. They would not return to the river until the next morning.

Half Tarahumara Indian by birth, the old man had become a mestizo by choice some thirty years before (about 1950), when he decided to accept a modicum of Western technology and started speaking in Spanish. He took up residence with his family in San Pedro de Batopilas, an ancient mining center once called the Comstock of Mexico. His younger counterpart claimed descent from mestizos and a Yaqui miner who had come to the pueblo in its heyday in the second half of the nineteenth century. By the middle of the twentieth century, the Batopilas they lived in was smaller than it had been 100 or even 300 years ago. By 1980, it counted fewer than 1,500 souls, less than a quarter of the more than 6,000 workers who came to this remote place from all over the world in the 1880s and 1890s to take part in one of the largest silver bonanzas ever known.

The first silver booms took place in the seventeenth and eighteenth centuries when Spanish owners began to pay their workers with real money in lieu of the barter exchange that had prevailed. The wealth attracted a diverse population that included a heretic who questioned the divine right of kings and that even brought the Holy Office of the Inquisition to Batopilas. Most of the citizenry, however, freely joined the missionary church established by the Jesuits, who dedicated it to Saint Mary of Mount Carmel (Santa María del Carmen) and Saint Peter. In the eighteenth century, the town was under the fathers of the mission at Moris, a settlement some 85 miles (140 kilometers) to the northwest, on the edge of the canyon country. At that time, the native silver ore, assayed at 80 percent silver, attracted a series of Spanish wealth seekers, who were followed by officials who placed the region within the political district of Nueva Galicia.[1]

Now, in the first years of the new millennium, most of the foreigners in Batopilas are American tourists drawn by stories of lost missions and the grandeur of the Copper Canyon complex. Life is very hard for the *bato-pilenses* today; their difficulties are compounded by an active marijuana industry, toward which they take a live-and-let-live and, for a few, a participatory approach. Despite their hardships, the farmers, part-time miners, artisans, and most of their neighbors have a love of community, a sense of place, and a distrust of the outside world that makes thoughts of leaving their canyon homes very difficult. Some Raramuri communities in the area now raise marijuana for export on small plots. (*Raramuri*, the name preferred by the people themselves and many scholars, and *Tarahumara*, the name most frequently used by the general public and some scholars, are used interchangeably in the text.) Young men, even children, deliver it to brokers and transport specialists. The guns and spending of these men represent a potentially significant cultural influence on the youth of the region, although how significant is still unclear. Outsiders have been here before, yet most of the 45,000 Tarahumaras in the canyons and the women of the hamlets have never left the rugged mountains. They have a sense of place rooted in their pueblo cooperatives, their religion, which blends Catholic with indigenous beliefs, their clothing, tools, and family lineages; they have little desire to experience what seems to be a hectic and violent outside world.

Between 1860 and 1921, however, American and other miners came to them and were a major influence on life in the barrancas. Although the Americans maintained their own community across the river from Batopilas, they mixed economically and culturally with the townspeople. Some lived among the residents of Urique and Cerocahui, towns in the neighboring barranca. Owning the mines, enforcing the law in the region, and introducing science through an assortment of supervisors, mining engineers, mechanics, and other skilled workers (as well as a doctor and nurse, who were available to provide limited care for local citizens and miners), the Americans far outweighed the other foreigners in importance. The other outsiders presented a wide range of influences: an accomplished French photographer, English engineers, Chinese merchants and launderers, prostitutes, and mine workers of mestizo, African, Chinese, Yaqui, Mayo, and Asian subcontinental backgrounds.

During the Revolution of 1910–1920, the foreigners, miners, and a colorful array of adventurers, prostitutes, drunks, pickpockets, and duelers began to leave the barrancas in search of safety and better opportunities. And in 1921, when the price of silver in the world market fell far below the point of profitability and the wealth ceased to flow, they were followed by those who had hung on until then but who were now driven away by the area's harsh climate and other hardships.

Batopilas settled into an eerie serenity. Later, in the 1980s, the only visible remains of the past were the hulks of the gaunt and abandoned former mine headquarters and owner's residence, known as the Hacienda San Miguel, located across the river from the town. A half mile upstream stood the remains of the once powerful turbine that had driven the giant grinders at the mouth of the Porfirio Díaz Tunnel and provided electricity to the company and town. Supposedly the longest mine shaft in the world, the Díaz Tunnel ran through the heart of the mountain at its base, enabling the miners to excavate the silver ore on a massive scale from vertical shafts and to load it onto the mining carts that waited to haul it outside. From 1921 to the present, the company headquarters, hospital, turbine, and castle lay silent.

Beginning in the 1860s, and continuing until the Mexican Revolution of 1910, the owners, miners, citizens of Batopilas, and people of the canyons created a legend. Some of them produced as much silver and human drama as any group in the world; others preserved ways of life and worldviews dating from prehistoric and Spanish colonial times.

The silver deposits took shape in the region during the late Tertiary period when most of the Earth's mountain ranges were formed. The area's andesitic rocks and rhyolites were created by volcanic activity in the Cenozoic era. Whereas the andesitic deposits range from 70 to 80 million years old, the rhyolites are only 20 to 40 million years of age, but neither compares to the strata found in the Grand Canyon, which are over a billion years old. The fine-grained rhyolites at Batopilas, however, contain high percentages of silica, aluminum, and silver, the deposits of which approach one mile in depth. For tens of millions of years, water moving down the hillsides and the Río Batopilas at the bottom of the formative canyon eroded the ash falls, exposing the silver. In the last 300 years, the miners of Batopilas have produced approximately 300 million ounces of the precious metal.

Silver normally occurs as a chemical compound in association with copper and gold. It appears as one of the three metals that form group IB of the periodic table and is usually obtained as a by-product of copper mining. After refining, silver is usually presented to the world as sterling, which contains 92.5 percent silver and 7.5 percent copper.

During the 1860s and 1870s, however, most of the silver mined at Batopilas was found in its rare, nearly pure native form and in high-grade argentite ore. The area around Batopilas still holds immense quantities of this rich ore, although they are now hidden from view. Even after centuries of removal by hand and decades of intensive removal by industrial machines between 1861 and 1910, the shallow and surface deposits of native silver and argentite ore occurred on a scale comparable to those of the Comstock Lode in Nevada, the Cerro de Potosí in Bolivia, and the Aspen mines in Colorado.

During the 1840s and 1850s, Raramuri Indians sat on hard stone platforms at the mine entrances using heavy stones to crush the ore by hand into grain-sized pebbles and dust. Merchants in San Francisco began to trade with the miners of Batopilas at least a decade before Judge John Riley Robinson of Mansfield, Ohio, and a syndicate of New York City financiers purchased the mines in 1861. During the early 1860s and again at the end of the 1870s, the important American financiers who became owners of the area's mines initiated a process that tied the people of the barrancas directly to the economies of the United States and China and revolutionized local society. That process was part of an ongoing global economic expansion that began in the Western world with the Spaniards and Portuguese. By 1861, American entrepreneurs had joined their British and other European counterparts in seeking natural resources beyond their frontiers. Mexico's Sierra Madre Occidental was one of the first places they looked.

A trusted supervisor with the Wells Fargo Overland Company, a doctor, a judge and gristmill operator at Mansfield, and later an inventor in Maryland, John Riley Robinson initiated the American presence at Batopilas. In the late 1850s, he recruited partners for the venture from among the most important bankers in the United States. They included Wells Fargo Bank Directors William G. Fargo, Danford N. Barney, and Ashbel H. Barney, at the forefront of financiers from San Francisco and New York who moved quickly to purchase silver mines in Mexico.

By the late 1850s, the discovery of new mines in California had nearly stopped, while the legends of Mexican lodes had correspondingly grown among speculators. By the late 1860s, Robinson was able to include the new Wells Fargo chairman, Lloyd Tevis, in the enterprise. Robinson enjoyed the directors' confidence because he had been a leading figure in the development of the Wells Fargo transportation network in the upper Midwest. In 1860, he explained his plans and their significance: "Office of the Overland Co. Friend Rumfield: . . . I have been raising a company to work a silver mine in Mexico . . . Batopilas, for $50,000. Fargo, myself, and the Barneys are the purchasers, so you see I have the strength of the Overland. This enterprise will be the commencement or introduction of Wells Fargo & Company into Mexico in their express and banking business."[2] In 1861, when they purchased the mines, Robinson, Fargo, and the Barneys each held a quarter share in the enterprise.

For nearly two decades, the new owners developed the connection between local and global processes. They employed American, Mexican, and Native American miners, who extracted uncounted tons of native silver, which they hauled downstream through the Sierra Madre to the Río Fuerte and across Sinaloa to the deepwater port of Mazatlán, where they shipped it to the U.S. Mint in San Francisco for final processing. They sold silver to the mint, but during the Civil War, they shipped most of it to New York and some to China. The Pacific Mail Steamship Company of New York provided most of the transportation from Mazatlán to San Francisco and Asia; the Wells Fargo Overland and Union Pacific Railroad provided cartage to New York.

His diplomatic skills in negotiating with the state and local elites in Chihuahua, his managerial experience, and his connections to Wells Fargo personnel in San Francisco made Robinson an ideal choice for the task of overseeing development of the mines. He was ambitious, hardworking, and creative. The Wells Fargo men who joined him in creating the Batopilas Consolidated Mining Company were equally ambitious. They pioneered the financing of the California mining industry, land development in the San Francisco Bay Area and later in the San Joaquin Valley, the development of transportation and communications infrastructure in the Midwest and West, and shipping on the Pacific Ocean. As the California mining industrialists settled into a more regularized extractive mode of operation, they applied their experience and capital in a search for new opportunities in the northwestern United States, the Pacific Basin, and northwestern Mexico.

Thanks to the complex support system organized by Fargo, the Barneys, Tevis, and other directors of Wells Fargo, Robinson was able to transport, process, and market the vast riches found at Batopilas. For eighteen years, his men stripped "pillars" of native silver from the fissures in the rocks. Sometimes these emerged as thin slivers and sometimes as grotesquely shaped monoliths. The directors generated millions of dollars in profits from the company's overland and oceanic express service and from its banking, smelting, and minting operations.

By the late 1860s, Mexican Vice President Sebastián Lerdo de Tejada complained to President Benito Juárez that the Americans were extracting vast quantities of silver ore from the region to be processed elsewhere, without employing or training Mexican labor and without paying any taxes. Indeed, he reported that ore was being removed in strips so large it took several men and mechanical hoists to load them onto ships bound for San Francisco at Mazatlán and other points on the Sinaloa coastline. Lerdo de Tejado wanted the Americans to pay custom duties and to employ skilled Mexicans in smelters and mints as assayers, coiners, and auditors.

Finally, in 1871, President Juárez and, in 1872, the newly inaugurated President Lerdo de Tejada moved to force the issue by requiring that the silver pass through a mint being enlarged and modernized at Chihuahua City, Chihuahua. From there, it could be shipped to the border at Paso del Norte, opposite El Paso, where a soon-to-be-completed transcontinental railroad would transport it in whatever direction deemed convenient by the exporters. The Chihuahua mint did not become fully operational until the late 1870s, however; in the meantime, most of the silver from Batopilas continued to pass through Mazatlán. In the decades that followed, the American mine owners would continue to send contraband silver out of the country from remote shipping points in Sinaloa.

When the Chihuahua mint finally began its modernized operations, the miners at Batopilas melted the silver into ingots and hauled it out of the barrancas by means of well-guarded mule trains known collectively as the Conducta. The mules took slightly more than a week to reach the Chihuahua City mint, owned and operated by Americans Henry Muller and Frank MacManus and Mexican citizen Enrique Creel.

The son of Reuben Creel the American consul and former New York financier, Enrique Creel enjoyed connections to people in high places in both Chihuahua and New York; his mother, Paz Cuilty, was a member of the Chihuahua oligarchy. Frank MacManus descended from the steel manufacturing MacManus family of Philadelphia and Camden. During the 1860s, the family patriarch, John MacManus, had lent active support to the effort of the leaders of the Pennsylvania Railroad Company to create an American-owned rail system extending from El Paso to Chihuahua City and from there to all of Mexico.

At the Chihuahuan mint, employees, mostly Mexicans, assayed, weighed, molded ingots, and stamped the treasure, and Mexican government officials then levied the appropriate taxes. There was only one catch. In the late 1860s and early 1870s, bandits, many from the hamlets in the canyons, disrupted mining operations and even occupied and worked the sites for months at a time.

In response, during the late 1870s, the newly installed national government of Porfirio Díaz imposed a strong rural police and army presence in the barrancas. But before that happened, Robinson had already lost two sons and two grandchildren to typhoid fever, which periodically ravaged the people of the canyons. Given the higher level of police protection, a demoralized Robinson was finally able to return to the United States. He left operations in the hands of assistants, but production declined dramatically. By the late 1870s, Robinson and his partners were ready to sell their controlling interest in the mines.

In 1879, Alexander Robey Shepherd, the last governor of Washington, D.C., began negotiations for the purchase of the Batopilas Consolidated Mining Company. From 1879 through the epoch of the Mexican Revolution, Shepherd and his son Alexander Jr., who succeeded him, headed a continuous effort of exploration and applied high technology at Batopilas. Their efforts combined with those of other foreigners and people from all over Mexico including the Yaqui and the ambivalent Tarahumara. Although many Raramuris continued to live in cliff dwellings, and most refused to work in the mines and mills, some did not. The mining industry would change their lives dramatically, not least of all by bringing axmen to cut and clear the neighboring forests for the beams needed in the shafts.

Financed by capitalists in New York, Chicago, and San Francisco, Alexander Shepherd greatly expanded the mines, extracting and processing lower-grade ore on a massive scale along with the ever-harder-to-find native silver and argentite ore. The endeavor stimulated a sudden increase in population at Batopilas and its environs and led to the creation of an alienated working class. To maintain political stability and ensure the growth of his operations, Shepherd quickly established control over the area. Initially, he issued his own scrip currency and employed seventy mine and plant guards, who also served as a cavalry, escorting the silver ingots over the mountains via the Conducta. Later, through his connections with the Chihuahua state and Mexican national authorities and the New York financial community, Shepherd became the dominant political force in the Sierra Raramuri.

Using his wealth, armed might, and connections, Shepherd created what his son Grant called a feudal regime, a company town in which, as the Patrón Grande, he controlled local politics, wages, and working conditions and suppressed Mexican protests against deforestation and water pollution. At times, he served as a beneficent godfather, but his abuse of power in keeping wages low and the workers and townsfolk under rigid control presents another picture. In doing these things, Shepherd anticipated American overlords elsewhere in Mexico, Chile, Cuba, Peru, and Liberia. Until his death in 1902, the Patrón Grande exercised authority over a region embracing 35,000 square miles. Indeed, it was not until the Revolution of 1910 that Mexican challengers were able to put an end to the authority of the Batopilas Consolidated Mining Company.

When John Robinson first arrived in Batopilas, both the town's elites (like those elsewhere in Mexico and the Third World at later times) and its miners hoped for the creation of vast local wealth. Their Tarahumara neighbors in the surrounding heights and barrancas viewed the outsider with suspicion, but even some of them chose to provide timber and join the thousands who came in search of work in the mines. The newcomers included Mayo and Yaqui Indians from the nearby states of Sonora and Sinaloa, African Americans, Africans, and Asians.

This is the saga of the Americans, Mexicans, Yaquis, and Raramuris who made history by coming together at a remote locale in the Sierra Madre Occidental. The isolation of the people, the wide mix of cultures, the fabulous wealth and natural splendor of the place, and the prodigious undertakings there combined to make Batopilas and the region known as the Copper Canyon special.

Spearheaded by aggressive entrepreneurs and the directors of the Wells Fargo Bank, the activities in and around Batopilas anticipated later forays of American capitalism, led by the First National, National City, and Morgan Banks, into other remote areas of the Third World. The New York financial institutions that controlled the silver mines at Batopilas would later control gold mines in Burma, kaolin mines in China, iron mines in Liberia, copper mines in Chile and Peru, and, in part, the diamond and gold mines of South Africa.

Our tale involves the eternal search for wealth and power, the divide-and-conquer strategies of empire, the contrast between mimesis and arrogance, the encounter of the powerful with the weak, environmental respect and degradation. It is a tale of adventure, tragedy, triumph, and survival.

CHAPTER 1

Robinson's Quest

> The White Whale swam before him as the monomaniac
> incarnation of all those malicious agencies which
> some deep men feel eating in them, till they are
> left living on with half a heart and half a lung.
> —Herman Melville, *Moby-Dick*

The Beginning

WHEN JOHN RILEY ROBINSON EMBARKED by train and headed southwest for Chihuahua from Ohio in 1861, most Americans would have considered the journey across Texas the adventure of a lifetime. After all, he was leaving the most rapidly developing region in North America at the time and traversing west Texas, where forces loyal to the Confederacy at the onset of the Civil War were taking loyal Union men prisoner, and where Comanche and Apache raiders were resisting the incursions of outsiders by striking wagon trains, stagecoaches, and ranches with often devastating success. But Robinson's adventure exceeded even those possibilities.

His destination was Batopilas, the site of the ancient Real de Minas de Acanasaina, a fabled but remote silver mining town deep in the Sierra Madre Occidental. In those mountains, bands of Yaqui warriors replaced the Comanche who roved the plains below and augmented the groups of Apache warriors who sought survival by relieving miners, muleteers, and ranchers of their wealth. In addition, small bands of highly mobile bandits were especially active in the mining regions of the Sierra Madre.

Robinson, a doctor, railroad superintendent, gristmill operator, inventor, and future patent holder for the J. R. Robinson Dumping Car, thought he had a fairly good idea of what to expect. At 51, he was already a veteran of the American West and had worked throughout the Midwest during an illustrious career with the Wells Fargo Express Company. As a member of upper management, he had planned and helped establish a network of Wells Fargo stations throughout the region and south into Missouri. In 1850, he claimed an estate valued at over $25,000 and had opened a gristmill at Mansfield, Ohio. But the late 1850s were a bad time for business; by 1860, Robinson's estate was worth only $10,000, not counting $1,000 cash on hand.

John sought to recoup that loss by using his high-level contacts at Wells Fargo to create a powerful partnership for a silver mining operation at Batopilas. Acting as agents for the owners, the firm of Belden and Stearns of New York and Monterrey, Mexico, had issued the equivalent of an earnest money sales contract to Robinson. He left the family business and his difficult position in Ohio to undertake an incredible adventure, a search for treasure in the Sierra Madre Occidental of Mexico. From the outset, President William K. Fargo and Directors Ashbel H. and Danford N. Barney of Wells Fargo joined him in the endeavor. Later, Lloyd Tevis, who succeeded Fargo as bank president, a certain "Mr. Cheney of Boston," and other financiers, would join the project.[1]

Before his departure, Robinson obtained a visa and a certificate from the Mexican consul in New York that attested to his power of attorney, issued by Belden and Stearns, on behalf of Fargo and the Barneys. Joined by his twenty-three-year-old son Asher, Robinson carried $1,200 worth of "Mexican doubloons" to cover the estimated expenses for the trip, a Sharps rifle, 300 rounds of ammunition, a pair of blue blankets, a rubber pillow, mining compass, tape measure, medicine, and "other necessaries." As he prepared for travel, John, a northern Democrat, was preoccupied with the news of impending civil war not only because the future of the nation was at stake but also because his plans included stops in potentially rebel territory at Forts Chadborne, Belknap, and Davis in Texas while en route to El Paso.[2]

The Journey

Robinson headed south from Mansfield on February 27, 1861, probably traveling by carriage. He purchased supplies in Cincinnati before leaving the next day on the Ohio and Missouri Railroad for Saint Louis. He

John Robinson, circa 1861. (Courtesy of Pamela White)

suffered an overnight delay when the locomotive ran into a "drove of horses and killed 4 of them throwing the engine off the track[s]." After reaching Saint Louis, Robinson waited for other members of his party to arrive, including his son Asher. In the meantime, Abraham Lincoln took office as president of the United States; John took great interest in a special Missouri State Convention that was meeting in the city to decide the issue of secession. In the end, the delegates announced their "strong support" for the Union. By then, Robinson had decided to enter Mexico at Presidio La Junta (today Ojinaga) rather than El Paso because of the growing threat of fighting in west Texas between Unionists and rebels.[3]

On March 11, he and six other men left Saint Louis for Fort Smith, Arkansas. At Smithton, Missouri, the party boarded a stagecoach, which, after toppling over, reached Fort Smith on March 14. The party then set out across Texas. The roads were rough, and the stage toppled over once again. On March 20, the men arrived at Camp Stockton (now Fort Stockton), Texas, where they were joined by Frank MacManus, whose prominent New Jersey steel family had interests in the Pennsylvania railroad that was seeking to extend its rails into Mexico through Chihuahua, who had helped found the Chihuahua mint, and who was now a part owner of that important institution. The new acquaintances dined on buffalo meat and rested overnight.

In the morning, the now-enlarged Robinson party headed south on the Chihuahua Trail, which began at Camp Stockton, continued beyond the border across the fierce Desierto Oriente of northeastern Chihuahua, and ended at Chihuahua City. They spent their first night at scenic Fort Davis, at the foot of beautiful cliffs with a forest and natural springs nearby. Here John met Lieutenant James Judson Van Horn, the Union officer who would soon surrender the fort to a superior Confederate force. The U.S. Army had established a post there to deny the Comanches a resting and watering place and to provide its troops with a base of operations for interdicting Indian raids to the south on the ranches around La Junta and Presidio, which faced each other across the Rio Grande near its junction with the Río Conchos, where it flowed out of Chihuahua.

On March 26, the Robinson party left Fort Davis on a stage headed for Presidio. During the first two hours, they enjoyed the view of the pine-covered Davis Mountains to their north and Paisano Peak to the south. As they continued to the south, the lands became ever more desertlike, and the orange-tipped ocotillo and Thompson's yucca replaced the prairie grass that predominated around Fort Davis. Halfway to their destination, they dined on venison and stopped to rest at the Spencer Ranch (probably El Cíbolo, now known as the Cibolo Creek Ranch and owned by Iran-Contra figure Admiral John Poindexter). John Spencer lived in a large adobe house north of Presidio and not far from Shafter in a valley between the Three Sisters Mountains to the east and the even higher Chinati Mountains to the west.

Thirty-two million years earlier, the Chinati Volcano had exploded in an eruption that displaced even more earth than the Mount Saint Helens explosion in the late twentieth century. The rugged terrain that resulted from that blast supported mountain lions, grizzly and black bears, golden eagles, deer, pronghorn antelope, badgers, black-footed ferrets, and an infinite variety of snakes, including copperheads and western diamond-back rattlesnakes. The trees on the ranch joined the wildlife in enjoying the benefits of several small streams. These ran southeasterly to the Rio Grande.

Spencer's Mexican wife prepared dinner while Robinson enjoyed the antics of the couple's children. In addition to ranching, the Spencers were endeavoring to find and develop silver, gold, and copper mines in the mountains of the Big Bend, although those efforts would ultimately prove fruitless. As he showed John samples of ore, Spencer exuded the eternal optimism of the prospector, but like most of the miners in the American Southwest and northern Mexico, he lacked the mining engineering skills, adequate technology, capital, and the transportation and marketing network that Robinson and Wells Fargo had at their command. The next day, the travelers followed the ranch road into Presidio, a town of 800 souls and humble adobe homes, directly across the Rio Grande from La Junta. Although the townspeople relied on corn, beans, and wild game for their diet, Robinson managed to find eggs and coffee for his breakfast. At 4 p.m. on March 30, the travelers left Presidio and headed southeast downriver for several miles to gain the most favorable crossing point. Choosing the best trail possible, they pushed forward into the Desierto Oriente. They traveled until midnight but covered only twenty-eight miles because of the rough terrain. The following morning, Easter Sunday, they arose at dawn and traveled until 10 a.m., when the intolerable heat forced them to stop.

In 1857, the population of the state of Chihuahua (from the Tara-humara word for "workplace") totaled just over 164,000, with one city and 136 pueblos. It had not changed much in four years. The party covered long distances without encountering anyone, while circling hawks and vultures watched them. Following an L-shaped route, they halted at La Mula, only fifteen miles southeast of Presidio as the crow flies, named for the heavily burdened animals that watered and rested there. Today it is an immigration checkpoint, where drivers and their eighteen-wheel semi-trucks heading north and south from the border find brief respite.

It was noontime and the temperature hovered at 90 degrees. The northerners had not yet adapted to the grueling heat of the day, but they were not the only ones affected. The dry desert winds and hot sun left even the mules in a state of exhaustion. As the men and mules rested, Mac-Manus bought ham and eggs at a nearby ranch. They spent Easter Day in the shade of some huts. The desolation of the place overwhelmed them.

John noted the terrain but evinced absolutely no interest in its inhabitants, including their poverty and the near total absence of men, who were away working on nearby ranches. Then the party set out again across the Desierto Oriente, headed for Chihuahua City the capital of the state. They walked through a vast but thin forest of sotols, ocotillos, agaves, and cacti with long trunks and many branches, the white-spined *cordón* and the black-spined *pitaya*. Lacking fresh water supplies, the travelers walked on, while the vultures and hawks still circled.

The Chihuahua Trail followed a course at some points only a few miles south of the present highway that runs east–west from Ojinaga to the state capital. They pushed on until midnight, when they encountered impressive agaves, yuccas, cacti, and huisaches and, in between them, the less obvious peyote and smaller plants. The yuccas reached thirty-five feet in height with white flowers, and the huisaches offered the travelers beautiful yellow blossoms and a fragrant aroma.

They could not have missed the large flights of doves etched against crimson skies evoked by the setting sun, nor the howling of the Mexican wolves, which began their hunt at the fall of darkness. Weighing 120 pounds at maturity, the wolves roamed the land in small packs, searching for luckless coyotes, rabbits, mice, peccaries, and mule deer. The reclusive mountain lions and wildcats that also roamed the area were less likely to announce their presence except at sundown, when the lions let out a territorial scream. At that hour, bats seemed to be everywhere. Robinson would complain about the tough day- and nightlong treks, about the dust, prickly bushes, wolves, and rough terrain, calling the land they had entered "wild country."[4]

On April 1, to avoid the heat, the party broke camp at 2 a.m. and reached the settlement of Chupadero (meaning "snail," after a nearby rock formation that looked, if not like a snail, then at least like a turtle) by nine that morning. The mules were "almost knocked out," but the travelers enjoyed another repast of ham and eggs and coffee, again provided by MacManus. The handful of people at Chupadero appeared to be entirely mestizo. They had a simple church (*capilla*) and lived in small mud and adobe houses and in shacks (*chozas*) made from sagebrush and mesquite branches. The next day, the travelers, fearing the lack of water, left Chupadero at 2 p.m. and "drove all night."

The land was flat and well traveled. As a result, the party pushed forward sixty miles until they reached San Antonio de Julimes, a pueblo of a thousand people that featured fresh water and trees. In 1691 the Spanish had formally recognized Julimes, an even older Native American settlement. They used it as a base from which to colonize and Christianize the Julime Indians, who had dominated the region. Situated on the banks of the Río Conchos at 3,900 feet above sea level, Julimes marked the boundary between the western edge of the desert and the less extreme climates of central and western Chihuahua. It included the marvelous plant life the party had witnessed near the Rio Grande.

By 1861, the Native American residents of Julimes were a small minority that included ten Tarahumaras, or Raramuris (meaning "those who run well"), who served mestizo landowners as agricultural workers. The heat of the day was again stifling, and the Robinson party sought relief under the tall cottonwood trees that dominated the embankments of Ojo de Julimes, a hot spring "said to possess great medicinal virtues." The water temperature in the spa stood at 150 degrees. The Río Conchos and the Río Chuviscar, which joined with the Conchos nearby, provided Julimes with ample irrigation for fruit, beans, corn, herbs, and shade trees. The animal life included small groups of collared peccaries, ocelots, and bobcats. Some believe the Río Conchos was named after the Conchos Indians, who once flourished in its network of fertile river valleys; others attribute its name to the smooth, rounded, oblong rocks strewn about its edges and riverbed, which reminded the area's inhabitants of *conchos*, or large sea mollusks.

The people of Julimes enjoyed more of life's comforts than did those of Chupadero, including at least a few commercial goods. A priest paid regular visits to celebrate Mass and hear confessions at the pueblo's seventeenth-century church, dedicated to Saint Anthony of Padua, who offered miraculous cures and comforted the ill. As a *cabecera*, or county-like administrative center, Julimes boasted a civic building, which stood across the central plaza from the church. The pueblo also had two other hot springs, El Tanque and El Pandeno, already being visited by *chihuahuenses* from other parts of the state. Among the spa's many visitors was Robinson's vulnerable son Asher, who was able to soothe his "sore eyes," irritated by the heat, dry air, dust, and pollen. The Americans had just missed Saint Joseph's Festival (Festival del Señor San José), held on March 19, a celebration that has continued into the twenty-first century. Finding such a pleasant, restful stopover and easier terrain ahead of them vindicated the party's decision to proceed southeast along the Rio Grande and to cross the desert on the southern branch of the Chihuahua Trail.

At 2 p.m. on April 2, they broke camp and, enjoying a carriage ride with a team of horses provided by MacManus, headed straight for his recently purchased Hacienda Bachimba (which would be a major battle site during the Mexican Revolution some fifty years later). Located only twenty miles southeast of Chihuahua City, the estate consisted a *casco* (big house) with a fine garden in an enclosed patio and 60,000 acres of land, including irrigated fig, peach, pomegranate, and other orchards. The trees bore fruit in great abundance. The house and grounds were much in need of restoration, which MacManus eagerly planned to undertake. Having rested for a day, the Robinson party left for Chihuahua City at midnight on April 3, arriving eight hours later at the Fonda Riddle, an inn owned by an American of the same name, after an uneventful trip.

The state's capital, its only major city, and the hub of its trade with central Mexico, Chihuahua City pleased and amazed Robinson, who started the morning of April 4 with something like the breakfast he would have enjoyed back home in Mansfield. The city's population numbered about 15,000, most of whom, John noted, were "very poor." In its picturesque though run-down center, the narrower, often cobbled streets were crooked and irregular in width but managed to accommodate horses, carriages, and wagons. Nearby stood the Spanish colonial houses of the elites, designed in the Spanish-Moorish style, with wrought-iron gates and window guards, heavy carved wooden doors, interior patios, porches, floors, and often arched windows outlined in laminated tiles, spires, and red-tiled roofs. Although many of the houses were more elegant on the inside than outside, Robinson appreciated their beauty. The patios, the main plaza, and well-placed squares were planted with palms as well as with bougainvillea and other flowers.

The Cathedral of Chihuahua, dedicated to Saint Francis, patron saint of the city, was completed in 1789 at a cost of $800,000. With two towers standing 146 feet and an ornate façade of intricate stonework and bas-reliefs, it was the most impressive structure in the capital. The interior measured 109 feet by 86 feet and was dominated by the main altar, with its sixteen Corinthian columns clustered in groups of four around a statue of Saint Francis. The apses featured statues of saints, the Virgin of Guada-lupe, and Christ on the Cross. Open to the public, the towers offered a commanding view of the surrounding countryside. Having climbed one of them, Robinson noted the distant clouds of dust raised by mule and burro trains carrying goods to and from the city.

The doctor from Ohio was a keen observer of people and quickly sized up those who interested him. He was intrigued by the "strange sights" of the city's central market and enthralled by the variety of smells, garbs, and people, Tarahumara, mestizo, and criollo, he found there. "The market is principally kept by women, except the butchers," he noted, "and the articles for sale are so very strange to an American—corn, beans, chili and other singular productions of cacti and fruits. The women all wear re-bosos or long shawls—no bonnets, and but few dressed as Americans with hoops."[5] John watched with fascination as they shouted out the virtues and prices of their wares in singsong voices while forever cleaning the hopelessly worn and dirty floors.

Robinson was less impressed by the spectacle of a bullfight he wit-nessed in the Plaza de Toros that Sunday. He appreciated the enormous size of the arena and the large crowd, but the matadors proved inept, and seeing the picadors impale the beast with their "sharp hooks" put him in an ill humor. His mood in no way improved when one of the two female clowns challenging the bull was charged and knocked over, "exposing the unprepared portion of her body and linen, which were not the cleanest or most inviting in appearance." The bull was even more put off than John and refused to fight, to the "great mirth of the crowd."[6]

When MacManus led him on a tour of the newly improved Chihuahua mint Robinson was surprised to find it in "perfect condition" and able to coin $150,000 in silver pesos per month. John appreciated that Mac-Manus had important partners among the Chihuahua elites. One of them, the extremely able General Luis Terrazas, was the governor of the state and the one politician who could maintain order through the reconciliation of the violently opposed Liberal and Conservative political elites as well as the rival Liberal generals in the region. In 1852, Terrazas had made a strategic move in this regard by marrying Carolina Cuilty Bustamante, the daughter of a wealthy hacendado. By 1861, he was already well on his way to becoming the owner of the world's largest landholdings, approximating 7 million acres. In 1866, Terrazas would lead the Mexican forces, newly equipped with the latest armaments by General William Tecumseh Sherman at El Paso, to victory over a powerful French force sent to conquer the state.[7]

During Robinson's meeting with him, Terrazas proved to be deeply interested in developing Chihuahua's ties to the U.S. economy. The governor already owned a complex of gristmills and other enterprises in addition to haciendas around the state. In the tradition of the Mexican elites, the prosperity of the Terrazas extended family was central to his personal success. One of his daughters would marry Enrique Creel, the son of U.S. Consul Reuben Creel. Reuben, a banker from New York, was almost certainly acquainted with Fargo and the Barneys. Paz Cuilty, Reuben's spouse and Enrique's mother, was one of the wealthiest members of the Chihuahua elite and maintained close ties with the governor.

During the decades that followed, the evolving Terrazas–Cuilty–Creel family alliance remained the core of the increasingly wealthy Chihuahua oligarchy. The American owners of the Batopilas mines would enjoy the advantages of close relations with the members of this alliance. Those advantages included critically important political and military interventions on Robinson's behalf against challenges from local elites, workers, and rebels in the barrancas.

John also met several mine owners during his stay in the city and found them to be a "different" lot. On the one hand, they were dreamers, constantly speculating on the discovery of untold riches. On the other, they were obsessed with what might be considered a justifiable paranoia, an abiding sense of insecurity regarding their claims and land titles. But they openly welcomed and offered advice to new strongmen willing to join them in their perilous undertakings in the Sierra Madre. They were truly "pioneers for profit." Don Mariano Sáenz, who operated the Morales mines in the mountains, volunteered his knowledge of the trails through the wilderness and specifically the alternative routes to Batopilas.

Robinson was surprised to learn from Sáenz that the route he planned to follow through the Setenbrión Canyon complex to accommodate E. Quimby, a traveling companion who had joined him at the outset of the journey, would take him far to the northwest of his destination and entail another week of travel. Realizing that Quimby had misled him, John decided the two should part company at Bahuichivo, high in what is today called the Sierra Tarahumara region of the Sierra Madre. From there, Quimby would follow the high ridge on a more westerly course, and the Robinson party would turn south and enter the Barranca de Urique.

The outlying areas of Chihuahua City were decidedly less pleasing to John than the central area. The dwellings consisted of one and two rooms made of adobe, over dirt floors, with only one or two openings in the walls in order to provide protection from the extreme temperatures of summer and winter. Crude wooden shutters and cloths covered the windows and doorways to provide further protection for the inhabitants. Outhouses were too few and ill maintained. As one moved away from downtown, the streets widened but became deeply rutted and lacked pavement. Strong winds in the afternoon compounded the malaise by blowing the dust in large, dense clouds, while stray dogs, garbage, and other items of waste plagued pedestrians.

Robinson noted the disease amid the flies and filth, but what he did not understand was that as the dry winds blew fecal bacteria about, they turned mere discomfort into a situation injurious to pulmonary and intestinal health. The people living on the periphery of the city appeared to be uneducated and poor Indians and mestizos. Educational and health care services were almost nonexistent, and most of the people resorted to various forms of home medical treatments, including marijuana, peyote, prayer, and herbal cures derived from Tarahumara and Mexican experience. The sickliness of the children and their high mortality rate must have shocked the American doctor.

The commercial economy of Chihuahua was almost moribund at that time following years of civil wars fought between the Conservatives and Liberals at the national level and by their adherents in the state. As John gathered experience, he learned that Chihuahua City was the only major city in the state and the hub of trade with central Mexico. But he also realized that the rich mining, timber, and farming areas of western Chihuahua had great economic potential when they were connected by railroad to the U.S. marketplace.

After a short time, Robinson made ready to leave the city and investigate the mines at Batopilas and nearby sites in what is popularly known in the twenty-first century as Copper Canyon (Barranca del Cobre). He also encountered the first, still unrecognizable, sign of serious trouble. Quimby, who claimed limited financial resources, proved reluctant to meet his share of the expenses in the purchase of pack mules at $160 per animal. In John's mind, this compounded Quimby's duplicity about the route to be taken. When Robinson forced the issue, Quimby backed down but agreed to buy only a single pack mule, and a barely adequate one at that.

In their first full day of travel, the Robinson party covered dry, rolling country to the southwest of Chihuahua City, following the route that would be adopted a few years later by the Chihuahua, Sierra Madre, and Pacific Railroad. Built by Chihuahua railroad owners and U.S. steel industrialists Charles Schwab and Grant B. Schley of New York, the railroad would link the western half of the state to its capital and, later in the century, Chihuahua's western mining, timber, and grain regions to El Paso, though it would not span the Sierra Madre.

The travelers stopped for breakfast at Rancho La Peña, some thirty miles from Chihuahua City and just three miles before reaching Santa Isabel de Tarahumares. Abandoned during the great Raramuri rebellion of Tapomare, a century before the missions reincorporated almost all the Tarahumaras in western Chihuahua, the mission settlement of Santa Isabel had been restored by the Franciscans in 1668. By 1861, it had become a regional ranching and trade center dominated by the Terrazas family, into which Robinson's grandson Charles would later marry. Santa

Isabel would become infamous on January 10, 1916, when revolutionaries loyal to General Francisco Villa and under the command of General Pablo López executed seventeen American mining engineers en route to John's next stop, the silver mines at Cusihuirachi.

Situated alongside a stream at an elevation of 5,450 feet, Santa Isabel had less than sixty days of rain per year, most of it in summer downpours. In April, the weather there was quite mild and dry. By the time of Robinson's arrival, open-range ranching had already curtailed the ability of wolves and coyotes to roam freely in the area. The cowboys hunted them down or poisoned them, while cattle grazed in the extensive fields of Buffalo grass and hay (*zacate*) that lay interspersed amid larger fields dominated by shrubs, agaves, yuccas, and chaparral. Santa Isabel held little interest for the travelers: it would not celebrate its saint's festival until November, and its modest deposits of iron, manganese, marble, and kaolin could not compare to the real and imagined treasures to be found in the Sierra Madre.

John rested at the nearby Hacienda Juanita, where the wealthy "Spanish" owner received him gracefully and even provided musical entertainment through his ten-year-old daughter, who played the harp and danced. In the mind of Robinson's host, the performance demonstrated his commitment to high culture and separated him from his less sophisticated mestizo neighbors.

After breakfast the next morning, the party set out at 8 a.m. for the ancient Tarahumara village of Cusihuirachi, a small settlement located to the southwest at the headwaters of the Río Conchos just inside the first cluster of hills before reaching the Sierra Madre. The trip entailed first crossing the gentle, rolling slopes of the valley. The tall buffalo grass, already two feet high, spread out before him in the morning light and helped accentuate the dark green pine forests that covered the higher ground and mountains to the west and south and the azure blue sky sprinkled with salmon pink cirrus clouds above them. The mountains facing him reached elevations well over 9,000 feet above sea level and extended from east to west on the southern side of the valley before turning north and disappearing beyond the horizon.

During the course of the day, the intense blue of the sky changed, interdicted by the thin cirrus clouds and the changing angles of the sun's rays. Robinson arrived at Cusihuirachi at 3 p.m., where he quickly noted that the population was predominantly mestizo rather than Tarahumara. He found a corral for his animals and a not dissimilar residence for himself. Surrounded by the rocky slopes of the foothills, Cusihuirachi was located in a small valley at 6,500 feet above sea level. Robinson was some seventy-five miles southwest of Chihuahua City. Because of timbering, the hillsides had already lost most of the original mix of the 200 oak and 23 pine tree species, including the distinctive Chihuahua white pine, found throughout the 28,000 square miles of the Sierra Madre.

"Cusihuirachi" literally means "place of the standing stick" in Tarahumara, most likely in reference to the 30-inch cane of authority once wielded by the chief or perhaps to the white pine. In the seventeenth and eighteenth centuries, Cusihuirachi had been the head settlement in that part of the Tarahumara world. In feathered soldierly attire with animal skin quivers on their backs, the men had learned the arts of war: how to frighten their enemies with rattles made of deer hooves and bones and how to slay them with bows and arrows or spears.

The nearby San Bernabé and Huizache Springs provided both settlement and river with water. For many centuries, the Raramuri residents had hunted game and exploited the wild plants and trees there, including prickly pears for food, mesquite for cooking and warmth, and ebony and palms for building houses, silos, and corrals. They also had domesticated and evolved distinct varieties of chickpeas and corn from their wild counterparts. In addition to herbal cures, the Tarahumara were also masters at preparing *atole*, a sweet, energy-providing, nonalcoholic beverage made from high-quality corn.

The Spaniards recognized Cusihuirachi as a mission settlement in 1673. Immediately upon their arrival, the Jesuits had put the Tarahumaras to work constructing the Santa Rosa de Limón Mission. Shortly thereafter, the discovery of silver led to an influx of miners, who then found modest amounts of gold, copper, lead, kaolin, pumice, lime, and sand. In the 1680s, the Spanish authorities designated the settlement a *real de minas*, which meant that government officials would reside there to regulate mining activity.

In 1861, Cusihuirachi was a pale reflection of what it once had been. Overwhelmed by the flood of Mexicans and other outsiders, whom the Tarahumara called Chabochis, Tarahumara artisanry went into a rapid decline. Nevertheless, a few of the women continued to fashion clay pots, or ollas, from the high-quality white clay (kaolin) found in the region, to give them a distinctive green hue with dyes and repeated rubbings, and sometimes to cover them with decorative markings. And they continued to weave gray, white, black, and sometimes red zigzag designs into their homemade blankets, which the mestizos used as bedding, and which Raramuri men and women wore as shirts and as wraparound pants in cold weather.

During the late seventeenth century, when the Spanish authorities began to draft ever greater numbers of Tarahumara men for cutting timber and making adobe bricks, the indigenous people gradually withdrew from Cusihuirachi. They would be replaced by mestizos, who arrived intermittently over the next two centuries. By the time Robinson arrived, the mestizos constituted an overwhelming cultural and economic presence. Most of the Raramuris had retreated to higher ground, as had the groves, forests, and wild plants, the last replaced on the bottomland by the mestizos' watermelon patches, and peach, apple, pear, and fig orchards, which were irrigated with the small amount of spring and stream water available.

By the 1860s, the town lay amid orchards and small fields of bear and deer grass and daisies, known as *coronillas*. Yuccas, agaves, cacti, and other spiny plants thrived in the drier parts of the valley. The once ubiquitous bighorn sheep and grizzly and black bears had already grown scarce. Although the Mexican wolves (*nariguris*) still dominated the night with their haunting calls, they were being driven to the edge of extinction by the mestizos, who hunted them for sport or poisoned them to protect livestock. The wily coyotes flourished in the early 1860s, but by the middle of the twentieth century they would be nearly extinct, and the grizzlies entirely so.

The scattered townsfolk found Robinson and his entourage a curious sight. Although most of them were mestizo and spoke Spanish, some were still Tarahumara, shy and reticent with strangers, yet inquisitive. They were still capable of mimesis, ready and willing to puzzle at and then accept the introduction of at least some mannerisms, tools, and beliefs. The Robinson party, in contrast, was singularly focused on silver mining; they were unconcerned with "primitive" beliefs, practices, or attitudes toward nature.

After taking care of the animals, John set out with some local miners to examine their workings. He noted that the mine owners were under-capitalized, using obsolete technology, and had little chance of success. Although he saw some potentially profitable sites, he offered the locals little encouragement, advising them only to acquire modern machinery and to seek outside capital.

In the late afternoon, the cirrus clouds, reaching out from a lower mountain range to the east and stretching westerly in thin lines across the sky, changed first to brilliant salmon pink, then to crimson and finally to purple. It was John's first taste of the stronger colors of a Sierra Madre sunset. After dark the sounds of the night took over. The howls of the wolves in the mountains seemed to intimidate the yipping coyotes.[8]

In the morning, the Robinson party set off again, this time for Carichi, the next Raramuri settlement on the trail, fifteen miles to the southwest, surrounded by fields but with the mountains in full view to the south. Arriving there at 4 p.m., John could not help but notice the scattered, timber-roofed Tarahumara houses. Most had stone and adobe walls, although a few were made of logs, boards, and caulking. The people of Carichi and other Raramuri settlements customarily helped build each other's homes. The work usually entailed six or seven days and included stockpiling a large quantity of rocks and timbers at the construction site.

First the builders set eight-foot upright posts into the ground in two rows 18 to 30 inches apart along a rectangle about fifteen feet long and ten feet wide. Then they stacked stones between the posts to form walls, sometimes using chisels to shape the cornerstones and carefully preparing openings for the door and sometimes a window. Next they squared the usually pine lintels with axes and placed them above the openings to support the enormous weight of the stones above them, which extended another three feet upward. They made a sloping roof from a cross work of pine timbers and boards known as *canoas*. And, finally, they sealed the walls and roof with a durable adobe to shut out the harsh winds of summer and winter and installed a flue and a door made of two boards held together with pegs or nails. The flue and ax were but two of the concessions the Tarahumara made to Spanish and mestizo influence while maintaining as much of their way of life as possible. A third was the steep-sided gable roof with false ceiling featured by a few of the Tarahumara houses.

In contrast to Tarahumara flexibility, John evinced no interest in the

Raramuris during the journey. Most contemporary Americans scorned or ignored the culture of their predecessors in the United States. The shyness of the Tarahumara in the presence of others, both among members of their own community and toward outsiders, widened the already deep gulf between them and the newcomer. To his loss, and ours, John underestimated, indeed all but ignored the Raramuri. He was unaware of their complex religious ideologies, their profound sense of morality regarding public behavior, their sensitivity to the feelings of others, and their wide range of beliefs about unexplained phenomena. Despite deep moral, religious, and political differences, Raramuris rarely disagreed in public. They reserved their personal views for community discussions and for private moments among intimate friends, a practice that encouraged outsiders to underestimate or even disregard them.

Raramuri cosmology focused on the sun and moon as the father and mother deities. Other celestial objects and phenomena also carried supernatural significance and required various forms of reverence or respect. But the Raramuri sense of the human soul or souls was even more developed. Probably a majority agreed that human beings possess seven souls. Three major souls were found in the head, heart, and midsection of the torso, corresponding to the way we "think with our heads," "feel with our hearts," and sense fear and anxiety "in our stomachs." Four lesser souls resided in the body, one in each limb.

The departure of souls from the body explained the onset of illness and the severity of the affliction. It also reflected the interconnectedness of mind and body a concept that at that time was still not appreciated in Western culture. Animate objects, including the bears, wolves, and elk, also had souls and should not be killed for "sport." At Carichi, the Raramuris had already adopted the three wise men of Christian belief, whom they still celebrate with a procession and dancing on the second weekend of January.

By the 1860s, most of the Tarahumaras, despite their capacity for mimesis, were already grieving at the loss of wild animals gunned down by mestizo outsiders. The most offended of these Native Americans fled the villages to join their brethren in the hamlets (*aldeas*) and caves above Urique and Batopilas, deep in the Copper Canyon complex. The Raramuri attachment to animal life, however, had another side to it. Though they rejected *nagualismo* (animism), their deep and open reverence for animals was seen by others as animal worship as recently as the 1930s, and the Batopilas town council found it necessary to publicly decry that activity within the town limits.

Raramuri medicine men and community presidents disseminated religious and political beliefs and ideals on the larger scale through ceremonies and rituals. In times of illness, however, the medicine men offered personal explanations and cures for the affliction consistent with local beliefs that called for herbs, prayer, and atonement. Sometimes the source of the trouble was an unintended offense that may have caused one or more souls to depart the flesh of the suffering patient. These minor violations could stem from something as innocent as unknowingly stepping on a peyote button growing in the ground. More serious diseases were attributed to major offenses including such transgressions as violent acts committed during one of the frequent *tesquinada* festivals, when *tesquino* (corn beer) was frequently consumed to excess.

During ceremonies performed on saint's days, the presidents offered speeches that conveyed theoretical knowledge to those in attendance. The attendees, especially the young adults, generally accepted the overriding philosophical outlook of their leaders, including ideas about the meaning of life and death, but they individually interpreted those insights, providing the Tarahumara community with a wide tapestry of beliefs.

One example of that diversity was the pragmatic but varying degrees of adoption of practices and tools offered by the Chabochis (outsiders). Another was the partial acceptance of the outsiders' religious beliefs, which many Raramuris attached to their own, creating a syncretic religion. The integration of beliefs allowed for the construction of imaginative new theories such as the Tarahumara tale of the toad that helped invent death. This folklore, woven into their cosmology, relates that long ago, Toad, who was then not a toad but a fat and slow Raramuri man, believed that the world would soon be overpopulated. So he asked Onoruame (God) to invent death to prevent overpopulation. Onoruame did so, but gave the man, perhaps as punishment, the form of the toad. When John arrived, the Raramuri frequently portrayed toads in their artwork. Like one of their incarnations of the Christian Devil, the toad was fat and slow with a big belly.

Most of the time, Onoruame, as a father, was good to the Tarahumara.

He and his fellow deities provided water, rich soil, warmth, trees, and soft breezes. In contrast, the Christian Devil, Onoruame's rival, did evil things. He joined his helpers, like Coyote, to roam about at night seeking to commit bad acts such as attacking the souls of sleeping dreamers. Some Raramuris used Christian images to reject the outsiders, especially the Americans later in the century, as sons of the Devil, and, while taking some tools and even ideas with them, they retreated from "the evil ones who killed animals for sport and aspired to wealth and personal power versus their neighbors." The resisters, who retreated into the most remote canyons and mountains, exactly where Robinson was heading, did not adopt violence as a tactic, but after seeing the actions and hearing the cultural, economic, religious, and political views of the outsiders, these Raramuris rejected them.

The name Carichi is derived from the Tarahumara meaning "alongside streams." Flowing past the town from a sizable lake, the Río Carichi, like the streams near Cusihuirachi, drains into the Río Conchos. Carichi lies on the eastern edge of the Sierra Tarahumara at 6,600 feet above sea level and experiences extreme temperatures, ranging from a low of 10 degrees to a high of more than 100 degrees.

Jesuit missionaries first arrived at the settlement, then known as Guerocarichi, in about 1648. Following common strategies, they put the Raramuris to work constructing a mission that was formally named Jesús de Carichi on November 18, 1675. In the eighteenth century, the local people finished the construction of El Templo del Sagrada Familia, intended to serve the burgeoning and more diverse population that had developed as a result of mining endeavors in the region. Just twenty-five years before Robinson arrived, in 1836, Comanche raiders had overrun the village and sacked it, robbing, killing, burning, and carrying off women and children. By 1861, its people and culture were a mixture of local and outside influences, but the population was still predominantly Tarahumara.

Following Raramuri custom, the men at Carichi hunted rabbits and deer by spreading out and moving forward in a single rank, eventually exhausting and encircling their quarry. In addition to protein, the rabbits provided fur for ropes, while the deer offered a variety of services including antler decorations for masks and headdresses, and skin for quivers and moccasins. When Robinson arrived at Carichi, Tarahumara cuisine featured snake as one of the dining pleasures, while local brewmasters added tesquino, the popular and highly intoxicating corn beer, to the ever-present atole as a drinking option. Wild turkey, which the Raramuri called *guajolote*, a word from Nahuatl (the language of the Aztecs), fish, rabbits, and deer provided other wild food sources to complement the growing number of cattle and goats.

If the Robinson party had arrived at Carichi during Holy Week (Semana Santa) the members would have witnessed an exhibition of rain dances called Tutiyuri, acted out with the assistance of "traditional" Raramuri music produced by a combination of violins, drums, and flutes, which were introduced during the Spanish colonial era. As it was, they found lodging with Don Patricio Borja, a member of the local elite, who had been recommended by his counterparts back in Chihuahua City. Borja recognized an opportunity and provided John and his cohort with anything they requested but at exaggerated prices. Robinson knew what was going on, but the pleasures rendered by civilized conveniences clearly outweighed the small insult incurred by his host's underestimation of him. John took advantage of the situation, staying over for a day and shooting snipe for his dinner.[9]

On April 16, the group departed Carichi for the Tarahumara settlement of Sisoguichi at the civilized hour of 8 a.m. As they mounted the rocky trail and reached higher ground in the Sierra Madre, they entered what seemed like an endless pine forest comprising three distinct kinds of trees, the taller *pino*, the *pinavete*, shaped more like an equilateral triangle, and the thorny *tascate*. They followed the trail at the lower elevations between the heights, which reach 8,500 feet in that area, through the forests and rugged terrain toward Sisoguichi, located on a hillside and small valley. After some twenty-five miles, they encountered travelers moving east from the forestry camp of San Juanito. Robinson, ever seeking knowledge of the region, if not of the Raramuri, spent an evening camped out with them sharing stories of his travels and theirs in the Sierra Madre. On the morning of April 18, the Robinson party continued moving west-southwest, covering some fifteen miles through rich pine forests and the relatively level terrain of the highlands toward Sisoguichi and the even higher terrain that lay beyond it.

Between 1648 and 1684, the Jesuits had struggled to maintain a mission at Sisoguichi, located at the northeastern edge of the canyon country. They persisted in their proselytizing despite the attempted murder of a padre by an angry Tarahumara in 1732. The Raramuris of Sisoguichi continued to use poisoned arrows well into the eighteenth century to stun or kill human rivals, especially Spanish soldiers, and to bring down game.

Despite its more remote location, in comparison to Cusihuirachi and Carichi, by the eighteenth century, the Sisoguichi area supported over 200 head of cattle, in addition to burros, chickens, goats, and the sizable number of sheep essential for the making of wool shirts, wraparound pants, and blankets. The introduction of goats, which consumed grass to ground level, contributed to the further retreat of wildlife. Situated on the Río Sisoguichi, a small stream that also fed the Río Conchos, the native people survived on a spare cuisine based on corn and beans, sometimes supplemented by goat meat and wild game including fish, turkeys, other birds, deer, and rabbits. The locals hunted with bows and arrows, spears, and clubs. The latter were used by groups of men after running down rabbits and even coyotes. The spears served them well in their perfected art of fishing. Their drinks, like the rest of the Tarahumaras, included tesquino and atole.

Unlike the more Mexicanized settlements the Robinson party had passed through, the Raramuris at Sisoguichi still played *rarachipa*, a pre-Columbian game best described as a kickball relay race. Two teams, kicking distinctively marked balls called *gomakaris*, usually made from the durable, locally found Arizona madrone (*Arbutus arizonica*), in front of them, would race along a course beside the river, marked out and sometimes monitored by men standing at intervals. People from the surrounding small settlements would watch the race from the slopes of the river valley. Almost always played in conjunction with a tesquinada festival in honor of a saint's day, harvest, planting, or other ceremonial event, a rarachipa could last "a few minutes, a day, or several days," depending on the importance of the occasion. The travelers did not stay for the tesquinada afterward and therefore did not witness the drunken violence that all too often ensued.

At 8 a.m. on April 19, John's party set off for "the Indian town" Bocoyna, only a few miles as the crow flies but more than fifteen hard miles by mule because of an intervening ridge. Indeed, the travelers needed a guide to help them find and follow the trail. After proceeding two miles west, they rode three miles south along a rugged arroyo before turning west again and crossing the ridge into the next canyon. There they struggled north for another ten miles along a second, boulder-strewn arroyo.

The terrain became more difficult by the day. At this point, the elevation averaged 7,200 feet. Their rest at Sisoguichi had paid off handsomely. At noon, the group arrived at Bocoyna, a small outpost on a trail that ran southwesterly in somewhat more gentle terrain for about thirty miles before it, too, became rough. Bocoyna was a largely Tarahumara settlement with a few mestizos, who farmed and cut timber. It was nominally under the legal jurisdiction of Sisoguichi.

In 1702, Jesuit missionaries christened the Raramuri settlement and the Native Americans constructed a small mission called Nuestra Señora de Guadalupe de Bocoyna. It stood in a comfortable valley surrounded by higher ground with a number of higher peaks hidden from view. The Raramuri attached spiritual significance to some of the prominent mountains in the region, including Nechupiachi, Rumurachi, Sayahuachi, and Sojahuachi. But, in a few days, John would be above precipices that would make all that he had seen to this point seem tame in comparison. Since it was April, the air at the higher altitudes was cold, even freezing, at night.

In 1861, Bocoyna was at the hydrographic center of the Raramuri world. It lay on the east side of the Río Bocoyna, a mere twenty miles from the most remote point of origin for the Conchos before it begins its long journey across Chihuahua into the Rio Grande and then on to the Gulf of Mexico. The Robinson party was now near the Continental Divide. The next canyon to the west contained the easternmost headwaters of the Río Oteros (meaning "coming from high places"), which drains into the Pacific Ocean. Bocoyna was also the easternmost center of the receding Tarahumara culture. Surrounded by rich pine forests, it attracted a few mestizo foresters, but the extreme cold in winter and the lack of mineral wealth and soil suitable for farming and grazing had spared it the effects of the larger foreign invasion that the Americans had witnessed at Cusihuirachi, Carichi, and Sisoguichi.[10]

The travelers found a suitable campsite two miles from Bocoyna, where they slaughtered, cooked, and ate the ewe John had bought in town, then rested for the night. At 7:45 the following morning, the party headed southwest, toward a series of high ridges, still out of view, that embrace one of the most challenging and beautiful landscapes in the world. En route, Robinson paused near Cruces, a crossing where the trail west from Bocoyna to the mission settlement of Cerocahui intersected the trail from the mining center of Parral in southern Chihuahua. Cruces was about ten miles south of the later settlement of Creel, named in honor of Enrique Creel.

At 7,600 feet above sea level, Cruces lacked a river but enjoyed the benefit of a nearby lake fed by springs and a wide and level valley. After lunch, the party continued onward and in the late afternoon encountered the first of what seemed like an infinite number of sublime scenic displays. As the Robinson party reached the first high point on the increasingly difficult trail, they looked down into the rugged Barranca de Tararecua, a major part of the wider Copper Canyon complex. In the changing late afternoon sky, characterized by ever more vivid salmon and reddish colors, they saw seemingly endless lines of ever higher arêtes extending with darker shades of purple to the southern horizon. The travelers had covered about thirty miles that day and stopped to rest near the mesa of Pitorreal. The view of the cliffs and sunset was awe inspiring.

The altitude, the lack of grazing grasses, and heavy burdens on the pack animals, however, overtaxed man and beast. The result was a wholly unnecessary crisis on the trail. The travelers were pushing their animals too hard and they had reached the highest and most rugged terrain imaginable. The loss of burros or mules at this point would put in jeopardy not just their expedition but their very lives. Fortunately for John and his party, the Mexican looking after the animals found a spot for grazing and water and lost only one animal.

The next morning, the travelers rose before light and struck out on the trail by 7 a.m. The scorching heat and high altitude required the early departure. They were now in the Sierra Tarahumara, one of the most rugged areas of the Sierra Madre. Inching along the northern edge of the Barranca de Tararecua, they followed roughly the same route as the modern railroad from Creel to Los Mochis on the Sea of Cortez. In addition to the grand vistas one might expect in a mountain range and the vivid sunrises and sunsets, the canyon complex offered sublime, majestic scenes of canyons, with walls that reached down vertically as much as 6,200 feet to bottoms where one encounters a semitropical climate. "We found the mountains almost inaccessible, and very high," wrote Robinson, who knew the American Rockies well.

The mules were tired. Very hard in the steep ascents. Tortuous windings and narrow paths. In many places the roads were made by the ledges of rock, and the mules would barely have room to pass the projections, and sometimes actually hung over the edges of the precipices from 5,000 to 10,000 feet perpendicular. We are now in the midst of the mountains, and they are the most grand and imposing I have seen, often rising into the clouds in masses of granite, in the most fantastic and wonderful shapes.[11]

The pine forests in the higher altitudes starkly contrasted with the parrots and subtropical flora the travelers would soon find on the canyon floors. On many days of the year, the peaks soar above the clouds and during the winter they collect snow. In April, on the rim of the canyons, temperatures fell below freezing at night, whereas deep in the barrancas they would rise to 100 degrees or higher.

At 1 p.m., the Robinson party arrived at the Tarahumara pueblo of Cuiteco or "neck-shaped hill." Located on the edge of an arroyo of the same name, at 5,600 feet above sea level, Cuiteco had a long pre-Columbian history. Its earlier inhabitants have been identified as Cuiteco Indians. By 1601, however, Jesuit missionaries described it as a Raramuri settlement, which suggests that Tarahumaras, retreating before the Spaniards and mestizos who occupied the eastern valleys, had displaced the less numerous Cuitecos.

Padre Juan María de Salvatierra, the founder of the first California missions, established one at Cuiteco in 1684 and saw to it that the place was incorporated and given pueblo status by the civil authorities at the same time. By 1861, there were a number of subsidiary settlements around Cuiteco, while the place itself claimed several hundred souls. The Raramuris raised goats and worked small farms, while a cluster of mestizo entrepreneurs cultivated apple orchards giving the place a broader basis for contact with the outside world.

The Tarahumara residences in Cuiteco were significantly smaller than those the Robinsons had encountered to the east around the headwaters of the Conchos such as Cusihuirachi, Carichi, Sisoguichi, and Bocoyna. Here the Raramuris constructed much simpler one-room residences, some with stone walls and others of logs. They measured only six feet by twelve feet, with sloping roofs made of timber frames and canoas attached to the upright posts. The stone walls caulked with mud, however, were almost as impressive as those in the eastern towns, measuring as much as three feet in width but about a foot shorter on average. The walls of the log buildings were solid, based on notched planks.

Despite the simplicity of their homes, the Raramuris of Cuiteco viewed them, as did the people in the more accessible areas, as the center points for all things, practical and mystical. Besides a corral, grain silo (*troje*), and toolshed, for workday activities, each house had an *ahuiritzi*, a ceremonial yard with a small altar bearing three crosses, consistent with both European Christianity and Native American religious symbolism. The family prayed at the altar, carefully aligned with the rising sun, to fend off ailments, bring rain, and ensure other benefits.[12]

John's party rested at Cuiteco and did not leave until one in the afternoon. It turned out to be a wise decision because they immediately faced a steep climb before turning south and following the northern ridge of the Barranca de Urique, a southwesterly continuation of the Barranca de Tararecua. They made their way amid Apache and Chihuahua white pine to the settlement of Bahuichivo. They then headed directly south and descended into a beautiful valley, where they encountered pochote trees with their magnificent white flowers and octopus agaves. The descent was perilous in places because of the steep slopes and volcanic scree on the trail. It was 9 p.m. when they arrived at the ancient Raramuri mission settlement of Cerocahui. Surrounded by cliffs once again, they set up camp in the abandoned mission.

The town, situated at 6,100 feet of elevation, was yet another Native American settlement that had been slowly reorganized by the Jesuits. Padres Pecoro and Prado visited Cerocahui in 1676 and then Padre Salvatierra founded the mission in 1681. It was the first religious outpost established in the remote and rugged region that counts the mining centers of Batopilas and Urique as its neighbors. Exhausted, the Robinson party cooked a dinner of beans and dried beef and slept "on the ground as usual." In the morning, they fortified themselves with a hearty meal of beef and corn tortillas, washed down with coffee, witnessed the nearby waterfalls, and encountered more than a few of the over 200 species of birds.

Surrounded by curious Tarahumaras, who took a special interest in the strangers, the Robinsons decided to visit the local mines, which had been discovered only sixteen years earlier by Ignacio Arriola and Mariano de Valois. The Mexicans invariably suffered from a lack of technology and capital when they undertook mining operations in this remote area of the Sierra Madre. They traditionally depended on Native American manual labor, which, although cheap when measured against the wages paid a few hundred miles away north of the border, was prohibitively expensive when measured against the value of the product. Yaqui and Mayo Indian workers from Sonora provided most of the labor because the vast majority of Raramuris resisted being incorporated into outsider undertakings. Arriola and Valois had recently sold their claims to a foreign company, the local representatives of which included a Scotsman and two Americans. One of the latter was the sort of pilgrim John would learn to appreciate in the Sierra Tarahumara, an unnamed American medical doctor living in Cerocahui while serving his mining concern as a "clerk."

Robinson, seeking mineral wealth, unfortunately lacked interest in the Native Americans who lived there and therefore deprived us of his insights regarding the people of Cerocahui. His keen eye would have been invaluable in narrating Raramuri practices and technology. However, the dwellings of the indigenous people at Cerocahui revealed a tremendous versatility. Their homes, while more compact than those found to the east in the richer and milder region around the headwaters of the Río Conchos, or even those in the highlands above them, were constructed so low to the ground that the occupants had to bend over inside of them. They included cooking, sleeping, and dining areas in one small room, and required minimal fuel to keep warm in winter.

The cooking area occupied one of the short walls and included a slight depression lined with stones in the earthen floor and, in the stone structures, a rock and clay flue that went through the wall. They constructed the flues by placing small stones secured with clay around a log that extended halfway up the wall, and then another log placed at a right angle that exited the wall. After removing the logs, they sealed the cracks in the rocks with more clay. In the winter, the Tarahumara closed the flue with a wood flap or plugged it with a stone. They usually placed shelves made of pine planks on the same wall for the holding of cooking utensils and supplies.

The utensils included an iron griddle measuring about eighteen inches across and tapered to a depth of about two inches in the center. The locally made clay eating bowls measured about eight inches across and three inches in depth. They also used clay ollas for water storage and clay pots for cooking. They made these items by flattening balls of kaolin into tortilla-shaped pancakes, molding them around gourds to give them different shapes, and then kneading them with wet hands. They then placed the work in the sun to dry and followed that up with a one-hour firing in flames generated from dung, an expendable fuel not suitable for cooking or indoor use. In addition, the native people at Cerocahui made a single-handled jar suitable for transport, which they carried by simply attaching a fiber cord to it and hanging it around the neck.

Their in-house storage also included marvelous painted gourds, adapted to serve as bowls, containers, canteens, and dippers. They decorated some of the gourds with images of deer, rabbits, coyotes, and birds. They used the gum of *guru* roots as a glue and filler in order to repair cracked and even broken gourds. The guru gum dried quickly, and sometimes they held the broken pieces together by hand until the adhesive set. At other times, they tied fragile objects with fiber strings or strips of hide to hold them together and prolong service. Their spoons often measured fifteen inches in length and were sometimes carved from madrone wood.

Household furniture was often limited to pine sleeping boards covered with homemade blankets, woven by the women from the wool yielded by the family's sheep. The beds measured five feet by eighteen inches and sometimes featured headboards. Just outside the abode John must have seen hollowed *wisaro* trunks used as feeding troughs and for the processing of hides. At some homes, he might also have noted the careful placement of plows, tools, and troughs aligned to please Onoruame (God), his wife, and other deities as represented by the sun, moon, and the stars. The Raramuris at Cerocahui also used extracts from madrone bark as a cure for kidney infections and the juice of the pitaya and the fruit of the giant saguaro cacti, to treat nervous ailments and circulatory problems.[13]

After visiting the mines and mildly complaining about the curiosity of the Tarahumaras, John had his party set off at 10 a.m. for the famed mining settlement of Urique at the bottom of the barranca. But the terrain misled the travelers After they ascended the Cerro Gallegos, which separates the valley in which Cerocahui is found from the Barranca de Urique, John thought the journey from there to the town of Urique and the river below would be relatively easy and rapid. The town appeared much closer than it actually was from his vantage point, 1,500 feet above Cerocahui and 4,500 feet above Urique, which lay at the bottom of the barranca. Strung out along the north side of the Río Urique, the houses looked small but easily accessible and the stream looked like a silver snake in the clear air and bright sun.

Precipitous cliffs faced him towering thousands of feet above steep slopes sprinkled with the red flowers of the pitaya cactus. At the bottom, he would encounter a subtropical climate. Beginning in the pine trees at the rim, the party traversed three ecological zones in one day from a pine forest to oak trees to the subtropical canyon bottom. As he gazed into the barranca, the dry, almost desertlike terrain on its sides reached beyond the limits of his vision to the southwest. Looking directly south, the arêtes rose in successive and seemingly never ending silhouettes until they blurred in the distance. Despite the beautiful vistas, the rugged and treacherous trail proved to be "the worst mountain we had yet met." The downward trip began at 2 p.m. and ended at nine that night when Robinson encountered another American pilgrim: "Our mules became desperate and ran head-long down the mountain in the dark, and lost themselves and the luggage. There was some tall swearing at everybody and everything in the country, but about 10 o'clock, by the help of one of the natives, with a pitch torch, we housed ourselves with an American across the river, of the name of Beecher, who received us kindly."[14]

Beecher managed the principal mines at Urique for a "Company of California capitalists." Two hundred years earlier, the Raramuri had pointed out the gold in Urique to the Spaniards, as they had the silver at Batopilas. In 1684, Padre Salvatierra visited the site for religious reasons, but it was not recognized until January 12, 1690, when Spanish prospector Juan Tarango Vallejo filed gold claims in the area and settled among the Native Americans already using the site. Because of its wealth, Urique attracted Spanish gold miners and became a center of trade. By 1861, the authorities in the town exercised the powers of law enforcement, including a court of law, and recorded vital statistics. Now the California capitalists had directed the local miners to dig a tunnel that would run into the mountain to a vein that carried an estimated $1,000 in gold per cubic yard. John's ready acceptance of this high figure reveals the highly contagious nature of "gold fever."

Robinson also visited the Rosario tunnel of the Guadalupe Mining Company and found the workers had dug some 390 feet into the mountain with only ninety feet left before intersecting the vein and, he recognized the importance of the tunnel as a strategy to be employed at Batopilas. Writing to the Barneys in New York, John, in contrast to his lack of interest in the Native American people of the canyons, focused on the history of the Urique gold mining industry and faithfully repeated romantic gold discovery stories with their exaggerations as truth. He retained the acumen, however, to note that a mine was being "badly managed" and, in the case of the Guadalupe, he critically measured profits against costs.[15]

On April 30, the party left Urique for Batopilas. First, they headed downstream for twenty miles through pitaya, jicama, pochote, *palo blanco*, *amapa*, and other trees to a ranch owned by "our muleteer." The heat must have been unbearable, as May and June are regarded as the most unfavorable times in the bottomlands of the barrancas because drought conditions prevail and there are no rains to offer relief from the heat. The climate had already taken its toll forcing them to replace their mules in Urique with fresh animals. The following day, they hiked until noon before resting and then continued on to a rancho where they arrived at 5 p.m. Pedro, the Mexican translator, "gave out" earlier in the day and finally caught up with them at 9 p.m.

The news of Robinson's arrival preceded him, as it usually did for newcomers among the people in the barrancas. Guadalupe Ramírez, a co-owner and interested seller of the Batopilas mines, sent his son and a companion out to guide Robinson for the remaining two days of the journey. The two parties met at the rancho and spent the night. On May 2, they headed up the last mountain between them and Batopilas. The trail was exceedingly rocky as they climbed past the oak trees upward some 4,200 feet to the top of the ridge, where pine trees covered a distance of about twelve miles. The pack mules were kept at the bottom to await cooler temperatures for the ascent. John's party then followed an easy, rolling trail easterly through the virgin pine forest across the mesa until they found a suitable resting place.

The view from the top of the ridge was fantastic. The high ground of the Barranca de Urique was to their rear and in front of them they could see the towering Cerro Colorado (Red Mountain) and the southeastern rim of the Barranca de Batopilas. Since they had not yet reached the edge of the barranca, they could not see the Río Batopilas, which lay some 3,800 feet below the edge.

When the Robinson party arose at daybreak on May 3, the sky was red and orange with the edges of the colors fading into ever-lightening blues. In May and June, there is little cloud cover in the canyons. The sun rose as they crossed the remaining rolling land that lay between the two barrancas. It was an area noted for its grizzly and black bears, jaguars, mountain lions, lesser wildcats, Mexican wolves, coyotes, elk, eagles, macaws, and the brilliantly colored, now extinct Sierra Madre woodpeckers, giant birds that stood two feet tall and lived throughout the lower elevations of the Sierra Tarahumara.

After only two hours on the crest at 5,800 feet elevation, they left the pine forest that covers the higher parts of the sierra and entered a narrower elevation zone, once again characterized by oak trees. Then, as they crossed the ridges and high points above the ravines adjoining the great Barranca de Batopilas, they could make out the river shimmering and convoluted. Like the Urique, it looked like a silver serpent in the distance. Their descent quickly placed them among *higueras* (prickly pear cacti) and among *nacapules* and *camuchines* (wild fig trees), some of which approached 1,000 years in age and stood out in the wide variety of vegetation.

As John and his companions descended, they encountered a growing number of pochote trees, brandishing their white flowers. Looking up during the course of the day, they saw the rock strata above and opposite them changing colors in the light, moving from basalt and sandstone red colorations to purple and finally gray. After three hours of descent they reached La Junta, the junction of a tributary and the Río Batopilas, some three miles upstream from the town.

As they neared Batopilas, their surroundings presented a romantic image, including a relatively quiet but still impressive river, measuring some fifty feet in width and as much as three feet in depth. The group approached the town from the west side of the canyon. On their right, the canyon wall that was so dominant farther upstream had tapered off into a steep hillside. At first only a few jacales, or shacks, and seemingly abandoned mines could be seen there.

Across the river, they could see the San Antonio mine workings, named in recognition of Saint Anthony of Padua, the patron of miners. They lay just upstream from the Hacienda San Miguel on the same side of the river. Saint Anthony was a force in opposition to the fevers such as typhoid, which afflicted the people of Batopilas, and he also fought the diabolic obsession that some of the townspeople believed afflicted the Tarahumara. A cart bridge made of wood connected the hacienda and the San Antonio mine to the Batopilas side of the river. The cart trail ran from the bridge up the hill on the Batopilas side of the stream to a complex of mine shafts named for San Miguel, in which John was most interested.

On the outskirts of Batopilas, the travelers encountered a series of jacales, which had been built out of branches and larger pieces of wood by Tarahumaras and outsiders unable to obtain more permanent materials, and which, John could see, were vulnerable to the floodwaters that cascaded down the barranca when it rained in the upper reaches of the sierra.[16]

Batopilas

The Raramuri named Bachotigari (meaning "alongside the river") long before the Spaniards arrived in 1623 to mispronounce it "Batopilas." They were searching for gold deposits they found soon enough at Urique. Then, in 1708, Pedro de la Cruz filed a claim to a silver mine in the vicinity, which he named the Guadalupe. As the miners uncovered more and more silver, the town grew in importance throughout the colonial era.

When the Robinson party rounded a bend in the river a half mile or so from the center of Batopilas, they caught sight of the Hacienda San Miguel, whose stone, adobe, and timber buildings stood on a terrace that, reinforced by a stone fortification and retaining wall, faced the river. Named for the Archangel Michael, who with Gabriel defeated the Devil and protected Moses, the hacienda was a bastion against the dark and evil forces of nature and humankind for mine owners, past, present, and future.

Nestled amid a series of volcanic hills named Las Animas, San Néstor, Los Frailes, El Púlpito, and Algarín, the Hacienda San Miguel and Batopilas together featured tropical trees and flowers, including the ubiquitous bougainvillea. San Miguel stood some thirty feet above the river and had a retaining wall that made it safe from even hundred-year floods, to which all but the higher part of Batopilas, away from the river, was vulnerable.[17]

During the 1740s, Don Juan José de Rivolta had enlarged and improved the original San Miguel Hacienda, which had been built in the

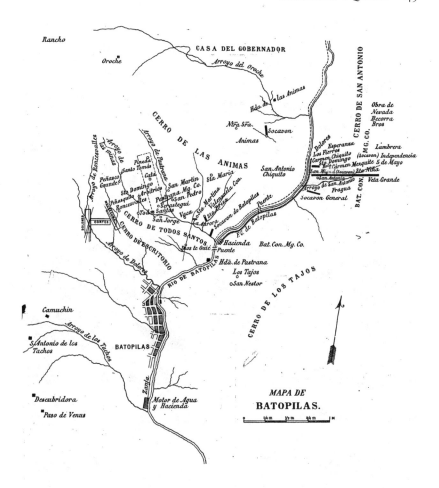

The Batopilas area. (Courtesy of the Library of Congress)

middle of the seventeenth century. An old soldier and man of action, Rivolta made a fortune in Batopilas from the labor of mestizo and Indian *barreteros* (miners who work with a pick or pry bar) after he retired from his military career. Adding a newly discovered piety to his long-standing claims of racial purity untainted by Native American blood, he used a sizable part of his wealth to successfully promote the white Virgin of Mount Carmel (Carmen), alongside the dark-skinned Virgin of Guadalupe worshipped by the Indians and most of the mestizos.

Bearing the titles of *capitán de guerra* (military commander) and

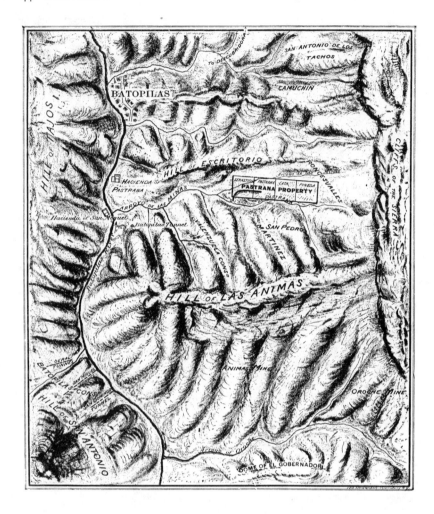

The northern portion of the Batopilas region, showing the Pastrana property. (From the 1881 report of John C. F. Randolph; courtesy of The Bancroft Library, University of California, Berkeley)

alcalde mayor (political chief), Rivolta wielded political and military power over several thousand square miles of the Barranca del Cobre complex. He transformed San Miguel into a medieval-style castle, complete with guard towers and a surrounding defensive wall. He made certain that the side facing the river could withstand floods and that the opposite side, facing a steep hill, could withstand attacks by Indians, bandits, and rebels. His buildings and fortifications would later be enlarged upon by Alexander Shepherd.

Following Rivolta's death, Don Rafael Alonzo Pastrana, a man of more common origins, had discovered several silver bonanzas. The Pastrana vein produced silver valued at 48 million pesos between 1730 and 1750 and made its owner one of the richest men in the world. The Pastrana mine remained productive a century later, at the time Robinson arrived. Pastrana took over San Miguel and most of the mines around Batopilas. By the 1750s, his opulent lifestyle and silver exports to Álamos, Sonora, and to Mexico City had drawn the attention of outsiders. When the bishop of Chihuahua announced he would come to the Barranca del Cobre to visit Batopilas, Pastrana ordered his workers to pave the street from the cathedral to the rectory with silver ingots.

The bishop decided to stay on in the town for several weeks, ostensibly to bless marriages and buildings. In the end, he left with a valuable collection of gifts from Pastrana, including large nuggets of native and "ruby" silver. So impressed was the bishop that he only mildly reproached Pastrana for his all-too-evident vanity. Throughout the rest of his life, Pastrana would make improvements to the 13-acre San Miguel estate, adding to its already expanded living quarters and patios and to its facilities for ore processing and storage.

Later, near the end of the eighteenth century, when millionaires in New York were still rare, Don Ángel Bustamante took over the hacienda and the Carmen mine, which produced 30 million pesos' worth of native, ruby, and other silver ore between 1790 and 1820. (The native silver from the Batopilas mines had a silver content of 75 percent, instead of the widely accepted 80 percent.)

Bustamante's gifts to the Spanish Crown earned him the title of marquis. Following his death and the transportation disruptions caused by the Wars of Independence (1810–21), however, Batopilas fell into disrepair and continued to deteriorate until the middle of the nineteenth century.

Then came Manuel Mendazona, an energetic merchant of Basque descent from Mazatlán, who first visited Batopilas in 1852 and was enraptured with it. Motivated by the money and the challenge, Mendazona wanted to restore both the town and the mines. He bought and rebuilt the dilapidated Hacienda Pastrana near the cathedral. For Mendazona, the center of Batopilas lay in the town itself and in its people, not in the

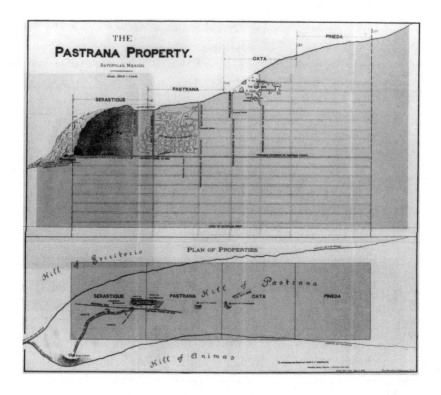

Plan of the famous Pastrana mines. (From the 1881 report of John C. F. Randolph; courtesy of The Bancroft Library, University of California, Berkeley)

Hacienda San Miguel, isolated with its mine workshops across the river. Mendazona died suddenly in 1856, however, before he could carry out his plans. Men from Batopilas and the neighboring towns of Álamos and Guadalupe y Calvo purchased the mines and leased them to *gambusinos*, experienced miners who paid the owners in kind, working a full shift and taking as wages their last load of ore at the end of the day, often after regular hours. Then, in 1861, the doctor from Ohio arrived at the town "alongside the river."[18]

A half mile from the center of town, the Robinson party entered a narrow road lined with one- and two-room houses, shops, and a few cantinas made of adobe and timbers, squeezed between the road and the river and about ten feet above it. Above the road stood the old cemetery. As they entered the center of town (three short blocks at its widest), they could see abundant fruit trees and masonry buildings, including a few elaborate ones such the cathedral, in a highly dilapidated state, which stood on the town's main plaza, and two blocks northeast of it, the restored Hacienda Pastrana, where they would stay. The hacienda was a walled-in complex that included a main house, patio with fountain, a garden filled with banana, mango, papaya, and orange trees, and smaller outlying buildings, enveloped in bougainvillea and other tropical flowers.

Between the hacienda and a bend in the river, and vulnerable to floods, lay the sizable Plaza del Taste, named for a tree with flamboyant blossoms and wide leaves. The plaza was a center for relaxation and revelry, featuring small shops and cantinas, as well as a few two-story houses owned by local merchants. Two parallel streets extended two blocks southwest from it and from the hacienda to the town's main plaza.

There the Robinson party passed the cathedral, dedicated to Saint Peter, the patron saint of Batopilas, and to the Virgin of Mount Carmel (Carmen), the town's protector. Just as Saint Peter served as the undisputed head of the Roman Catholic faith, so Batopilas was the region's cultural and administrative center. And just as Peter was a teacher and leader, so the town was a center for teaching and steadfastness in the faith. The white Virgin stood for the hegemony of Europeanized culture but also for feminine nurturing, love, and charity at the same time, significant elements in the consciousness of the townspeople, the indigenous workers, and the Tarahumara.

The municipal building faced the river from the northwest side of the main plaza, the farthest removed and safest part of town. Shops and cantinas lined the other three sides, with those on the southeast side backed up to the river but somewhat above it and, unlike the Plaza del Taste, safe from all but the worst of floods. A solid but unfinished masonry school building, which served as the jail, stood on the northeast side.

Batopilas had suffered the effects of the recent War of the Reform (1858–60); its parish church, like many others in Mexico, had lost much of its financial support. Led by President Benito Juárez, the Liberal Party had won the fight to privatize the properties of the Church and force it out of politics by placing the government in charge of health care, education, and welfare. The Church hierarchy fought long and hard, as it did during the Wars of Religion in Europe, to retain its position. Many of its Conservative advocates denounced the Liberals as "agents of Satan" while the opposing armies devastated entire regions of the nation and committed atrocities. The struggle left lingering hatreds and resentments on both sides.

Because of its remoteness, Batopilas had escaped direct violence but suffered from disrupted trade ties with the outside world, as well as from the lingering hatreds and resentments the war had left in its wake throughout the nation. Though practicing Catholics, most batopilenses supported President Juárez, the inspirational leader of the Liberal cause. The Liberal leaders claimed that their program would provide individual freedoms, equality of opportunity, regardless of class or ethnic background, and better care for the needy, who, they asserted, had been ignored by the Conservatives and the Church.

The local priest had confined himself to his ecclesiastical duties, keeping, as much as possible, out of public view. Nevertheless, the lingering political conflict had driven most of the men away from church attendance and contributions. The cathedral would remain in disrepair until that conflict was resolved.

The road downstream and out of town was also lined by the jacales of the poor. Heading toward the Mission of Satevo, it soon narrowed to a foot trail; the mountains closed in, reaching straight down to the river. On higher ground lay another rugged area of the barrancas and more silver mines.[19]

In his search for wealth, John Robinson entered an isolated place rich in mineral wealth and dramatic cultural diversity. He had initiated what would become a historic and revealing encounter of nineteenth-century American capitalism and culture with the people of the Third World.

CHAPTER 2

The Invention of the Fritter

Some were bitten by snakes; others by venomous scorpions or
tarantulas; others contracted rare skin diseases that never
healed, . . . which nobody, . . . could explain . . . whoever was
spared attack from reptiles and mysterious diseases died from
the different kinds of fevers that abounded.
—B. Traven

The Background

JOHN ROBINSON AND HIS POWERFUL BANKING and manufacturing associates had no intention of limiting themselves to the small-scale operations of the principal Batopilas mine owners, Jorge Lebrun and Guadalupe Ramírez. Robinson's Wells Fargo partners included some of the
leading mining impresarios of the American West. As major figures in
banking, transportation, and industrial production, they enjoyed limitless
opportunities to sell their silver in the eastern United States and Asian
markets and to hold it in their banks in San Francisco and New York.

During the 1860s and 1870s, Robinson, as the active partner in Mexico
of the Batopilas Mining Company, would become a prominent member
of the Chihuahua and Sinaloa elites. By the 1870s, he had amassed enormous wealth and in 1873 his son Charles married Carmen Torres, a
member of the Sinaloa and Sonora oligarchy. Their wedding took place
at Choix, Sinaloa. Two of their infant children died at Batopilas in 1875,
but a third child by the marriage, Charles Louis Francis Robinson, married Esther Francis Terrazas in Chihuahua City in 1906 and lived in the
United States until his death in 1944. Esther was the only granddaughter
of General Luis Terrazas, the greatest landholder in Mexico.[1]

Between 1861 and 1879, the silver Robinson delivered from the Batopi-las mines, his transportation network, warehousing facilities at Choix, Mazatlán, and Chihuahua City, and his trade with the regional elites made him the most important mine operator in Mexico and a wealthy man. But the horrible health conditions at Batopilas shattered his life. His sons Asher and James Willshire Robinson both succumbed to typhoid fever at Batopilas in September 1861 and June 1862, respectively. Then the passing of his two grandchildren, Fred and Lena, victims of the same disease in the same place a little more than a decade later compounded his grief.

Mimesis and Adaptability

After his arrival in Batopilas, Robinson found that the town offered scenes of human drama comparable to those of nature presented by the wilder-ness and topography of the surrounding mountains. Located miles away from the 6,200-foot high and almost vertical cliffs upstream, Batopilas possessed diverse geographic features. First, only three miles upstream the junction of a tributary and the Río Batopilas at La Junta offered a wide plain that provided views of the spectacular Barranca de Batopilas to the east and the rugged Cañón de Roncesvalles to the north. The open area provided space for the cultivation of crops and the economic benefits of a seemingly endless supply of sand that could be excavated for con-struction projects.

Second, downstream, the Indian settlement of Satevo, almost four miles to the south of Batopilas, offered another wide expanse of sand, tropical flowers, blue water, and a dramatically beautiful carved stone and adobe brick mission building. The Tarahumaras built the mission for Jesuit missionaries, and it was still standing after more than two centuries of earthquakes and weathering. Finally, closer to Batopilas, several rivu-lets fed by springs cascaded down the mountainsides on the upstream edge of town, offering pools of water, shade trees, and the potential of electricity. The area around Batopilas, considering all of its physical and cultural attributes, displayed tremendous potential.

The town itself featured an array of people comparable to the centuries-old architecture of the place. A mix of native-born mestizos and criollo shopkeepers constituted the small upper segment of the social order. The handful of Spanish men who had lived there invariably chose mestizo wives and lived with their Mexican counterparts near the two plazas. The batopilenses mixed on a daily basis with itinerant miners from the Sinaloa coast and from other parts of the Sierra Madre creating some variety in music and cuisine, but the manner of dress was extremely limited. The miners dressed in white muslin with a consistency best described as parochial.

John demonstrated his considerable social skills, education, and business acumen to the Batopilas elites from the moment of his arrival. During his first stay, between May 3 and June 11, 1861, he introduced the fritter, invented a miner's lamp, performed two operations on a woman's abscessed breast, visited most of the mines in the area, found silver for Lebrun in the latter's own excavation, and purchased the mines he deemed desirable at bargain-basement prices.

The miner's lamp promised a savings of 50 percent on the considerable amount of money spent on candles to illuminate the mines. The gambusinos as well as the mine operators were duly impressed and adopted its use. Robinson's operation on the abscessed breast, however, did not go well. He lacked the proper utensils and, aside from alcohol, the means to properly sterilize the wound or anesthetize the patient. Because of an unsatisfactory result, he tried again a few days later and described the outcome as a slight improvement but still "very bad."[2]

In contrast to his medical dilemma, John scored a major success with the fritter. He introduced the delicacy because he found tortillas detestable and they were the basic staple of consumption. He used the kitchen facilities at the Hacienda Pastrana (Mendazona mansion) to blend wheat flour, water, sugar, two eggs, and a dash of bicarbonate of soda together. Then he deep-fried the dough in *manteca* (lard) and, voilà, the assembled guests enjoyed a completely new repast. The word quickly spread throughout the town that the American had brought them a marvelous addition to their diet. Robinson shared his recipe and cooking technique with a number of housewives reinforcing his initial popularity based on his friendliness and good looks. Fritters became the rage and then turned into a Batopilas staple.[3]

During John's stay, he was probably surprised at the depth of religious belief in the community but none too impressed. On May 30, Corpus Christi Day, following a special Mass at the run-down cathedral, the parishioners sang hymns as they carried a heavy statue of Christ from the cathedral, located near the Hacienda Pastrana, to the civic plaza and then back again. They held their Savior firmly in place with parallel beams held up by four of the men, two in the front and two in the rear. They stopped every fifty yards or so and fresh participants replaced the tired bearers without lowering the sacred image. John took no notice of the ceremony.

In addition to Church calendar holidays, religious ceremonies celebrated special events, people, or Church undertakings. One such ceremony paid homage to La Misión, the Jesuit missionary effort undertaken in the Sierra Tarahumara some 250 years earlier. In the parishioners' view, the missionaries had devoted their lives to bringing the word of God to the people of the world and to the Barranca del Cobre. The whiteness of their Saint Mary of Mount Carmel (Santa María del Carmen), the protectress of the town; and their veneration of Saints Anthony and Michael, after whom they named their outlying mining complexes, and Saint Peter, the founder of the Roman Catholic Church and for whom the town was named, gave a sense of how they defined themselves and the deep effect of European and Catholic influence.

They believed that San Antonio represented education against the hosts of darkness and savagery in addition to his better-known role as a protector and lover of children. Many Batopilas residents at that time shared the more generalized belief of the Mexican elites that the cave-dwelling Raramuris and violent Apaches and Yaquis represented those very forces in their midst, as did the bandits of the barrancas. The miners especially worshipped Saint Anthony, the patrón saint of their profession, while they held San Miguel, the Archangel, in special esteem because he protected humanity from evil forces. The saints encouraged them and created an alternate reality as they genuflected at the mine entrances before entering the darkness. But Miguel's place in the cathedral was also warranted, given the continuous challenge presented by hostile Apaches and bandits.

The ceremonies reinforced the batopilenses' deeply held religious beliefs. The most common ceremony commemorated beloved members of the community on the first anniversary of their deaths. Seeking blessings for a deceased neighbor or family member, mestizo and Indian (Yaqui, Mayo, and Raramuri) men, women, and children paraded the

The archangel Saint Michael in his role as defender against the forces of evil and darkness. (From the author's collection)

Saint Anthony in his role as protector of miners. (From the author's collection)

three miles from the settlement at La Junta to the cathedral. Dressed simply, some of them in rags and barefoot, and bearing the wooden image of Christ, they would sing of their belief in the Trinity, the Virgin, and the relief that followed the suffering and pain of death. Typically, the priest would greet them in front of the cathedral and tell them they were "welcome in this place of God." The pilgrims would then sing yet another sweet song of devotion and enter the cathedral, still bearing their Savior, which they would place a third of the way toward the altar, where it would remain during a special Mass.

As a businessman, John must have worried about the loss of workdays: in 1861, the batopilenses celebrated some ninety to a hundred saint's days, which they observed as work holidays. Inherited from Mexico's past and reinforced by isolation and poverty, these precapitalist observances conflicted dramatically with his economic ambitions. During his short initial visit, Robinson noticed that Corpus Christi was a labor holiday, which even included fasting. He would find that, combined with alcohol-related incapacitation on Mondays, absenteeism among mine workers because of religious observances during the week would create a serious challenge to the smooth operation of his capitalist enterprise.[4]

To some extent, Robinson understood the problems of the Batopilas mines even before he arrived. As a Wells Fargo and railroad superintendent, he had witnessed the larger issues that faced the silver mining industry in the American West. During his first trip to Batopilas, he carefully noted the labor arrangements and manner of operations at the mines his party had encountered while in the Sierra Madre, as well as the mine operators' responses to the challenge of realizing the potential of their holdings in an almost inaccessible wilderness. In the cases of the San Miguel and San Antonio mining complexes, that potential included some of the richest veins of silver in the world.

The problems of mining at Batopilas, however, only began with a lack of owner capitalization, tools, and mining know-how. Of the two principal mine operators, only Ramírez lived in Batopilas, and he had never been a miner. (John had even located a rich vein for Lebrun in the latter's own mine.) Lebrun resided at Álamos, a far more comfortable mining and mercantile center in the western foothills of the sierra, forty miles away as the crow flies but a three-day trek from Batopilas over rugged mountain trails.

While Lebrun had some business contacts in the outside world, they fell far short of what was needed to guarantee stable prices and bring the mines to their full potential. Lebrun, recognizing the problems and possibilities of what would later be called the Mexican Comstock, wanted to sell some of his properties while keeping a few claims around the rich Pastrana and Cata veins of the San Miguel complex. In the short term, these would provide him with steady income through a mix of gambusinos, free wage laborers, and rentals to other operators. In the longer term, if Robinson turned Batopilas into a bonanza, Lebrun would have a share of it.

Later, during the 1870s, Robinson acquired additional mining properties from Lebrun. He visited Álamos in order to purchase some but not all of the Frenchman's remaining Pastrana and Cata holdings. The lack of witnesses from Batopilas and detailed descriptions of the acquisitions would lead to disputes over ownership with Shepherd in future decades. Meanwhile, John did not disturb the gambusinos and renters who still worked at those sites, the old ways continuing alongside the new ones characterized by wage laborers or peons.

Ramírez, in contrast to John's sophistication, had little knowledge of the outside business world. He and Lebrun owned some mines separately and others in tandem. Ramírez, as the resident partner and caretaker, jealously guarded his properties, but neither he nor Lebrun could do much to modernize or vertically integrate operations. As a result, the partners lost a lot of money in the production and marketing process. Undercapitalization meant costly labor-intensive mining and milling. At some mines, Lebrun and Ramírez hired peons (servile laborers), but usually they had to use the more skilled and expensive gambusinos because most of the miners demanded that arrangement, and labor was scarce.

The gambusinos and peons worked by candlelight in the mines. Their labor was costly because they loosened the solid mass "in the most primitive manner, drilling with bars, and blasting with gunpowder." Then, using picks and shovels, they loaded it onto carts and used a *malacate* (windlass) to pull it out of the shaft. In the vertical extractions from the ever-deepening pits, Yaqui, Mayo, and Tarahumara *tamenes* (carriers) hauled the ore in packs supported by the forehead via a strap and their backs. These loads weighed up to seventy-five pounds. The laborers then performed the first phase of reduction, using stones instead of hammers, on esplanades at the mine entrances "to pound the ore until it was reduced to the size of beans."

Following that success, they carried the ore to an *arrastra*, a round construction about ten feet in diameter" with a stone-and-cement floor and elevated sides made of the same material as an outer rim. A yoked mule, tied by a rope to a heavy vertical post in the center of the arrastra, walked in circles pulling a grinding stone that crushed the pellets into powder. The workers then shoveled the ore onto another esplanade, where salt was added to the pile and thoroughly mixed with the powder by the trampling of bare feet. Next the laborers spread out the mass and allowed it a *repaso* (rest) for one day. The most dangerous step in the process ensued when the workers added mercury (quicksilver) to the mass. The mercury came from the canyons near Batopilillas, a Raramuri town in the Sierra Madre about 100 miles north of Batopilas. The workers mixed it into the ore, where it attached to the silver. In previous eras, they had mixed the mercury with the ore with their bare feet, a practice that led to agonizing deaths years and sometimes only months later.

Next, they placed the mulch in an agitation tank about six feet deep by ten feet wide. They ran water across the top of the mass from a neighboring water tank, a step called *lavado* (washing), while a mule, again attached to a strong vertical post, walked in circles and turned agitators inside the tank. The water and the separated pyrite and silica exited a hole in the tank, while the heavier mercury-silver amalgam sank to the bottom. After draining off the water by opening ever-lower holes in the side of the tank, which caused it to carry off additional quantities of loose soil, the refiners took what remained out by hand and carried it to a trough, where it was washed until only the combined mercury and silver remained. Lavado, because of the precious metal lost in the operation, was the most serious inefficiency in the entire refining process.

The metal was then placed in strong, finely porous bags and beaten with paddles in order for the quicksilver to run out. The workers then placed the remaining amalgam in vats with heavy lids and exhaust holes on the side enveloped with water and started fires under them. The mercury vaporized, exited the outlets, condensed and settled to the bottom of the water to be used again. Exposure to mercury, especially in a vapor-ized state, was extremely dangerous. "The silver was then taken out and molded into bars."

During the processing, the owners lost about one-half of the silver content, creating slag heaps of considerable value, which could be re-worked later, when methods of extraction improved. The runoff of min-ing chaff, however, contained mercury, when it entered the Río Batopilas just downstream from the hacienda. Therefore drinking and irrigation water should have been always obtained upstream from the point of entry. That, however, was not the case. Some batopilenses did not understand the aggregate effects of mercury poisoning and the four-mile distance downstream to the next settlement at Satevo did little to dilute the pollu-tants. The effluent undoubtedly affected the health of the people in Satevo—accounting for its near abandonment—and, to a lesser degree, the residents of Choix and other towns toward the Pacific Coast.

After the ore had been refined at the Hacienda San Miguel, the smel-ter workers melted it into ingots and loaded them on mules. In addition, they often shipped native silver in untreated chunks and sheets. The sure-footed animals then carried the silver out of the wilderness to the Pacific littoral because Batopilas was in the far western part of the Sierra Tara-humara and steamships offered rapid connections with the world market. Lebrun and Ramírez could not handle the export process because they had no buyers abroad. Thus they sold the ore to brokers. Those middle-men, headquartered in the port city of Mazatlán and in the smaller towns along the Sinaloan coastline, provided their own mule skinners (*arrieros*) for transportation. They relieved Ramírez and Lebrun of the risk of ban-dits robbing the mule trains of their cargo and also found foreign buyers, but they exacted a high price. They paid Lebrun and Ramírez only 50 percent of the world market price for their silver by weight.

John felt he could readily solve the production, transportation, and marketing problems. His plan included the renovation of the mining equipment and arrastras to increase the rate of ore extraction from the mines and the level of silver extraction from the ore. This included new hand tools, sluices, aqueducts, arrastras, and settling ponds. Then he would create his own transport system, hiring his own mule skinners and protection from the bandits all the way to Mazatlán. From there, he and his partners would secure the Pacific Mail Steamship Company and others to provide discounted cartage rates on ships capable of hauling the extremely heavy cargos to the new U.S. Mint at San Francisco. Finally, the raw silver would be converted into currency and stored by the Wells Fargo Bank, which could hold the ingots or coins for the best market opportunities and then transport the silver safely across the United States to New York or the Pacific Ocean. His partners already had customers in Korea, China, and India, and they enjoyed the low cartage rates consistent with the Wells Fargo Bank directors' leadership role in the shipping industry.

When John arrived in Batopilas, he carried the cash needed to purchase the Hacienda San Miguel and its mines. In his negotiations with Ramírez, Lebrun and a less important group of owners, the Ochoa brothers, who lived in Guadalupe y Calvo, a mining town sixty miles to the south, he was careful not to share the details of the enormous potential for profit through vertical integration. The Mexican owners could not imagine the effect that new tools, such as giant shears for cutting sheets of native silver and large sledgehammers for smashing ore rocks, new arrastras and refining equipment, and the network of modern shipping and outside support would have on profits.

On May 25, Robinson bought not only the San Miguel mine group and hacienda but also the San Antonio complex on the hacienda side of the river and upstream from both it and Batopilas. The price, a mere 27,700 pesos, included $4,000 for the Ochoa Brothers, $1,200 for personal property, and $1,200 in agent fees for his intermediary in Guadalupe y Calvo. Since in direct transactions a peso valued slightly less than a dollar in those days, the price he paid was less than 60 percent of the $50,000 advanced by his partners for the purchase of the San Miguel mines alone. It should be noted, however, that Lebrun and Ramírez understood the sale to consist of most of the mine shafts but not all of them. That discrepancy would become apparent some two decades later.[5]

Ramírez had figured Robinson out, well in advance of the sale of the mines, as a hard-driving American businessman bent on profits. He hoped that Robinson would get along well with the local folk, and he wanted to facilitate that outcome. His ambitions, however, were only partially fulfilled. With the passage of time, Robinson and his surviving son would integrate to a greater degree with the regional elites of northwestern Mexico than with the locals. Meanwhile, Ramírez and his sons maintained a friendly relationship and provided a solid basis of communications between John and the local business community. The enduring friendships of the Robinson and Ramírez families and the ensuing marriages of Robinson's surviving son, Charles Sherman Robinson, to heiress Carmen Torres at nearby Choix in 1875 and of his grandson Charles Robinson with Ester Terrazas, the granddaughter and principal heiress of General Terrazas, demonstrated the depth of American and regional elite integration and the limits of intimacy with the local folk. Some of the working-class citizenry of the barrancas, meanwhile, would grow to resent Robinson's wealth and power and contribute mightily to his final departure.[6]

After concluding the purchase agreement with Ramírez, Lebrun, and the Ochoas, John set off for the United States to make arrangements for supplies and exports, leaving Asher and the engineers and supervisors who had come with them to supervise the initiation of production. Under a Mexican government mining export permit, John and his partners would not have to pay federal taxes on the silver they exported, other than token duties imposed at the port of Mazatlán, for the next decade. How the American impresario obtained the permit, whether as a concession in purchasing the mines, through the firm of Belden and Stearns, or from the appropriate officials in Mexico City, is unclear.

Robinson returned to the United States via Mazatlán, where he stopped over before sailing to San Francisco. Robinson chose that port for his exports and imports because it was a regular stopping place for ships of the Pacific Mail Steamship Company and other oceangoing vessels. It offered the deepest channel on the Sea of Cortez, had a large warehouse facility, and was the most modernized. Those advantages were complemented by the notably lax tax impositions made by local federal officials, who accepted personal donations in lieu of tax payments.[7]

John lived in Batopilas for extended periods from 1861 until the late 1870s, directly supervising operations on behalf of the BMC's owners. In addition to his prowess in long-term planning, Robinson demonstrated a high level of social skills. During his first trip, he befriended the leading businessmen and miners of Chihuahua, including MacManus and Terrazas, and then the local leaders along the trail from the state capital to Batopilas. Once there, he achieved the same level of acceptance from local leaders, who sought both profit and civic improvement from him.

He consistently took his American compatriots and mestizo workers to task when they did not perform up to his high standards. Meanwhile, he continued to ignore the Raramuris, even those working at the mines and hacienda, and never recognized the rich diversity of their culture.

John's blending of capital resources, technology, politics, and transportation and marketing infrastructure was crucial to the project's successful beginning. During the 1860s, he chose two experienced miners from Batopilas, Jorge Hernández and Achilles Morris, to serve as foremen in charge of the two crews assigned the task of exploring for new deposits of native silver and "pay dirt" and of working the already discovered deposits. Both crews would work the older deposits when more silver was needed to fully load the Conducta.

During the 1870s, John and his partners recruited George Hearst, Lloyd Tevis, and James Ben Ali Haggin to the Batopilas Mining Company. Veterans of the Comstock Lode and Anaconda mine, these men had substantial real estate holdings in San Francisco, the San Joaquin Valley, New Mexico, and Chihuahua. Alongside Ashbel and Danford Barney, the three men would provide Robinson with much-needed financial backing, Tevis through his control of Wells Fargo in the 1870s and Hearst and Haggin as major investors. Haggin would later join New York financiers J. P. Morgan, James Stillman, and George Baker in enormous copper mining operations in Chile and Peru. Between 1861 and 1879, the Batopilas Mining Company would make an enormous amount of money. But health conditions at Batopilas and continued political strife throughout Mexico would turn Robinson's life there into a nightmare.

An Ordeal for Both Sides

Robinson's dreams of great wealth in Batopilas quickly turned into the utmost tragedy. On September 24, 1861, his son Asher, who had stayed on in the mining town to oversee operations while his father returned to New York, died of typhoid fever. Robinson received the bad news only a short time after returning to the United States. The following year, on June 12, James Willshire Robinson, who went to Batopilas to replace his brother, also died of typhoid.

Both brothers almost certainly contracted the disease from contaminated food or water. The effects of the typhoid bacterium (*Salmonella typhi*) are devastating. Victims first experience aches and pains as the wall of the small intestine becomes infected. In the second week, typhoid bacteria infect the spleen and lymph nodes, causing loss of appetite, nausea, and distension of the belly. A fever of 104 to 105 degrees sets in, accompanied by diarrhea. From the lymph nodes, the bacteria pass through the bloodstream to the liver, gall bladder, and bone marrow. Victims usually die an agonizing death when their intestines burst.

Ridding their town of typhoid fever was one of many changes the batopilenses sought to bring about by attracting American capitalists. Although unsure of its exact causes, they had long since concluded that the disease was connected with their drinking water. Ramírez, a leading merchant and political figure in Batopilas who saw Robinson as a source of both personal and community enrichment, stood at the center of a movement to bring improvements to the municipality. Chief among these was the construction of an aqueduct to bring in water from the river well above the populated area of the barranca. Ramírez also wanted to build a sewage disposal system to carry human waste to a point well outside the town and to renovate the run-down buildings on the main plaza, including the school-jail. He and other town leaders welcomed Robinson as a source of the capital needed to make these improvements and to bring greater overall prosperity to Batopilas.

The relationships established between the elites of Batopilas and Robinson reflected similar relationships established across Mexico after General Díaz seized power in 1876 (and indeed across Central America and the Caribbean in the late nineteenth century). The sale of Mexican assets by well-placed politicians and elites to wealthy Americans capable of enriching the few at the expense of the many became national policy.

John's efforts and accomplishments upon first coming to Batapilas reinforced the town leaders' hopes and earned him their good will. When a pharmacist opened for business soon afterward, Robinson's presence was given partial credit for that as well.

Ramírez would serve as *jefe político* (district head) until his death in December 1882. With their $10,000 share from the sale of the mines, he and his sons lived in opulence. Enlarging and creating sumptuous houses, they bought up large tracts of range and farmland, which went for pennies an acre in the barrancas at that time, while continuing their roles as respectable merchants. They solidified their relationship with Robinson by enlisting their friends in Mazatlán to help him with shipping, warehousing, and customs arrangements and with securing government permits and licenses. More important, they served as his allies in the many confrontations with local miners, bandits, and rebels that would ensue.[8]

The batopilenses received Robinson with high hopes because he represented the redevelopment of the mines. The local citizens and Ramírez took him at his word and their imaginations did the rest:

> They envisioned the investment of millions of silver pesos in the mines along with the opening of wide, well-built roads crossing the rocky divides and chasms to the outside world. The silver would pay for palatial mansions, provide the basis for the establishment of a mint and bank, steam-powered energy, and support a local drama company as well as visiting theater groups. The [now flourishing batopilenses] would take trips lasting several days into the picturesque and beautiful mountains, build comfortable and well-furnished houses, lack no conveniences, and enjoy the sweet sound of music.
>
> They would create a place comparable to the fantastic palaces of Las Hadas (the Arabian Nights). Everyone would employ several well-paid domestic servants attired in elegant uniforms. Their [spending], in turn, would represent even more wealth. The batopilenses would also own magnificent thoroughbred horses. In other words, they would enjoy an eternal oriental paradise.[9]

In this settled place, everyone would be baptized, married in church, and educated. The antithesis of this dream would be a mining boomtown.

Everyday Forms of Making Money

John initially shared the batopilenses' big ideas for the mining of the fabulous silver lode he had acquired. But, as it turned out, the extraction of the wealth entailed virtually no major investment at the site, and the deaths of two sons early in the endeavor undoubtedly changed his outlook. He was able to keep his costs down by extracting native silver from extensive surface deposits; removed from cleavages in the rock with large levers and shears, the sometimes massive strips did not require much on-site refining. The batopilenses, not finding large-scale employment, lacked the sovereign power to impose levies that would give them a share in the profits.

In some first steps, Robinson, his engineers, and supervisors took advantage of the shady copses and springs to establish rest areas for the men working in the nearby mines, with shacks for those exploring undeveloped areas. They also hired men to excavate the sand deposits at the junction of the rivers to provide the cement necessary for arrastras, sluices, and a three-mile-long aqueduct from La Junta to the San Miguel Tunnel, and settling ponds and buildings at the Hacienda San Miguel. They also constructed a smaller waterway between the San Antonio mines and the hacienda, which were across the river from Batopilas. The men who performed these tasks were largely *jornaleros* (day laborers), not the semi-independent gambusinos.

The American engineers rationalized production through technology and labor reform and continued the process with the excavation of two tunnels, one reaching 1,172 feet under the San Antonio mines, and the other extending 689 feet under the Pastrana and Cata veins. Historically, the Pastrana was the greatest producer of native silver in the region, but like the other veins, it had been mined too deep for profitable extraction. The tunnel allowed the miners to dig upward and extract the ore by moving it downhill. Then they built large arrastras made of cement and stone at the mouths of the tunnels to crush the rocks. That reduced the weight of the ore that had to be moved to the hacienda by at least 50 percent.

They used new large hammers to break up the ore outside the tunnels and upstream between the San Miguel Tunnel and La Junta. Then they used a sluice and aqueduct to move it as much as three miles to the San Miguel Tunnel entrance, where they subjected it to grinding at the new arrastra, sifted it, and loaded the concentrates on burros and mules for the one-mile trip downstream and across the swing bridge that spanned the river to the even larger arrastras at the Hacienda San Miguel.

The American improvements in transporting the ore from the points of production back to the Hacienda San Miguel began when the workers at the San Miguel complex placed floats in the stone-and-cement aqueduct that carried the ore downstream to the hacienda smelter. Then John ordered an even larger and longer aqueduct on the Batopilas side of the river. This aqueduct, which would be enlarged and lengthened later, extended from a point upstream near La Junta some two and one-half miles to the arrastra at the mouth of the San Miguel Tunnel. The workers then broke up the rocks and placed the ore on mule carts, and the animals hauled it across the river to the refining site at the San Miguel Hacienda.

The Hacienda San Miguel's processing equipment remained small and obsolete by the enormous scale and cutting-edge standards being employed in the silver mines of the American West, but with modest improvements to the arrastras and settling areas, it was good enough to handle the high-quality ore coming from the mines.

Robinson only minimally changed the refining process, now pouring the ore into wider cement arrastras, in which a pair of mules, rather than one, hauled a much larger grinding wheel in seemingly endless circles. The workers moved the powder to a shallow cement pool, where they added water and salt, making it a doughy mass in the old manner. The salt ate at the pyrite deposits in the silver. After allowing the mud to settle for one day in the traditional repaso, they added more water, washing away the loose earth and the salt. The removal of the pyrites gave the silver a cleaner appearance, but many of the impurities remained on the now more-visible metal. To separate the other metals, they still added mercury. The most important change then took place. They replaced the vats where heated water boiled out the remaining salts and pyrites and separated the mercury-silver amalgam. Now pressurized boilers operating at unprecedented high temperatures brought about a higher level of purity. This last step, although faster and achieving superior results, was primitive in comparison to the enormous boilers used by smelter workers in the American West.

The larger-scale refinement and improved technology achieved a 64 percent improvement in the silver retention rate, but the improved method still lost 18 percent of the valuable metal. The silver was then placed in small ovens made of iron and steel imported from the United States The smelter workers used hand-operated bellows placed on one end of each firebox to send air into the chamber in order to increase the heat and more quickly render the molten mineral into dies for 75-pound ingots. Significantly for Batopilas, the new motor-driven technology that would save even more time, revolutionize capacity, and retain the 18 percent of the metals still being lost would not be introduced until the 1880s. The Batopilas refiners largely ignored second-class ore.[10]

Utopian dreams faded fast for the batopilenses as mining realities set in during the course of the 1860s and 1870s. Batopilas stretched along the river for well over a mile, but for most of its length it was less than fifty yards wide. The houses along the narrow upper reaches of town were exposed to cart and horse traffic over dirt roads from early morning until after dark. Flies swarmed over animal dung in the road and seemed to proliferate in the stifling heat, which soared over 100 degrees for five months of the year.

The small downtown area was somewhat more hospitable but still primitive. Until the late 1870s, only one water pipe, extending from the aqueduct running from La Junta to the San Miguel Tunnel, bypassed the pollution exuding from the Hacienda San Miguel and reached the center of town. To a considerable extent, the townspeople depended on well water. The masonry buildings, small shops, and dozen or so multiroom houses alone could not provide the local elites with the conveniences of civilized life that they wanted. Some owners of multiroom dwellings provided room and board to miners but most of the miners and the smelter workers earned too little to afford such extravagance. The small shopkeepers and semiprofessionals barely lived better than the miners. One found elegance only at the Hacienda Pastrana, the Ramírez residence, and in a few other homes. The public school cum jail and the civic building maintained a run-down appearance. Only a few structures featured cornices, perhaps a legacy of the wealth that had come to the town during previous bonanzas.

Despite its beautiful locale, Batopilas presented a miserable spectacle during the Robinson era. The number of shacks along the waterfront and the edges of town somewhat increased, occupied by miners, prostitutes, half-starved transients, and Raramuris. These sights could not help but inure the mining engineers and other professionals who visited the place to its social malaise. Under Robinson, dozens of miners found employment and better conditions in the short run, but as we shall see, the long-term prognosis, even for them, was not good. The miners and marginalized populace had little hope for material betterment between bonanzas, and the zones they inhabited could not help but shock and force a sense of resignation upon the newcomer.

During the 1860s and 1870s, a multicultural population emerged, comprising a few Americans and Tarahumara, hundreds of Mexicans, and a scattering of Chinese, Europeans, and Africans. Some of the more commercial-minded among the small Chinese population began to offer laundry and small-scale retail services. They presented an image of working hard and charging high prices, while living largely separate from the rest of the population. In the larger towns in the Mexican north, the *pequeña burgesa* Chinese merchants maintained even more isolation from the miners. While this strategy helped maintain a degree of Chinese cultural integrity, it caused the Mexican workers to view them with distrust as price gougers.[11]

The presence of children of mixed Asian, African, European, Mexican, and indigenous lineage, however, provided incontrovertible evidence to John and other observers that romance and prostitution in this isolated place transcended ethnic and cultural barriers. The process of racial mixing offered a microcosm of Mexico at large.

The Mexicans, like the Americans, also held stereotypical ideas about the identities of the Africans and British newcomers and about the Tarahumaras who came to Batopilas as residents. They noted that the Africans "strutted about" and were "arrogant," prone to crime and to the use of prostitutes. They deemed the British to be arrogant as well but skilled and withdrawn in haughty isolation, highly intelligent, and selective in their choices of the young women with whom they chose to have sexual relations. The Americans bewildered the batopilenses by fulfilling all of the partial images earned by the other outside groups, while John's son Charles married into one of the richest families in northern Mexico. Robinson eased the negative reactions among the local population by continuing to offer medical services and the espousal of progress toward a more civilized way of life. The batopilenses' disappointment with Robinson was that he did not do enough.

Others of the In Between

The Raramuris who stayed for part of the year at Batopilas presented a sense of the "wild" and hunted. Many of them feared the Americans, Mexicans, and other outsiders in their territory, and for good reason. In 1909, author and tourism promoter T. Philip Terry revealed the situation that had evolved around them when he attempted to explain the virtues of military action against hostile Native Americans in Chihuahua:

It was not until about 1830 that the Mexican army awoke to the necessity of inflicting severe reprisals on these red degenerates. By the proyecto de guerra (war project) of 1837 the state government offered a bounty of $100 for every Indian warrior's scalp, and $50 for that of a squaw. This proyecto had the effect of promptly lessening the number of [savages] in the region . . . and when the bounty for a buck's scalp was raised to $250 the Apaches decided that life in Chihuahua was not conducive to Indian longevity.[12]

In 1870, while "Indian hunting" was still going on in Chihuahua, Ignacio Pesqueira, the governor of the neighboring state of Sonora, offered a 100-peso bounty for Apache scalps. Because no one could tell the difference between Apache, Yaqui, Raramuri, or other Native American scalps, and because ruthless bounty hunters were everywhere, life for the Tarahumaras in the Sierra Madre became at least as dangerous as travel by white men and mestizos in the territory of hostile Apaches and Comanches.

The Raramuris, caught in the beginnings of cultural, economic, and political change, reacted in multiple ways. In the higher parts of the mountains, they continued to live in the isolation that had served them so well in the past. They entered the lower and hotter climate near Batopilas in search of economic survival. In doing that, they lived on the margins of the local economy. They built small one-room jacales (shacks), covering about 100 square feet each, along the riverbanks and hillsides, above the town, made of branches at no cost. Single men with only a few belongings resided in even smaller shacks, some of which were only wide enough to accommodate their bodies when lying down or when crouched. Those dwellings provided adequate air movement to relieve the buildup of heat.

They also maintained a mix of pre-Columbian and more modern Mexican implements in and around their homes. They continued to use pottery fashioned and fired through traditional means and tools made of stone, wood, and flint. Only a few cooking utensils were made from iron and steel. They still employed bows and arrows, native poisons for the killing of rattlesnakes, and herbal remedies for a wide range of internal and contagious maladies. The remedies were usually as effective as the contemporary medicines offered by John and the Mexican pharmacist.

Some of the Raramuris still placed their cooking materials, tools, and riding equipment in sequence and pointed at the deities that appeared in the night sky and at the morning sun to pay them proper homage

A Raramuri family, circa 1890. (Photograph by Carl Lumholtz; courtesy of the American Museum of Natural History, New York)

and preclude bad luck brought by way of supernatural resentments. Others, in the midst of transformations that occur through natural encounters and overlapping narratives, were beginning to view these reverences as inconsequential. In a step toward *mestizaje*, Tarahumara spouses of mestizo men, and their offspring, accepted and employed crucifixes in their living quarters. On Sundays, saint's days, and the death dates of family and pueblo members many Raramuris attended services at the cathedral in Batopilas.

Most Tarahumaras in and around Batopilas still participated in the indigenous religious celebrations that sometimes went on for days. They still drank tesquino on these occasions and experienced outbreaks of violence. Stabbings and fights were not restricted to the drunks, but inebriates sometimes attacked women and children. The corporal punishment of children remained the norm in the rancherías. In Batopilas, the police simply threw Tarahumaras in jail when they exhibited extreme intoxication. The punishment for more serious crimes was often severe, but the details are not known.

During the lengthy hot season, the women wore modest garments, whereas the men dressed in breeches, and young children were often naked. When living with their men, the Raramuri women in and around Batopilas tended to be reclusive from the rest of the population. Some of them, however, worked as maids, lived in Mexican homes, and learned the higher standards of rural Mexican household hygiene. The mothers tended their children closely through infancy, but then, like their mestizo counterparts, they expected daughters to contribute by cleaning, while sons ran errands, gathered fuel, and tended animals. The less fortunate among the Tarahumaras in Batopilas suffered and died from typhoid, alcoholism, and dysentery. Venereal disease associated with prostitution acted too slowly to affect life expectancy.

Many of the Tarahumaras worked hard when they found the opportunity, but most chose to do so for only short periods of time. Although some of them remained after acquiring experience as jornaleros in the mines, the others left Batopilas in the spring to plant their crops and to escape the rising temperatures. The Tarahumara population around Batopilas was in constant flux, with some assimilating to town life and others leaving, returning to their settlements in the high country. Those who remained in town comprised two groups: the majority found employment as domestics or industrial laborers; a minority became addicted to alcohol and resorted to begging, petty crime, and both female and male prostitution.

When Robinson and his men hiked into the high country surrounding the barrancas, they encountered the Raramuri pueblos and rancherías.

The pueblos, more highly developed than mere settlements, and their elites governed areas with about a fifteen-mile radius in which several rancherías or smaller communities were found. The population of these places lived in small clusters of houses surrounded by more dispersed dwellings in such a manner that each could have a parcel of land adjacent to it. Each pueblo had an administrative center comprising all the symbols of civilization, a church, courthouse, and jail.

The people in the rancherías, sometimes scattered over several miles on a linear basis to accommodate the terrain, usually convened at the center for religious festivals that combined tesquino consumption and dancing, in order to adjudicate disputes, organize work projects, meet their friends and relatives, and attend the frequent footraces that the people enjoyed so much.

A hunter led the participants in the Yumari dance that was performed at the conclusion of festivals. The Yumari and Tutugari dances dated back to before the arrival of Europeans in America. The Tutugari was performed along with chants evoking magic. A better-known dance, the Matachines, introduced during the colonial period, had clear Christian linkages. It involved colorful costumes and was performed more frequently during festivals than the others.

Robinson found that the stories of Tarahumara long-distance running exploits were substantially true. During their footraces, the Raramuri usually ran from two to twelve miles, kicking a wooden ball in front of them, but a longer race could continue for a day and a night. Many of the races involved relay teams, and they bet beads, cloth, blankets, goats, and other animals on the outcomes. In the shorter races, run for speed, the contestants sometimes wore feathers. The macaw and peacock were preferred. The competitors ran across the mountains at altitudes of 6,000 feet and above. At the beginning of each race, the headman of the county-like *municipio*, the *gobernador*, spoke, underscoring the importance of the event and warning the contestants not to touch the ball with their hands.

The women also raced each other, but in their case a wooden stick was used to strike or otherwise impel forward a ball or a hoop made from maguey. The pueblo hosts wanted to win these races badly, and so they often employed a certain amount of deception against their opponents, usually from a neighboring district. One trick was the placement of animal bones on the trail, the spirits of which weakened the visiting competitors when they inadvertently stepped on them. Sixty years later, in 1926, three Raramuris demonstrated their abilities to the world in an exhibition race by running sixty miles in nine hours. In the 1928 Olympic Games at Amsterdam, two Tarahumaras complained that the twenty-six-mile marathon was too short. They ran second and third and lost by three minutes. Robinson employed Raramuris for the carrying of messages out of the barrancas and over the mountains.

The Tarahumara, like their Huasteco brethren in the Sierra Madre Oriental (Eastern Sierra Madre), used a variation of the slash-and-burn system in their farming. The nitrogen derived from the burning and their goats and cattle provided fertilizer. After clearing an area and burning the rubbish, they built a fence around it. The fence was usually made with a combination of cacti, rocks, and branches. They worked the land using wooden and a few metal-tipped plows and the *coa* (digging stick), planting maize and the small granular beans that do well in the harsh climate and poor soil.

In the more prosperous Raramuri pueblos, a pair of oxen might be shared by the inhabitants, but in most places the indigenous people did not have that convenience and had to break up the rugged and dry land on their own. In either case, as many as ten to fifteen Tarahumaras formed work parties and prepared one field at a time using six-day workweeks while moving from one site to the next, until all were plowed and seeded. They employed the same cooperative method when harvesting. Fertilized by animal manure, a new field could last for many years. Many of the Raramuris repeated this practice with some frequency because they were seasonal nomadic agriculturalists, living in the high country in the summer and in the canyons or near Batopilas in the winter. Many of them needed several residential sites to support their high level of mobility.

Those who went into the high country for the summer made their jacales of small boards and sticks, as was done around Batopilas. They built the shacks and the cabins in the open, surrounded by the dusty, cleared land. Those who chose to stay in the colder climes for the winter, however, built the standard one-room log cabins with steeply sloped roofs found elsewhere in the sierra. Above Batopilas and less often elsewhere, they reserved a small space alongside the house for dining, work, and even dancing. Adjacent to their living quarters, the Tarahumara in the highlands and sometimes the canyon bottoms built one or two bins for the storage of grain. These were tightly sealed to keep out rodents. The violation of the food storage bins by an unauthorized individual constituted a grave crime because they lived in chronic food shortages. The Raramuri authorities saved their most severe punishments for these miscreants, imposing public whippings, incarceration, or banishment.

With their limited food choices, the Tarahumara made maize their staple. In difficult times, they ate the lowest-quality grain, "Indian corn," which was otherwise fed to the livestock. They also ground and toasted high-grade corn and mixed it with water or dehydrated it into a long-lasting cake called *pinole*, which they complemented with beans, wild greens, herbs, and a limited amount of goat meat. *Esquiate*, a soup of corn and a few pieces of goat or cattle meat, somewhat like the heartier pork and hominy dish Mexicans outside the barrancas call *posole*, was the dinnertime favorite. Native drinks included the ubiquitous atole, made by boiling pinole, and the highly intoxicating corn beer tesquino. Cattle consumption was reserved for special occasions. When the summer ended, some remained in the settlement to wait out the cold weather in their log cabins. A larger number migrated toward the cave dwellings in the canyons, while a few moved to Batopilas, Urique or to cliff dwellings, usually overhangs that the Tarahumaras enclosed with rock walls.

They arranged the marriages of their children, with the groom paying the value of his bride-to-be by presenting goats to her father. As recently as 1980, a young man working in Batopilas from the small settlement of Yerbabuena, located in the mountains nearby, told me he paid eighty goats for his bride. He saved the money from his work and military service in Chihuahua City. Despite cooperative work practices, individuals held private properties in a community. Private ownership included pots, tools, weapons, clothing, fruit trees, and animals in addition to land. In the rare cases of divorce, the former partners took back what had been theirs before the union and divided the new acquisitions.

The deceased left their belongings to specific individuals or family elders, and the community authorities adjudicated disputes. When unmarried persons died, their belongings were given to the closest surviving relatives. Meanwhile, the Raramuri neonatal mortality rate ran well above 80 percent, and a large but unknown number of women found death as a result of their unremitting cycle of childbirths. Only a small minority of either gender lived beyond fifty. In Batopilas, they left little, if anything, to mark their passage.

The traditionalists buried their dead in caves in the area, whereas the more Christianized placed the deceased in cemeteries. These choices and the rituals that followed were a highly sophisticated manner of mourning helping the living through their period of grief and reverently dealing with the feared spirits of the dead. When a person died, he or she was wrapped in a blanket and placed in repose within the house. The mourners placed a crucifix or small wooden cross in the folded hands of the deceased that rested on the breast. The mourners then maintained a small fire near the head of the corpse with a one-foot-high cross, draped with a rosary of Job's tears, standing on the dirt floor immediately behind or to the side. "The dead person's important possessions are stacked near the cross along with a symbolic offering of three or four grains of maize for a man or a woman respectfully placed in a bowl or pouch." Sometimes the mourners added pinole or other foods to the offering. After one day of lying in state, the deceased was carried, while lashed to a pole, to the cemetery, still wrapped in the blanket. At the gravesite, the mourners recited prayers, removed the pole, and lowered the body into the earth.

The mourners took great care in these procedures because the spirits of the dead were watching. Indeed, the spirits of the dead hovered near the graves for months until they were "helped along on their long journey to heaven" by a cycle of four funeral fiestas for women and three for men. The bereaved held the first fiesta to placate the spirits of the dead on the third or fourth day after death. The second fiesta came three or four weeks later and the third in the third or fourth month. The fourth fiesta, for women only, came in the eighth month.

Failure to commemorate the dead carefully and with reverence was unthinkable. The Tarahumara knew that it led to disaster when irreverent individuals failed to meet their obligations to the departed. The rituals, however, involved much more than remembrance ceremonies. First, the bereaved had to feel and demonstrate the deepest possible grief for the departed while they purified the habitation and belongings of the dead person with the help of a shaman. In doing this, they chanted prayers and songs. The drinking of intoxicants including tesquino helped the celebrants through this difficult experience.

On some of the ninety to a hundred saint's days observed yearly and on other commemorative occasions, the Raramuris at Yerbabuena and at other sites in the Copper Canyon complex gathered to drink their own homemade intoxicants. The Jesuit missionaries, who arrived in the region during the late sixteenth century, had altered Christian practices and celebrations to accommodate those of the Tarahumara in order to get their message across. They compromised to get them to accept Jesus Christ as their Savior and Mary as his Virgin Mother, and many Raramuris adopted these more supportive figures in addition to their harsher and even threatening deities. They were also responsive to and even demanded supernatural explanations for their hardships and the other troubling aspects of the unknown, especially death and the issue of the afterlife.

Converted to a hybrid Christianity, the Tarahumaras at Satevo, downstream from Batopilas, built and later elaborated a magnificent cathedral for their Jesuit teachers. Their devotion to the missionaries led some of them to rebel in 1767, when the Spanish government expelled the black-robed disciples of Christ from Mexico and Spanish America. But the teaching of Christian doctrine had a lasting effect, and the Raramuri and mestizo settlers at Satevo maintained the mission on behalf of themselves and the Jesuits' successors for the next ninety-four years until an impressed Robinson arrived on the site.

American observers often regarded the Tarahumara celebrations as orgies because they did not understand the religious symbolism involved. They watched as the tesquino transformed the normally gentle and unaggressive Raramuri men. It was during those festivities, which sometimes went on for several days, that knife attacks and fights created new or perpetuated old grievances. The people of Batopilas rarely attended these affairs because they feared drunken challenges to explain imagined injustices or affronts, and they did not wish to participate in what they regarded as binge drinking. The greatest social skills were required in order to avoid offending their hosts when taking one's leave during the festivities. Outsiders needed to be sensitive when interacting with the Tarahumara. For example, joking was a form of interaction reserved for family members.

In order to exchange goods with a Tarahumara, an outsider was well advised to enlist the services of a *norawa*, or trusted middleman from

A Raramuri at mission ruins, circa 1890. (Photograph by Carl Lumholtz; courtesy of the American Museum of Natural History, New York)

the lowlands. Newcomers attempting to hurry transactions were considered forward and offensive. Christian Tarahumaras turned to compadres, trusted friends, and *padrinos* (godfathers) for extended support during emotional crises, friendship on a daily basis, and to help rear or care for their children in the event of a parent's death or incapacity.

Strangers avoided contact on the canyon trails, walking around each other at some distance if they could, and never asking where the other was going or why if they could not. A person entered a Tarahumara home only when invited and only after calling out in a friendly voice from some distance away. At social gatherings, host and guests greeted each other with handshakes and a murmured "kwira"("May God protect you"). The host expected his guests to refuse offers of food and drink at least once before accepting, but not to finally accept was an insult. Long stays violated the host's privacy except during tesquinadas, and, except then, even overnight visits were extremely rare.

Festive occasions required tesquino because of its supernatural powers. After opening each jar, the host offered a bit of it to the deities and to the spirits, good, bad, and those of the dead, by pouring some onto the ground in front of the household cross. He then gave the man he had chosen to serve the tesquino on his behalf three gourds full. After consuming his portion, the server offered the other guests the opportunity to join him by filling the three gourds for each man present and one gourd for each woman.

Shamans sprinkled tesquino on newborns to make them strong and on the ailing of all ages to cure disease. Raramuris consumed the sacred drink from birth, mothers blending it with their breast milk. Young men and women drank it in public for the first time when they celebrated their arrival to manhood or announced their readiness to become wives. No marriage was legitimate without it. Tesquino also provided good luck before hunting and fishing trips and before first entering new caves or man-made dwellings. When neighbors (vecinos) worked together on cooperative farming and construction projects, the host rewarded their efforts with tesquino.

The dead required tesquino offerings at their funerals in order to achieve eternal rest. Without it, the spirits of the dead would return and exact revenge on those who had slighted them. Good and bad spirits, and witches were everywhere, in the trees, wind, water, and celestial objects. Night and death constantly challenged the survival of the soul. Disagi and rusiwari, "malignant" and "small birdlike beings," came out at night and could hex those they encountered. Even worse were the korimaka (devil-like beings), and the wa?luduwi (a water devil), who lurked in the lakes and could "grab, detain, and eat the largest human soul causing illness and possible death." Whirlpools were their worst manifestation.

Witchcraft and sorcery caused the Tarahumara to be extremely careful not to offend others. One never mentioned the wrinkles and gray that characterized elders. Sins led to the appearance of evil spirits, who sometimes sprang forth as whirlwinds, whereas good spirits swept over the mountains in the form of cool breezes in the torrid barrancas. For the more wary Raramuris, evil underground spirits sometimes sent forth rainbows to trick people, while "sorcerers" used shooting stars to capture human souls. In those high altitudes and clear starlit skies, the moon served as the sun of a frightful night. While owls brought disease, even daylight beings such as the toad, snake, and lizard could do that.

In a parallel of Christian belief, Onoruame had created this world, and he regulated it. He animated human beings from clay and set aside heaven for the good and hell for the bad among them because they had free choice. If frail human beings followed the rules carefully, they could avoid many maladies while on earth, but their inevitable sins would catch up with them sooner or later, and they would then suffer bad luck, illness, or even the loss of the soul. That calamity was manifested by illness and drunkenness at unsuitable times. Extreme wrongdoing led to death, although the end came to everyone and the survivors could never be sure of what caused it and therefore feared the spirits of the dearly departed. The offerings of tesquino drinks, prayers, careful piety, and even the correct placement of implements outside the living space helped them avoid reprisals and punishments.

The Raramuri elites maintained a high degree of social control despite the dispersed nature of their communities, and they demonstrated relative material affluence through the ownership of animals, the ability to serve more tortillas and tesquino than others, and the wearing of the symbols of political office. The gobernador of a Raramuri municipio offered moralizing speeches or sermons each Sunday at the church in which he frequently shamed individuals by contrasting them with the way good people should be. He almost never named them during the sermon because everyone knew what was going on and it was neither necessary nor socially correct to use names.

The *tenientes*, *alcaldes* (mayors), and *suplentes* served at the community level beneath the authority of the gobernador. Other officials included the *capitanes* (police), the *dopiliki* (jail keepers), and the *fiscales*, who carried and delivered messages on behalf of the alcaldes and gobernador. Men filled all of these positions. The Tarahumara authorities used public trials, wooden stocks, and whippings, in order to punish wrongdoers.[13]

Everyday Ways of Doing Things

Robinson had reached Batopilas at a time when the mines were in a slump, undercapitalized, with production carried out by gambusinos, who fiercely defended their profit-sharing and wage-free independence. Some took the last load of ore of the day as their compensation, whereas others paid Ramírez and Lebrun a fee much like sharecroppers. Heavy mining had lapsed because the civil war between the Liberal and Conservative forces had raged around the barrancas since 1858 and disrupted commerce with the outside world. Even though the rival forces never attacked Batopilas, it was severely affected when rival bands invaded nearby towns in the low country, demanding contributions and threatening politicians with wavering loyalties. The Liberal Batopilas authorities were suspicious of outsiders. They accepted Robinson readily only because he carried written authorizations provided by Belden and Stearns and because Ramírez was expecting him.

John was lucky. He arrived in 1861, just as the War of the Reform came to an end. Although rebel bands, hostile Indians, and bandits still made it expensive and risky to bring in supplies or ship out the silver, the Liberal authorities in Mazatlán wanted more trade because it meant more prosperity at the port. Their interests coincided with the desire of the Batopilas elites to attract foreign investment in order to activate the moribund mines and stimulate employment.

In the few months that he survived in Batopilas, Asher ordered the excavation of cave-ins and restarted work on the surface mines. At that point, the men began to gather gigantic amounts of silver from obvious protrusions. Sometimes they did not even bother to smelt the thick native silver. Instead, they cut it into transportable pieces, some several feet long, placed the heavy loads on mules led by mule skinners under guard, and carried it out of the barranca to the Pacific littoral. At Choix, they loaded it on carts and hauled the treasure to nearby places on the coast and then carried it to Mazatlán in small craft before placing it on ships going to San

Francisco. The expense of maintaining the guards was offset by the economy of scale, that is, through the enormous amount of silver shipped. John's friendships with the customs authorities in Mazatlán paid off immediately and by 1863 large quantities of silver were leaving Mexico through the port.

Refining and digging operations remained on a small scale despite the overhaul of the Hacienda San Miguel because the rich surface deposits still did not require steam-driven rock crushers, let alone more sophisticated and expensive equipment. During the 1860s and 1870s, the number of workers rarely exceeded 120. As a result, although the mines remained the motor of the Batopilas economy, they did not foster a great deal of growth or a great upsurge of prosperity.

With enormous vertical strips of pure silver extending upward in the rocks and thinner branches following the many cleavages, Robinson's men broke the rocks at the site with sledgehammers and then cut the silver. The biggest problem with the native or pure silver was its overwhelming weight. It had to be cut, with large shears or chisels driven by hand-held hammers, into manageable units that could be carried downriver for storage at the hacienda. As the wealth of the treasure extracted increased, the company hired more armed guards and provided them with housing at the Hacienda San Miguel.

By putting the guards in their own barracks, with corrals, across the river from Batopilas, Robinson and the company officials could instill loyalty and discipline in them. The strategy gave the company and Robinson greater political power than the civic authorities, whose small police force could not compete. Robinson's political power grew as his economic power did. He began to pay his workers in scrip, which they could spend either in a well-supplied company store or in town, where Ramírez and the other local merchants also accepted it, redeeming it at the company at a discounted rate.

Explorations

After finding such rich silver deposits near Batopilas, the new mine operators immediately set out to explore outlying areas. A specialized team, sometimes headed by Robinson himself, undertook extensive searches of the Barranca de Batopilas and its adjacent canyons. From time to time, the floodwaters that rushed through the canyons, such as the Arroyo de Roncesvalles three miles north of Batopilas, had uncovered enormous veins of silver. It was reasonable to expect that such exposed veins might be found in other places nearby, especially upriver, in other arroyos that opened into the Barranca de Batopilas, where mines from the Spanish era lay hidden.

Some of these old mines were long abandoned and ripe for the taking by *denuncia* (denunciation or condemnation). Others were still being worked by *arrendatarios* (renters) and gambusinos, men unaccustomed to close supervision and mistrustful of outsiders, who might be claim jumpers. Many had not left the rugged area for years, even decades. Adding to the danger of John's explorations were unstable overhanging rocks, a multitude of poisonous snakes, gangs of robbers, and hostile Apaches.

On the first day, accompanied by a mining engineer and other support personnel, Robinson followed the barranca upriver to the Arroyo de San Antonio, where some of his own mines were located. He found exploitable silver outcroppings at the old Veta Grande site, deep in the arroyo. Continuing up the barranca itself, he found less and less to cheer about. As the cliffs loomed ever higher, reaching thousands of feet above him, the river became filled with giant porphyritic slabs, which had fallen there over the centuries, taking everything in their path along for the ride, but he found no sign of silver or other precious metals.

Robinson's team followed an ancient trail blazed by the Raramuris and miners of earlier eras and still traveled by Indians and mule skinners carrying supplies to the small mines higher in the mountains. With the scree from landslides everywhere and riding sure-footed mules rather than horses, the men carefully wound their way around endless washouts, taking several days to cover the fifteen miles to the most noted old mine at La Bufa (The Bluff), named for the steep mound of eroding, toxic tailings left at the mine's entrance.

To avoid the scorching afternoon sun, Robinson and his escort hugged the southwestern face of the giant cliffs of the barranca, getting what little shade they could from the stunted brush and trees. They almost certainly carried water bags filled at springs along the way, for the waters of the Río Batopilas contained arsenic, chromium, lead, and other toxic heavy metals, brought in by the miners or released from the earth they excavated.

The river carried these poisons downstream from La Bufa and lesser mines to Batopilas and then through Choix and on to the Pacific Ocean.

On his way to La Bufa, John explored the ever-smaller arroyos cut by streams that ran into the river, entering treacherous divides in search of precious metals but finding no deposits worth exploiting. Almost all the river's tributaries featured intermittent but spectacular waterfalls. Rainfall brought water to the edge of cliffs, where it fell in long streams even more beautiful than those in other parts of the barranca. Robinson would later explore the neighboring Barranca de Urique, which held, and still contains, large but hard-to-reach deposits of gold, but he would dismiss that possibility. Both barrancas offered spectacular views, but perhaps the most spectacular was at La Bufa, where the near-vertical green and gray canyon walls soared more than 6,200 feet from the river to the top of the Cerro del Pastel.

As John and his companions struggled forward, they could hear the Tarahumaras beating their drums on the high ridges above them, as the Raramuri had done for centuries to signal the arrival of outsiders. Though many were closer than it seemed, out of hostility or fear, they preferred to remain out of view. The Tarahumara lived in dread of hunters seeking the bounties for "Apache" scalps offered by the governor of Chihuahua. Even so, they presented no threat unless actually menaced by the intruders. During his scores of trips into the countryside in the nineteen years he ran the mines, Robinson made at least some effort not to disturb any of the Raramuris unduly, an effort made all the easier by the fabulous wealth he had encountered at Batopilas.

Despite the existence of precious metal deposits elsewhere in the barrancas, the richest lodes in the region were to be found within four miles of Batopilas and were, in John's estimation, the equal of those at Nevada's Comstock or any other mine in the world. He decided to focus his efforts on them, using the mining code in force at the time to "denounce" (condemn) inactive properties he found to have potential. Fortunately, he worked only a few of them and thus avoided many confrontations with the local citizenry. The problem was that many of these claims only seemed inactive. It was a custom among batopilenses to ignore certain sites for years until the labor and capital became available to work them.

Mining engineer John Randolph summarized the origins of the conflicts that arose between Americans and Mexicans after Robinson sold his holdings in 1879 to the more aggressive Alexander Shepherd. Randolph also addressed the problem that emerged from Robinson's purchases from Lebrun in Álamos. He "jumped claims that had elapsed and became possessed of the richest part of the Hill of San Antonio and then appealed to powerful friends connected with the Wells Fargo Company to aid him in the undertaking."[14]

By 1862, the first silver shipments had arrived in San Francisco, and it was only logical that rivals would emerge there and in Mexico as soon as their value was understood. "Junior" Almaden, the heir to a nascent California wine-making fortune, took note of the incoming precious metals and went to Mazatlán and Batopilas to investigate. Almaden liked what he discovered. He also saw in the French invasion and occupation of Mexico, which began in December 1861 and reached the Copper Canyon region and Sinaloa in 1864, an opportunity to gain control of the silver lode at Batopilas.

In 1864, as the French forces swept across the state of Chihuahua and most of the Mexican northwest, they dislodged Robinson's allies, the Liberal government officials in Mexico City and in Chihuahua, and drove the Liberal forces all the way to the border at Paso del Norte, across from El Paso. Although the French left Batopilas in Mexican hands, they established a temporary government in Mexico City under the nominal leadership of Hapsburg Archduke Maximilian, who assumed the title Emperor of Mexico.

Almaden became an avowed supporter of Maximilian and the Mexican Conservatives who had invited the French invasion. He then gained an informal authorization from Maximilian to take over the Batopilas mines. All he had to do was create an armed force capable of seizing the Hacienda San Miguel and Batopilas from Robinson's guards and the local citizenry. Almaden attempted to raise money in New York and San Francisco, but the vast majority of capitalists in both cities, consistent with the Monroe Doctrine, the interests of the Wells Fargo Bank, and the policies of Presidents Abraham Lincoln and Andrew Johnson, supported the ouster of the French and the cause of the Mexican Liberals.

Even though other rivals emerged at the local level, they were not able to mount armed attacks against John and his guards because he had the endorsement of President Juárez, and because nearby Sinaloa was engaged in a fierce and patriotic guerrilla war against the French. Then, in 1866, the Mexican Liberals, equipped with weapons delivered by aspiring investors from New York and the U.S. Army after the Civil War, inflicted two major defeats on the French army, driving it out of Chihuahua and out of the northeastern area of the country around the city of Monterrey. Robinson's friend General Luis Terrazas, the patriarch of the most important family in the Chihuahua oligarchy, led the victorious Liberal forces in the state. Terrazas's later alliance with John, cemented by the marriage of his only granddaughter to Robinson's sole surviving grandson, Charles, would prove important to the continued success of the Batopilas Mining Company.

By 1866, the French realized that the Liberals could not be defeated, announced "victory," and began a complete withdrawal from their short-lived Mexican empire. They turned over the military campaign to Maximilian and his Conservative supporters. During the rest of the year and early 1867, the Liberals marched south crushing the Conservative armies that opposed them. Maximilian went down to defeat and was taken prisoner at the city of Querétaro, north of Mexico City. Juárez ordered him executed in June 1867, at which point Almaden also acknowledged defeat. Robinson and his powerful American backers in San Francisco and New York were free to continue exploiting their silver lode at Batopilas.[15]

From the beginning of his operations in Batopilas, Robinson was keenly aware of the crucial role played by gang foremen and prominent citizens Morris and Hernández in maintaining worker discipline and morale. Being local miners themselves and understanding gambusino practices, they knew their men and could work with both jornaleros and gambusinos. They made sure every man knew exactly what was expected of him. Disrespect, refusal to follow orders, fighting, and theft all led to dismissal. Under their supervision, the crews excavated new mines, some as far as four miles upstream and others an equal distance up the aptly named Arroyo de las Minas.

Back at his headquarters, Robinson kept track of the smelting of ores and the books. He periodically visited the outlying mining sites but largely depended on the foremen to provide the needed leadership. To reduce travel time to and from the developed mines, John provided his workers basic on-site housing and company store items, including food, clothing, and tools, imported by way of Mazatlán, so that the men could stay on the job for a week or more at a time. In this manner, he maintained continuity with past practices in the mines while maximizing profits. He also assumed the role of a traditional Mexican *patrón* (dominant figure, patriarch), serving as godfather at baptisms, attending weddings and funerals, and handing out small sums to the families of injured, ill, and deceased miners.

Robinson initiated a more regimented work routine at the processing plant, smelter, and storage facility in the Hacienda San Miguel. To the "mozos" (unskilled workers and errand boys) John added assayers, furnace operators, and warehousemen, and increased the number of horsemen, mule skinners, and armed guards. The smelter workers produced identical ingots of silver, which they stored and kept under guard, along with the large strips of native silver.

Robinson faced continuous challenges until he sold the mining complex to Alexander and his associates. The political warfare between the Conservatives and Liberals continued to plague him. Finally, in 1870, his exports of untaxed ingots and unminted native silver attracted protest from the Liberal authorities in Mexico City. The long delay in their intervention resulted from the civil wars and the lack of a telegraph, which had not yet been introduced to the region.[16]

Secretary of State Sebastián Lerdo de Tejada complained to President Benito Juárez that "great strips of native silver" were being exported to the San Francisco mint without the payment of federal taxes. The government, Lerdo de Tejada argued, should require that the silver be shipped to a Mexican mint, to be established at Chihuahua City, where Mexican authorities and skilled personnel could assess, refine, and impose a tax on it. The mint employees could then transport the officially stamped ingots to the border at El Paso. Juárez agreed. But John was fortunate. The Mexican government could not afford to install its own mint, and nothing was done about taxing the silver for several years.

During the 1860s and 1870s, more localized political rivalries between the regional elites in western Chihuahua and the state oligarchy headquartered in Chihuahua City continually plagued Robinson. Rival groups roved the country claiming allegiances to Maximilian, Juárez, Lerdo, antagonistic elements of the Chihuahua elites, and finally, in 1876, to General Porfirio Díaz.

Before 1871, several roving bands raided Batopilas demanding "loans" and supplies. Robinson usually cooperated with the rebels to some degree in order to maintain his operations. In 1871 and 1872, however, *revoltosos* loyal to General Díaz, who was trying to overthrow President Juárez, seized Batopilas at least twice.

On the first occasion, Tito Arreola led a small force of men into the town. During their eight-day occupation, they forced Ramírez, his sons, and other merchants to "lend" them 10,000 pesos. They lacked the men and firepower, however, to seize the fortified Hacienda San Miguel. The estate, with its heavy stone walls featuring firing holes and turrets, presented intruders with the virtual certainty of heavy casualties. Across the river and backed up to a steep canyon wall, the fortified side of the hacienda faced the attackers. Arreola gave up and invaded Urique, where he seized the mines and even had his men extract gold from them.

But Robinson's problems were not over. Arreola joined forces in Urique with a larger band of pro-Díaz rebels, led by Felipe Arellano. Arreola became second in command of the stronger forces, numbering some 300 men, and in January 1872, the combined force occupied Batopilas. The rebels seized another 6,000 pesos from the merchants, and raised hell with the prostitutes and tavern owners. They later extorted 9,000 silver pesos from John under the threat of overrunning the Hacienda San Miguel, where they would have found far greater wealth. The value of the silver on hand at the time approximated 200,000 pesos because Robinson had been unable to send out shipments for at least two months.

In July 1872, the success of an even larger group of rebels revealed how great the accumulation of wealth could become. A large force led by Adolfo Ibarra, claiming loyalty to General Díaz during yet another attempt to overthrow the national government, seized both Batopilas and the Hacienda San Miguel. Ibarra took Robinson and his administrators Achilles Morris and Jesse Hernández prisoner. Meanwhile, his men sacked the stores of Englishman William Hooper and that of Ramírez and Sons. He even took over the operation of Robinson's San Miguel and San Antonio mines for two months. During that span, using his inexperienced men and as much of the normal workforce as possible, the mines produced 100,000 pesos in silver. Threatened by the arrival of federal troops, Ibarra finally marched off to raid Urique and never returned.

Intermittent attacks continued to plague Robinson and the citizens of Batopilas until 1877. The turning point in the struggle against chaos came

in January of that year, when Robinson and his guards joined the batopilenses to defend the place. Rebel chief Lorenzo Torres, leading 500
men, had already forced a "loan" of 2,000 pesos from the merchants, but
he decided to enter town anyway. The defenders set a trap and opened
fire from the surrounding hilltops using Remington repeating rifles imported by Robinson from the United States. The "small force" of resisters
demonstrated a high level of accuracy as they shot at the fleeing rebels,
who strung out on the narrow road below them in a panic, urging their
horses downstream toward Satevo.

Torres and his men took heavy casualties as they fled. The victorious
townsmen took up the chase, pursuing the rebels past Satevo and far to
the south, to the town of Guadalupe y Calvo, outside of the Copper
Canyon complex. There, a beaten Torres negotiated a peace and amnesty
agreement with the federal authorities and returned the 2,000 pesos collected from the merchants. John's shipment of modern arms and the
marksmanship of the miners gave the batopilenses their victory.

Meanwhile, General Díaz had finally overthrown President Sebastián
Lerdo de Tejada in 1876 with the financial support of Moses Taylor and
the Stillman interests of the National City Bank. Díaz was interested
in attracting more American investment and wished to establish a sense
of law and order in the countryside. That determination and the batopilenses' demonstration of fighting ability put a stop to the invasions of the
silver town by bandit gangs. But it was too late for Robinson in Batopilas.
He was worn out, two of his grandchildren had joined his two sons who
had died earlier, and he simply refused to invest the energy needed to
restore the mines. He returned to the United States, where he joined his
partners in the search for a buyer.[17]

A Forerunner of Things to Come

Over the sixteen years between 1861 and 1876, John had tried a variety of
tactics to maintain his operations in the face of rebels and bandits. Sometimes he paid the intruders who occupied the town and threatened to
disrupt operations. Usually, they were satisfied when he handed out provi-
sions and what for him were small amounts of cash, but the instability the
invaders represented forestalled any plans to expand his operations and
commit the capital of his investors to outlying sites.

While the larger rebel groups were beyond control at first, their ultimate defeat resulted from the integration of international and national processes with the local. During the 1870s, after John convinced them how much could be saved by the introduction of a hundred or more rifles, the financiers back in the United States finally acted. That small investment and the increased law enforcement efforts in the region after General Díaz seized power ended the uncertainty. The mining operations, however, remained limited until the enforcement of political stability and law and order could be ensured by the national government, and a new managing partner could be found. After 1875, a tired and demoralized Robinson limited his efforts to the San Miguel mines and spent much of his time in New York City, Washington, D.C., and Talbot County, Maryland, where he established a permanent residence.

Meanwhile, the miners in Batopilas returned to traditional labor, cultural, and political practices. The relatively casual work routines that had prevailed before John's arrival returned. Most of the miners went back to work on a gambusino basis for others who rented mines. A few of them worked alone, leasing small sites and processing the ore through manual labor. Robinson's minimal introduction of high technology largely left them on their own. Most of the miners opted to use the smelter at San Miguel because the higher yield paid for the cost and relieved them from a great deal of work.

For more than a decade, John had exposed Batopilas to more modern capitalist relationships: a wage-earning workforce that subordinated its time to the schedule of the employer, a reduced number of gambusinos who worked inside the mines and in search of new lodes, and specialists who processed the ore. Those steps encouraged the development of a small and salaried workforce at the Hacienda San Miguel.

A miniature corporate state emerged in the 1860s, run by the Batopilas Mining Company (BMC). For reasons of convenience and efficiency, John introduced scrip payments and a company store, supplanting in part the Batopilas shopkeepers and reducing the workers' independence at the same time. He used company guards to enforce order; he imposed fines on the workers for indolence and exacted damages from them for what he determined to be their carelessness.

To maintain a steady rate of production, he encouraged certain work procedures, which included fixing the times spent digging inside the mountains, establishing the methods of extraction and ore processing, and selecting the tools used. Some miners were forced to abandon their traditional work habits for the sake of increased productivity. Meanwhile, at the end of each *jornada* (workday), Robinson's guards searched the miners for stolen silver and flakes of gold. The mines became a closed social environment, in which Robinson was the ultimate authority. In response to the isolation, the absence of other businesses, and the necessities of the enterprise, John expanded his personal power, assuming the authority of a patrón over the workers and local officials.

As Robinson repaired and improved the fortress-like Hacienda San Miguel, he created a material form of isolation and power. He concentrated his armed men there in a barracks and guarded the bridge that crossed the river upstream and the hacienda entrance. Robinson, San Miguel, and the mining operation became virtually self-sustaining, separated from the town, interacting with it largely from a position of power, augmented when the state government assigned him a small detachment of troops. In the end, he had a hierarchical system with an American on top.[18]

Robinson gained influence with the Batopilas government through his importance to the local economy and his relationship with Ramírez. He represented a microcosm of a broader process taking place in Mexico, the assumption of political power in isolated workplaces by factory, hacienda, and mine owners, who were often foreigners. As a part of this process, Robinson became a cultural force. The need for an efficient workforce led to definitions of what constituted satisfactory performance. His goal of higher worker productivity redefined the concepts of competent work, poverty, and hardship.

John's attitude was informed by the concept of Manifest Destiny, an idea embraced by dominant society. He believed that he was "developing" the mines, providing wellness and a higher level of civility to the "backward" people affected by his enterprise. He would never concede what nationalist critics later claimed, that the removal of the silver in the absence of taxes and other forms of Mexican control over the process was theft. From Robinson's outlook, he provided employment and those who had the opportunity to work and did not do so were dissolute, in violation of the capitalist work ethic, and had disqualified themselves for sympathy and help.

The townspeople of Batopilas needed Robinson as a source of employment even if he never invested capital on the scale needed to fulfill their dreams. The limited commitment he did make, however, was crucial to the town's limited prosperity. Ironically, because the silver ore was so rich and easy to extract, he needed fewer employees than expected and invested less in technology. The smaller number of batopilenses employed in mining meant less benefit for the local economy.

Meanwhile, John's role as a capitalist and his American cultural practices led him into conflicts with his workers and neighbors that extended beyond their disappointment at not achieving a paradise on earth. Although a few muted critics saw him as a greedy robber, more subtle conflicts emerged. The batopilenses and people of the canyons, including the mining company employees and Raramuri, held complex, strongly religious, and individualistic, views of life. Their religious beliefs created powerful alternative realities and inherently conflicted with Robinson's project. Religion permeated virtually everything in their experience including the workplace and their expectations of others. Mestizo homes featured pictures of a tortured and bleeding Christ and a serene Virgin Mary. Their work had a religious connotation because of the doctrine of original sin. For mestizo and Tarahumara, the hardship of heavy labor was a part of the penance required of them in order to receive salvation and be delivered from evil spirits, the Devil, and hell.

The example of Jesus' suffering consoled them in their difficult socioeconomic condition. It provided them with a secure refuge, a belief that at some level they had self-worth, if not equality. The Savior had seen poverty as a virtue, and for many batopilenses his example offered them the resignation they needed in order to endure their hardships. In turn, they believed that the Church and the wealthy carried special obligations to help the poor through charity and to sponsor them on special occasions such as marriages, baptisms, and death. Since gods, spirits, and saints played a central part in Raramuri and mestizo thinking, any reduction in the day-to-day roles of these religious figures undercut the sense of public solace, increased feelings of guilt, and engendered negative sentiments among the citizenry toward those responsible for the change.

Most of the people in the region, including mine employees, treasured individualism and practiced it in myriad ways. That propensity also brought them into conflict with the Americans. In the case of the more independent Raramuris, when town and mining life became too oppressive, they simply left for a remote place. But when they sought the privacy of the forest and mountains, the American interlopers drove the forest back, cutting down trees for tunnel timbers and construction projects, and invaded the wilderness mountains, digging mines and fouling the streams. Meanwhile, artisans worked within their own areas of authority, the workshops, making products according to their own standards and schedules. The gambusinos extracted their income from the mines on the last haul of the day; the small shopkeepers decided when to open and close and what to sell.

All of them maintained a high sense of religious devotion but relied on their own resources because the Church charities were inadequate and state relief nonexistent. For some gambusinos, if the ore petered out or an owner insisted on the wage system, they asserted their independence by moving on to another mining site or settlement. Some of the artisans and small shopkeepers also moved. but for a different reason, following the mining booms from town to town.

The established artisans and most of the small shopkeepers, especially those in the downtown area of Batopilas, however, led more settled lives. They raised their own food and cut back production or inventories when there was no demand for their goods. Many of the miners joined these artisans and small shopkeepers in adhering to the emergent Liberal ethic of equality. They also believed they had the right to participate as citizens in politics and wanted to be treated as equals before the law, alongside the patrones. Their wishes for equal treatment in everyday human intercourse included the right to make free choices regarding when and where to work and when and where to move.

Their Catholic practices sometimes reinforced Liberal individualistic values by placing them in personal contact with their beloved saints. Batopilas identified itself with Saint Peter; Robinson's hacienda with Saint Michael. The mines were all named after saints: San Antonio, San Miguel, San Jorge, Santa Martina, Santa Teresa, San Néstor, Dolores, San Martin, Santo Domingo, Santo Tomás, and finally, Todos Santos. The rich mountain immediately north of Batopilas was named Todos Santos, while the Arroyo de San Antonio contained the San Miguel mines.

Each mining entrance had a *nicho* (wall recess) where a statue of the appropriate saint, San Miguel upstream from the town and San Antonio above the hacienda, waited each morning for the miners' prayers and genuflections before they entered the dark mines. Meanwhile, the priest taught the children to respect tradition, the local authorities, their elders, the foremen, and the *maestros* (skilled artisans), strengthening their sense of Mexican culture. The priest also defended Robinson indirectly by urging peace and respect for employers. During the late 1876, President Díaz joined the list of those meriting praise.

Major differences, however, separated the workers from their American employer. John had some idea of the subtleties involved in being a good patrón and the importance attached to it, but he sharply differed with batopilenses over issues like the importance of time. Most of the workers sought what they regarded as a satisfactory standard of living in a place lacking many conveniences. They wanted to enjoy their individual social and political prerogatives and, at the same time, lead lives consistent with their religious beliefs and customs. In contrast, Robinson sought higher productivity and profits for his stockholders and the self-esteem that came from success.

All too many of John's employees treated the ninety to a hundred saint's days as work holidays. The large numbers of miners who missed work on Mondays because of the drunkenness on the weekends left Robinson fuming because his expensive high-temperature boilers and rich mines stood idle. At other times, some workers arrived on the job late, and some left after lunch. Because they were expected to labor from dawn until nightfall almost every day, it made sense to some workers to skip workdays on occasion. Their heavy labor led not only to fatigue but also to accidental injuries and even death. Many workers left the mines because they simply could not face the ordeal.

The miners of Batopilas, in contrast to its merchants and semiprofessionals, realistically focused on day-to-day living, not on accumulating wealth. Meanwhile, many Tarahumaras disappeared from the mining center, sometimes not returning for weeks or months. The Raramuri relied on subsistence agriculture as the basis of their survival, and this often meant escaping with their families to the high country. Some of the otherwise tolerant batopilenses felt that Robinson pushed people too hard out of unbridled greed.

John attempted to reduce absenteeism and lateness through the use of scrip money that laid the basis for debt peonage, but that practice was minimized by the lack of stability in the region brought on by its remoteness and the absence of outside authorities. The use of debt peonage offered a temporary convenience to the employees followed by the obligation to continue working. While economically effective, it also violated the deeper Liberal precepts of freedom that were permeating Mexican society, especially in the North where the Liberal government of President Juárez had fought a protracted guerrilla war against the French invaders from 1863 through 1866. Liberalism was strong in Batopilas, as was Catholicism.

John's struggle to create a fully rational capitalist economy never succeeded because of these problems. The lateness to work and early departures of the Mexicans and Tarahumaras would continue throughout the American stay at Batopilas. His resort to debt peonage placed the American entrepreneur in the same position as his Spanish and Mexican predecessors and added another area of power to his already growing role. He became a debt collector, partially controlling the horizontal mobility of the workers. The conflict between Robinson's limited effort to create a more modern capitalist culture amid precapitalist practices and idealistic Liberal values was a prelude to the more intense conflicts that surfaced during Shepherd's reign.

The practice of debt peonage, however, was not an entirely negative phenomenon for the miners. The two administrators, their crew chiefs, and skilled workers, all enjoyed credit. In their thinking, the requirement to pay off the debt was only part of their contract, as long as they lived within their means. In contrast, for the unskilled laborers, who could neither read nor write, the debt became a trap they could not escape without breaking the law. Robinson favored retaining his workers as long as possible because the training of new men cost him time and money.

Meanwhile, John continued to adapt to local practices. By the late 1860s, his role of patrón included his attendance at the weddings of his administrators, some of his domestic and police employees, and a few of the townspeople, and the baptisms of their children. Most of the mine workers, however, continued to have differences with Robinson that were exacerbated by his failure to fully observe the obligations of a patrón. His long absences violated a long-standing custom in the local culture practiced by Rivolta, Pastrana, Mendazona, and Ramírez who stood in for Lebrun. The role of the patrón was rooted in cultural practices established during three centuries of Spanish imperialism and in the actions taken by the rich men who owned the mines. Those cultural performances still coincided with the expectations of the workers and residents of Batopilas.

The paternalism expected from him because of his role as employer placed him in a contradictory situation because, at the same, time an impersonal wage system was emerging through the employment of high technology supported by state intervention. As the combination of capitalist and state power advanced, it left the gambusinos marginalized and the workers in a weakened political position. The latter's reduced bargaining power resulted in lower income, about $75 yearly, despite greatly increased individual production. For example, in 1879, as Robinson was preparing to sell the mines to Shepherd, his workers struck a pocket of native silver and in a short period of time exported $200,000 in silver bullion to San Francisco. During eighteen years of challenge, exuberance, and utter despair, Robinson shipped almost $20 million in native silver and ingots from Batopilas to the United States.[19]

Conclusion

Because of the impoverishment that prevailed in Batopilas at the time of John's arrival and his prior experience with miners and merchants, he avoided virtually all organized labor unrest. The highest level of tension between Robinson and his workers occurred when he periodically moved to reduce gambusino practices. The high quality of the ore shipped and the division of labor in which veteran miners performed exploratory work rather than extractions, minimized the potential for conflict. The presence of troops rather than direct actions by the state in specific labor disputes was the only level of intimidation needed during his tenure.

John, despite his medical background, and the deaths of four of his own family members, did little to develop health care services in Batopilas. As company activities these undertakings would have constituted sophisticated mechanisms of social control. Instead, the batopilenses introduced them because the townspeople and miners needed relief from the myriad health problems that befell them as a result of the semitropical climate, fecal bacteria, poisoned water, silicosis, and mining accidents. During the 1860s and 1870s, a pharmacist in the center of Batopilas, perhaps with Robinson's encouragement, began dispensing a mix of manufactured drugs and herbal combinations, while midwives, herbalists, and medical practitioners without modern training offered their own services and treatments.

When Robinson arrived in Batopilas in 1861, he faced a cultural divide between his disciplined American business and predominately urban experience and the people of the barrancas. That divide was made even wider by the transitions under way in Mexico at large as people moved from the practices of the past to those of the Liberal era. Great tensions existed between the local, regional, and national elites and between most of the workers and Tarahumaras vis-à-vis Robinson. In this politically fractured environment, virtually all of the town leaders, except the company supervisors, wanted local prosperity while retaining their authority. Robinson, in turn, showed little interest in the town. He chose to develop his closest social ties outside of the barrancas, with the regional elites in Chihuahua and Sinaloa.

The local elites and miners sought progress in the form of better material conditions. From their perspective, that meant local investment in streets, buildings, utility services, a higher level of commerce, a hospital, a primary school, a mutual aid society for workers in distress, and the freedom to make personal and political choices. Meanwhile, the Tarahumaras in Batopilas sought opportunities for employment there in order to transport food, clothing, and tools back to their log cabins, caves, jacales, and plots of land. They hoped for dignified treatment while they were in town or working in the mines and insisted on their liberty to return to the surrounding wilderness whenever they wished.

In 1879, a tired and aging John Robinson and his partners sold their Batopilas mining concessions to Governor Alexander Shepherd for $600,000 while retaining a small share of the business. Robinson had helped lay the groundwork for the transformation of Batopilas and the mines. Shepherd would carry forward the capitalization and modernization of Batopilas beyond Robinson's wildest dreams. But it was the antithesis of a paradise modeled on the Arabian Nights about which the batopilenses had dreamed.

CHAPTER 3

Confronting the Wilderness

Being excellent judges, [the gambusinos] always selected the very
richest ore for themselves—ore so rich that a few pounds of it
often enabled them to imitate their master's carousing and
gambling on a small scale.

—J. R. Southworth

DURING THE MID TO LATE 1880s, the leaders and workers of the small
communities in remote western Chihuahua and the Sierra Madre had
learned that American capital, in conjunction with the growing political
authority of President Porfirio Díaz (1876–80 and 1884–1911), his temporary replacement President Manuel González (1880–84), and the state
oligarchy headed by the Terrazas family, would dominate their once-
independent region. The local people held mixed opinions about the
Americans and the Chihuahua oligarchy. The gambusinos needed jobs,
but they resented the efforts of American mining companies to rationalize
labor by converting them into wage earners. Town merchants and other
local elites recognized the opportunity to combine personal enrichment
and overall social betterment through the development of commerce and
industry, but they resented mine owner attempts to control the local
polity. As long as economic conditions remained at least hopeful, however, a relatively stable political climate could be maintained.

General Díaz's plan for political order and economic progress, called
the Porfirian Peace, began with a strong federal and state police presence
throughout the nation for the protection of private property owners. Díaz
then recruited foreign investment capital to modernize transportation,
communications, mining, and forestry technology, to commercialize
the agriculture industry, and to rationalize labor costs. The last step in-

cluded control of workers and the labor movement. In the mining industry, that effort included forced labor and the exaggerated rationale, so well expressed by J. R. Southworth, that the gambusinos were robbing the capitalists.

By 1910, America's leading financiers, including members of the Aldrich, Baker, Baruch, Cargill, Cheney, Danforth, Dodge, Guggenheim, Haggin, Hearst, McCormick, Morgan, Palmer, Pullman, Rockefeller, Rogers, Roosevelt, Schley, Schwab, Stillman, and Swift families dominated infrastructure, strategic resources such as oil, minerals, and timber, and landholding in Mexico. They, and fewer than one thousand other members of the American elites, held some 70 percent of the assets of incorporated businesses in Mexico. They controlled the nation's railroad trunk lines and communications companies, ports, copper and timber resources, and a major part of the oil industry. They also owned or leased 70 percent of Mexico's coasts and frontiers.

In Chihuahua, they controlled the major railroads, the telegraph and telephone company, 90 percent of mining production, almost all of the borderlands, and some 40 percent of all the state's land (18 million of 45 million acres). From 1880 to 1910, taking advantage of the land privatization program pushed hard by the Díaz administration, the American elites and Chihuahua oligarchy bought up virtually all of the timber, cropland, and livestock resources in the state. Their acreage, however, was concentrated in the most fertile and timbered areas. The government owned most of the desert wastes in eastern Chihuahua. Among the larger landholders, three of the Big Five American meatpacking houses held vast ranches in the northern, western, and southern areas of the state. By drilling several thousand water wells, they transformed their semiarid holdings into productive estates.

The Chihuahua oligarchy, a group of the largest landowners led by the Terrazas family, welcomed the railroad and land privatization program because it gave them wider markets in Mexico and access to the United States through brokers in El Paso. The innermost circle of the Terrazas clan alone gained ownership of 7 million acres of land during the time they consolidated political power in the state. Between 1880 and 1910, the Chihuahua oligarchy took part in a local replica of the closed polity that prevailed nationwide. Cronies, insiders, and family members of those in political power used their positions to move beyond blatant mineral and land grabs to develop a monopoly on lucrative government public works contracts. In these respects, the Chihuahua oligarchy was a microcosm of Mexican society.

At the national level, President Díaz helped the Americans by overriding both constitutional prohibitions on foreign ownership of land near coasts and frontiers and bans on regional monopolies through large estates. He also played a corrupt role when he approved land grants to American financiers connected to banks and railroads that supported him and to cronies such as his father-in-law Manuel Romero Rubio and Luis García Teruel, a regime insider who sold the properties to large American interests, including oil companies in Campeche. Influential Americans like William Randolph Hearst and Phoebe Hearst benefited from transactions in which valuable lands were sold at five to ten cents per acre. Those practices also prevailed in Chihuahua. Meanwhile, General Díaz crushed the labor unions attempting to organize the industrial and mine workers.[1]

Alexander Robey Shepherd, the new managing partner of the Batopilas Mining Company, was a prime example of the elite American entrepreneurs interacting with Díaz and Mexico's elites. His strategies for gaining power in Chihuahua changed the social dynamics of the region and duplicated those he had used in Washington, D.C. First, he sought to reorganize and centralize political control over the mining areas of the Copper Canyon complex by having the president approve large land grants and appoint sympathetic individuals as "the governing officers" to replace freely elected pueblo leaders. Second, he worked to achieve direct control over public works projects in the Batopilas area, such as roads and aqueducts, in order to further the development and industrialization of the mines. And, third, he moved to achieve racial segregation at Batopilas by enlarging the residential quarters in the Hacienda San Miguel and thereby maintaining the separation of Americans from the mestizos and Native Americans across the river in the town. Earlier, in Washington, he had prevented a "Black takeover" and averted a threatened move of the nation's capital by building wide boulevards, which drove the African Americans out of the center of the city to the east and northeast.

In the early 1880s, Shepherd acquired well over 122,500 acres in the

Sierra Tarahumara surrounding Batopilas for a nominal fee. A Chihuahua company controlled by José Valenzuela and his son Jesús had surveyed the lands concerned in order to make them available for sale by the Mexican government. Elsewhere, to the northeast, survey companies and the Chihuahua oligarchy sold vast tracts of land to American colonists, especially members of the Church of Jesus Christ of Latter-day Saints, or the Mormons. The survey company owners included the Valenzuelas, Frank MacManus, and the Asunsolo and Gómez del Campo families of the state oligarchy. By 1910, these sales had led to the creation of eight American colonies totaling over 3,200 relatively large landholdings.

Meanwhile, as President Díaz grew close to Shepherd and became the padrino (godfather) of at least one of the American's children, he also approved contracts for *enganchadores* (labor contractors) to take charge of thousands of Yaqui Indian prisoners captured by the army in Sonora. Although the vast majority of these Native Americans were placed on freighters and transported to the Isthmus of Tehuantepec and then marched overland into forced labor on plantations in the Valle Nacional, located in the southernmost part of the state of Puebla, and the Yucatán Peninsula, the enganchadores also sold some Yaquis to Shepherd, during the 1880s at least, to work in the mines. The Yaqui workers performed as ore carriers (tamenes) and as cleanup personnel, but the issue of how many of them were forced or free labor remains unresolved.[2]

Shepherd's struggle to reduce labor costs also led him to fight the persistent gambusino tradition of mining, still in vogue at Batopilas, by which miners extracted their share of profits in lieu of pay. That fight reflected a wider transition from artisan to capitalist practices in Mexico during the late nineteenth century, but at Batopilas it changed the way of life. Private entrepreneurs became wage earners. It also signaled the rising power of the national and regional elites and especially foreigners versus Mexican labor. That process was in motion throughout Chihuahua and Mexico. Elsewhere, some plantation and hacienda workers fell into de facto slavery, as did some Yaquis at Batopilas. At the hacienda new technology replaced skilled hand labor just as factory workers supplanted independent artisans in other industries.

General Díaz played a direct role in having press-gangs and policemen detain innocent poor people and petty offenders in Mexico City and the urban areas of central Mexico, who were then sent into forced labor on plantations in the south and Yucatán Peninsula. Yaqui prisoners were also dispatched from Mazatlán to the mines at Batopilas. The executive branch of the government directly issued the permits to the labor contractors for the seizure of "criminals." And it did nothing when the enganchadores in central Mexico resorted to press-gangs to obtain the workers. The hapless Yaquis probably received the same treatment at Mazatlán. Sometimes, along with pickpockets, thieves, and more serious offenders, the Mexico City police even took the impoverished victims who reported the crimes into custody. Shepherd and the landowners paid the contractors, who paid the police and army for their cooperation.

The leading enganchadores in Mexico City included Americans Edmund Kirby Smith, who worked for Shepherd from 1879 to 1882, and Isaiah Benton Miller. Both were tied to American capitalists with important agricultural holdings in southern Mexico. Miller and Kirby Smith worked as labor contractors in Tabasco, Veracruz, and Campeche. Kirby Smith, an engineer, was tied to Shepherd via his uncle General Edmund Kirby Smith, the last military commander of the Trans-Mississippi West of the Confederacy, a district that included Texas, West Louisiana, and Arkansas. In 1865, the general had fled to Mexico, where he developed large import-export connections during the Civil War, and then to Cuba, to escape possible prosecution by American authorities.

A year later, the general returned to the United States, after receiving assurances from General Grant, and served as president of the Atlantic and Pacific Telegraph Company from 1866 to 1868, when it was bought out by Western Union. He then took over as chancellor of the University of Nashville from 1870 to 1875 and served as professor of mathematics and biology at the University of the South (popularly called Sewanee) from 1875 to 1893. Linked to the Episcopal Church and a part of the apartheid system that characterized the postwar South, Sewanee attracted both Shepherd and his partner George W. Quintard, who sent their sons there. Quintard's brother, Charles Todd Quintard, the second bishop of Tennessee for the Protestant Episcopal Church, served as a regent at Sewanee and as a key founder of Fisk University, established for "Negroes." The younger Kirby Smith worked as a labor contractor and mine supervisor for Shepherd at the racially segregated complex at Batopilas where nonwhites lived on one side of the river and the Americans and British resided on the other. The only people of color allowed to live at San Miguel were the servants.

In Mexico City, Kirby Smith and Miller obtained the collaboration of the police, who held the *enganchados* (hooked ones) in a barracks located in the Callejón del Tesonatle, in the downtown area of the capital, until their departure for plantations in the south and Yucatán. The police collected payments from the labor contractors for hundreds of legally kidnapped people yearly. Most of the victims in Mexico City were sentenced, after processing, to forced labor on a selected group of sugar and tobacco plantations in the Valle Nacional of Puebla. Other urban police departments and press-gangs focused on different destinations. The workforce on the plantations of the south and Campeche included debt peons recruited from other cities in central Mexico with deceptive promises of "jobs" and then held against their will because of transportation charges they could not pay off. The enganchadores in Veracruz, for example, used that strategy and forwarded their victims to hardwood and chicle plantations, owned by some of the richest citizens of the United States, in Campeche. In Mexico City and Veracruz the press-gangs sometimes raided the poorest neighborhoods, literally kidnapping working-class citizens from the streets. The corrupt policemen of the capital joined in these activities while the press and public held their tongues, fearing the consequences of protest.

Similar conditions prevailed in Batopilas. Traffickers, including Kirby Smith, moved Yaqui prisoners dropped off by the Mexican army in Sinaloa into Batopilas for Shepherd. Alexander's method of procuring cheap labor, other than the Yaqui prisoners, paralleled but was less extreme than that used by the enganchadores in central Mexico: he paid a bounty to the men who brought him the "emigrant labor." Shepherd, however, also deducted 50 percent from the weekly salary of his free workers for the *tienda de raya* (company store). Meanwhile, it is charged, though unproven, that he locked up the impressed Yaqui in the San Miguel Tunnel at night.[3]

Cyrus McCormick, the head of the International Harvester Company, which dominated the henequen trade in Yucatán, and American and Mexican landowners in the notorious Valle Nacional all used Yaqui forced laborers. The Yaqui prisoners sent to Yucatán quickly died in the tropical climate; the much smaller number sent to Batopilas began dying after six months because of lung infections induced by the humidity and filth in the San Miguel Tunnel, where it is alleged Shepherd placed them at night. In the late twentieth century, International Harvester employed two historians who, it is alleged, purged the company archives of incriminating evidence. Meanwhile, the "official histories" of the Batopilas mines, written by Shepherd's son Grant and Walter Brodie, the chief mining engineer, make no mention of the suppression of labor organizers that took place there or of any other abuses. The suppression is well documented in the U.S. National Archives, however, as is the forced labor in Campeche and the Valle Nacional; descendants of Shepherd's employees personally recalled other atrocities that took place in the mines at Batopilas.[4]

In late 1879, immediately after taking charge of the mining operations at Batopilas, Shepherd established a force of about seventy well-armed men to protect the installation from marauders, escort the silver bullion out of the barrancas to Mazatlán or to the mint at Chihuahua City, and to establish himself as the most powerful man in the Sierra Tarahumara. In isolated Batopilas, several days from the nearest outpost of the Mexican military or federal authority, Alexander's power became unassailable, and he extended it over a large area of southwestern Chihuahua. In attitude, behavior, and power, he was the embodiment of a European feudal lord.

During the 1880s, Shepherd filed claims for and bought 122,500 acres, including virtually all of the land and mines in the canyons northeast or upstream, in the mountains surrounding Batopilas, and as far southwest as the small settlement and mission at Satevo, four miles downriver. The transfer of mine ownership from local to American hands during the 1860s and the consolidation of other locally owned mines during the 1880s into an American monopoly at Batopilas fit the emergent pattern found in Chihuahua. Mestizo pueblo claimants lost out to the state elite and Americans, who sought wealth by exploiting the land to provide metals, timber, cattle, and crops for the enormous and insatiable markets of the United States. The only hopes of the local citizenry for compensation from all of this activity lay in higher levels of employment in the mines and increased commercial exchange.

Meanwhile, because of the mining company's growing value, Alexander's armed men played an increasingly important role on behalf of the U.S. financiers. Díaz made Batopilas the cabecera (seat of government) for an enormous district that he dubbed Andrés del Río in honor of the director of the Antiguo Colegio de Minería in Mexico City. The district extended nearly 100 miles north to Tomochic in the mountains, forty miles east to Guachochic, and a hundred miles northeast to the more densely populated Papigochic Valley and the town of Guerrero. Whoever controlled Batopilas controlled the district. In Porfirian Mexico, sizable capitalization in mining usually meant American corporate ownership and the introduction of boilers, steam-powered stamping mills, electrical turbines, steel tracks, and locomotives.

In 1879, Shepherd's initial associates in the Batopilas Mining Company included Robinson, Fargo, and Ashbel Barney, who together retained a 20 percent interest. The new owners included railway car magnate George Pullman; General Edward M. McCook, the president of the Wells Fargo Bank; George R. Blanchard, the holder of several patents for the refining of aluminum from silicates identical to those of Batopilas; and Brigadier General Horace Porter, who was the vice president of the Pullman Palace Car Company and later U.S. ambassador to France. Blanchard was a prominent building materials manufacturer for the Philadelphia–New York–Boston region. Each of the four new partners held a 20 percent interest until 1880, when the company was reorganized.[5]

From 1879 to 1910, taking advantage of prevailing ethnic and labor divisions, the Patrón Grande, as Shepherd came to be called, and his son, Alexander Jr., who succeeded him as general manager in 1902, rarely had to apply draconian force against the nominally free workers and townspeople of Batopilas. After suppressing confrontations with the community elites and the workers in the 1880s, the Mexican army and the Patrón Grande's armed men held local dissent to a minimum. Meanwhile, they maintained armed escorts, composed of men with advantageous salaries and long-term employment prospects, for the Conducta, the mule trains carrying silver out of and supplies into the barrancas. For three decades, the imposition of armed authority in the Sierra Tarahumara by Shepherd and the government provided the political conditions needed for the success of the mines. The rebels, "renegade" Native Americans, and bandits who had plagued Robinson, Fargo, and the Barneys in the 1860s and 1870s had been virtually eliminated.

Alexander Robey Shepherd. (Courtesy of The Bancroft Library, University of California, Berkeley)

Enter the Boss

Born on January 31, 1835, in Washington, D.C., Alexander Shepherd grew up in a house on Rock Creek Road and attended the Presbyterian Church on New York Avenue. He attended Nourse's School on Indiana Avenue and then the Columbian College on 14th Street. He began his business career as an employee of John Thompson, the leading plumbing and gas line contractor in the city. In a few years' time, he gained Thompson's know-how in the business and succeeded him as the city's principal plumbing and sewer contractor. Following less than three months' service as a private in the Union Army between April and June 1861, Shepherd returned to Washington and was immediately elected to the Common Council of the city. He served as a councilman for three one-year terms and as president of the council in 1862.

During those years, Shepherd became an important player in the banking and media communities. He purchased the *Washington Evening Star* and befriended financier Henry David Cooke, whose firm, Jay Cooke and Company, had offices in Philadelphia and Washington. The bank served as one of the leading financial backers of the Union during the Civil War. Henry Cooke also held the presidency of the First National Bank of Washington. In 1869, President Ulysses S. Grant appointed Cooke as the first governor of the District of Columbia, and, two years later, Cooke named Shepherd to the Board of Public Works for the District. Alexander quickly became vice president of the board and a leader in the planning of urban development projects. He opened a publicity campaign in support of the projects, promising the public through his newspaper and others that "$4,358,598 will be the proportion of the expense to be borne by the treasury of the District in making these improvements."

Using his connections with President Grant, bankers, land developers, politicians, and contractors, Shepherd assumed de facto control of the district government, known by now as Boss Shepherd because of his style of governance. A land developer accustomed to insider dealing in the issuance of local government and public works contracts, he undertook a vast building program including 350 miles of widened and paved streets, 154 miles of curbs, sewers, drainage projects including storm drains, monuments, and 3,000 gas streetlights.

Boss Shepherd issued the contracts among his large circle of friends and then accepted payments for the "information" he provided them, a practice that his critics logically called kickbacks. Shoddy workmanship, defective materials, and gross overruns left most of the undertakings in a shambles, and poor political preparation for the street renovations turned the public against him. By 1874, the District debt for the projects had soared far beyond the $4 million-plus estimates and reached $26 million, while the overall obligation for the program had reached the wild total of $30 million. In contrast, the property tax base in Washington still only generated $1.5 million per year. Congressional aid and new taxes on the citizenry were needed in order to maintain the District of Columbia's financial integrity.

Critics railed at Boss Shepherd and the imperious arrogance of his administrators when two vendors died trying to save some of their goods after Alexander's men, without warning and in the middle of the night, began tearing down an old market building and caused it to collapse. In 1873, early in Grant's second term, the president appointed Shepherd to replace Cooke as governor of the District. By 1874, however, a growing financial scandal enveloped the Grant administration, and that included Alexander, who suffered exposure and disgrace. At that point, amid charges of criminal misconduct, the U.S. Congress undertook an investigation of his public works program and censured the District administration for exceeding its legal debt limit.

Despite mountainous evidence, the congressional inquiry deadlocked on the filing of charges against Alexander, perhaps because his Democratic critics had bigger fish to fry, including the president. Later in the 1870s, however, further congressional inquiries were threatened. By then, Shepherd's reputation in Washington had been so badly damaged that he felt the need "to seek business opportunities elsewhere." The evidence indicates that Alexander had issued contracts and handled monies in a manner beyond the very permissive limits of business ethics that prevailed in those times. Decades later, the myriad trees planted and the elegant elevated streets and traffic circles constructed during his administration remained, causing a grateful public to largely overlook his scandalous behavior.[6]

In 1879, severe depression as a result of his humiliation and fall from power and the possibility of prosecution drove Alexander to seek a place that offered the opportunity to recoup both his fortune, much as Robinson had done, and his self-esteem. In Shepherd's case, however, his relocation removed him from U.S. government jurisdiction but was close enough to home that he could return when the opportunity arose. Shepherd and his friends in Washington and New York knew about the troubles that Robinson and his Wells Fargo investors had experienced with political unrest and banditry in Batopilas. They also knew that General Díaz, an old friend of the United States financial elites and of former President Grant, had successfully imposed law and order in Mexico and desired American investments in Mexican natural resources. Díaz's connections with the American financial elites interested in Mexican opportunities dated back to the 1860s, when he commanded the military effort in southern Mexico against the invading army of French Emperor Louis Napoleon. Shepherd realized that the new regime would make it possible for him to restore the Batopilas mines to glory and make him richer than he had ever dreamed.[7]

On June 29, 1879, after finding an impressive array of financial backers, Alexander began his own journey to Batopilas and a life he could never have imagined a few short years earlier. Accompanied by New York shipping financier Lyndon H. Stevens, a director of the West Indies Shipping and Trinidad Shipping and Trading Companies, he sailed from New York to Panama. The two men then crossed the isthmus on the Panama Railroad, headed by David Hoadly of Phelps Dodge, and traveled up the Pacific Coast to Mazatlán on a liner of the Pacific Mail Steamship Company, controlled by New York financiers Moses Taylor, Francis Skiddy, and William Aspinwall. The Pacific Mail operated the principal shipping line between Panama and Mazatlán and extended its service as far as Cochin, India. The men then took a sailing ship to Agiabampo, located on a small bay 270 miles northwest of Mazatlán and 100 miles west-southwest of Batopilas, as the crow flies. They would later find travel to the Sierra Tarahumara through the choppy seas of the Caribbean to Panama, then north on the Pacific side to Mazatlán and on to Agiabampo even more wearing and dangerous than the overland route.

Agiabampo was a logical place to disembark. It provided the most immediate access to the Sierra Tarahumara and Batopilas. Mounted on *mulas de silla* (specially bred and trained riding mules), Shepherd and Stevens traversed the rugged terrain to Batopilas. Enduring temperatures above 100 degrees, they crossed the littoral of Sinaloa by way of Mocorito and followed the Río Fuerte to the district capital of Fuerte. After resting, they journeyed forty miles farther upstream to the slightly smaller town of Choix, named for the tar pits or pitch found in the region and located in the foothills immediately below the first high and steep sides of the Sierra Tarahumara. In the 1620s, Jesuit missionary Cristobal Villata had officially consecrated the town. Choix featured the historic and impressive Templo de San Ignacio de Loyola cathedral and some elegant housing for the Sinaloa and Sonora elites. During the seventeenth century, the citizens had built the cathedral on top of the original Jesuit mission. When Shepherd arrived, the residents were in the midst of a highly professional reconstruction of the building. The results of that work have endured into the early twenty-first century.

Choix had counted 3,438 inhabitants in 1873 and was noted for resins and other forestry products. It was also a gathering place for Raramuris during Holy Week and on other religious occasions. Red roses and stunning bougainvillea gave the town a distinct charm. A few American and Mexican miners had already opened operations there, but none would compare to the success and scale of operations that Shepherd planned for Batopilas. In 1879, Choix served as the western jumping-off point for journeys into the Sierra Tarahumara and the Barranca de Batopilas. Shepherd, however, like Robinson before him, took little notice of the cultural importance of Choix or of the complicated Tarahumara.

When Alexander and Lyndon struck out into the mountains, their party included two experienced mule skinners and their sure-footed mules. What they saw amazed them. Like Robinson twenty years earlier, they encountered a diverse range of fauna and flora. The hunters and timber men had not yet affected the more remote and rugged mountain habitats. After reaching the collection of huts called Ranchito, Alexander's party would most probably have headed east, traveling some six miles to Tazahers and then past Guamochil for several more miles, where they would have eaten a dinner of dried meat and tortillas, drank coffee, and camped for the night. The next day, they would have tried to reach a point near Culebra that lay twenty-five miles east of Guamochil on a rugged trail sometimes called the Camino Real.

After two hard days of climbing, they were beyond the oak trees and on top of the sierra, amid the pines. On the mountaintops, it was clear and cold. As they rested for the night, they heard the wolves howling and coyotes yipping in the distance. The stars hung in the sky like brilliant ornamental lights and unlike anything they had ever seen. In the morning, they broke camp after again eating dried meat and tortillas, chased down by coffee. Their sleep had been uneventful, uninterrupted by the ever present possibility of a bear entering the camp in search of food. The few grizzly bears remaining in the region were even more fearful of men now than they had been during Robinson's trek in 1861. The more cautious black bears only rarely intruded on camps. They had learned to fear humans. After thousands of years of coexistence with the Raramuri and other Native Americans, the bears, especially the larger and more aggressive grizzlies, were almost extinct.

As they climbed, Shepherd and Stevens looked down from the innumerable turns and folds in the trail and saw precipitous cliffs falling away below them on the opposite sides of the canyon, with their sprinkling of red pitaya flowers. These grew on the slopes that rose thousands of feet from the floors of the barrancas. Like Robinson before them, Alexander and Lyndon strained to make out the mix of increasingly desertlike terrain near the bottoms that were juxtaposed with the semitropical flora immediately adjacent to the Río Fuerte. The lines of the arêtes to the southeast reached beyond his range of vision.

The travelers headed directly for the Barranca de Batopilas, crossing some arêtes but avoiding the seemingly endless mountain peaks that they could see silhouetted row after row on the skyline to the east and southeast, which disappeared into the haze lit up by the myriad reflections of the rising sun. At sunrise on the third day, their last one on top of the canyon complex, the sky turned red and orange, with the edges of the colors fading into the ever-lightening purples and then blues that Robinson had witnessed. Soon they would be meeting the sun in the furnace-like terrain that stretched out far below them. After only an hour on a ridge amid enormous trees, higueras, nacapules, and camuchines, some of them more than a thousand years old, and the wide variety of other vegetation that comprised the virgin forest, they began the descent into Culebra.

Upon leaving Culebra, the party probably traveled the ten miles to Los Cueros and then kept moving in order to find water, finally stopping at a settlement called Tetanheca on the Río Fuerte. They would have covered about twenty miles of up-and-down terrain that day. That night, they would have used at least one watchman, alert for invasions of the camp-site by bears and jaguars.

The next, day they covered another twenty miles, stopping at Rancho Viejo to enjoy its water. The climate was decidedly drier. In the morning, they descended some 2,000 feet onto a relatively level valley some twelve miles wide, characterized by a desert flora of ocotillo, cactus, and mes-quite. They passed the ancient Raramuri settlement of Guasimas near the present-day site of El Rodeo. By late afternoon, they stood on the La Cumbre ridge, above and southwest of Batopilas.

From that commanding vantage point, the travelers could see three towns: Batopilas was strung along the river nine miles to the northeast and several thousand feet below them, Satevo was about four miles down the glistening river from Batopilas and about seven miles to their southeast, and Guasimas lay some ten miles behind them on the more gradual trail they had ascended from the west. As they moved down the steep and rugged trail and worked their way around the crevasses adjoining the canyon Alexander caught glimpses of the flora near the Río Batopilas, especially the bougainvillea and cottonwoods, and the water's reflections of the sun's rays. It shimmered in the light far below, and its distant convolutions once again, as it had to Robinson, made it appear similar to a silver serpent.

As they descended in the late afternoon light, the peaks and can-yon walls began to change colors. A curious atmospheric phenomenon takes place in the Sierra Tarahumara at sunset on all clear days. The sky displays an unusual purple hue that extends upward about 15 degrees above the horizon and surrounds the observer for 360 degrees. By the time the party saw this, the Camino Real had become little more than a steep sometimes-treacherous mule trail. The many different strata of rock showed purple, gray, and spectacular red and orange colorations. The party lost sight of Batopilas itself during most of the descent. It was tucked out of view behind a ridge on the west side of the river just upstream from them, at a point where it turned to the southeast. About halfway down, the famous Descubridora silver mine came into view in the upper reaches of a side canyon.

At this point, a geologic uplift had broken the crevasse into three shallower canyons. They crossed the two lines of hills from west to east and converged with a trail that led down from the mines in the area to the canyon bottom. It was late afternoon, but the temperature still hovered near 100 degrees. At the top of the third shallower canyon, the travelers stopped to drink water and rest. They had to drink frequently because the stifling heat of the barrancas can disable and kill unwary travelers through rapid dehydration. When they neared the historic San Antonio del Camunchin silver mine, Shepherd could see it off to their left as well as objects near the river, about one-half mile distant. They had descended rapidly and were now slightly less than one mile from Batopilas as the crow flies, but the rugged mountain that separated the Camunchin mine from Batopilas required them to cover two sides of a triangle.

During a tangled descent of about two miles characterized by repeated switchbacks, they encountered several more mine shafts. The worn and dusty condition of the trail indicated a high level of foot traffic. Most of the mines were idle, but a few showed signs of limited activity as gambusinos sought to make their living digging for silver in solitude and anonymity. It took them three hours to reach the bottom of the canyon. After a final stretch of steep drops that necessitated even more switchbacks on the trail they hiked upstream alongside the river for several hundred yards. As they followed the trail upstream, it widened, and they began to encounter jacales made of wooden planks, mesquite, and sage. After a week of rugged climbs and steep descents and fantastic views, they had completed the quickest and easiest route from the outside world into Batopilas.[8]

As they entered the town from the southwest, it presented a striking image. The jacales provided living spaces for Yaqui, Mayo, and mestizo barreteros, Tarahumaras, and transients who lacked the resources needed for more permanent constructions. Their dwellings were vulnerable to the severe floods that cascaded down the barranca from the upper reaches of the Sierra Madre during the rainy season. Passing the shacks, they encountered a row of one- and two-room houses stretched along the west side of the canyon and made of adobe and timbers, which faced the river and stood about ten feet above it. These dwellings extended about 200 feet to the center of town, and their occupants enjoyed shade in the late afternoon and the perpetual sound of running river water. Tropical vegetation of all kinds, including palms, mangos, and bougainvillea, offered considerable relief from the heat.

As Shepherd and Stevens entered the main plaza, they probably stopped briefly to announce their arrival to Guadalupe Ramírez, who served as the mayor in the two-story civic building that stood backed up against the canyon wall on the west side of the plaza. The downtown buildings featured whitened adobe walls, while a few claimed the harder shell provided by plaster. The still unfinished public school continued to double as a jail at the corner on the north side of the plaza.

One block up the street, near the Mendazona Mansion, where Alexander and Lyndon may have taken up temporary residence, stood the cathedral, still a victim of neglect. Two blocks up the street from the main plaza was the unchanged Plaza del Taste, named for its tree with flamboyant blossoms and wide leaves. That plaza extended westerly for one block from the river and halfway to the cathedral. The arriving party noted a few members of the town's merchant and mine-owning class sitting languidly on covered porches throughout the downtown area, out of the burning sun.

The Plaza del Taste, where young people performed nightly paseos, greeting and flirting with each other, featured palm, mango, bougainvillea, and cottonwood trees. The plaza was coming to life about the time the Americans arrived because the afternoon siesta had ended and the small shops were reopened. The mountain behind Batopilas covered the town in its protective shadow, and the temperature quickly dropped from about 100 to the low 80s. Tarahumara and mestizo women, their wares spread out for display on the paving stones, reminded passersby of their sliced pineapple and watermelon, halved pomegranates, oranges, and mangos, as well as simple utensils. Men sold tools and mining supplies. Small shops and a few two-story houses surrounded the Plaza del Taste on three sides, just as they had at the time of Robinson's first visit, almost twenty years earlier. The proximity of the river, however, left the entire plaza vulnerable to the terrible flood that would finally destroy it after severe deforestation upstream.

Two blocks farther upstream, the downtown area ended. The mountains closed in toward the river, leaving only a narrow road bordered on one side by whitewashed adobe houses and shops that extended upstream for a half mile. The next morning, Shepherd had to walk only a short distance upstream from the mansion to view the Hacienda San Miguel, situated across the river. Surrounded by beautiful trees, roses,

Batopilas from the north after a flood destroyed the Plaza del Taste. (Courtesy of The Bancroft Library, University of California, Berkeley)

mangos, and bougainvillea, the hacienda complex stood on a plateau some twenty-two feet above the river, safe from high water. Robinson had made some improvements in the seventeenth-century processing plant and housing facilities, but the Hacienda San Miguel was still largely a processing plant comprising mostly one-story buildings. Shepherd, however, did not want to live in the Mendazona home and had big plans for San Miguel as the site of a private residence separated from town by the river.

Alexander noted that the mines were in a state of neglect but saw rose-colored support pillars inside them containing large amounts of native silver. For Shepherd, this discovery indicated both the neglect and the potential of the place. He then studied Robinson's books, surveyed the town, the economy of which depended on gambusinos, and reported to his wife: "The thing has paid so well with slight effort . . . that the owners

Hacienda San Miguel from the north. (Courtesy of The Bancroft Library, University of California, Berkeley)

have been content to get out merely that which showed on the surface. . . . The managing people here have nice quarters and a good time. . . . An isolation of five years would be exile and banishment but I believe it would insure a fortune."[9] Shepherd returned to Washington by the overland route through Chihuahua City, Fort Conchos (now San Angelo), and San Antonio, learning that it was both quicker and safer than by sea, despite the possible raids of hostile Apache and Comanche Indians between the Sierra Madre and Fort Conchos.

Back in New York, Alexander met with his associates, and they agreed to purchase a controlling interest in the mines from Robinson and his partners, creating a new Batopilas Mining Company. They wanted control of the San Miguel and San Pedro mining complexes, that is, the working mines on both sides of the river. They also sought land claimed by the Díaz government to have long been in the public domain. That

The guardhouse at the entry to the Hacienda San Miguel. (Courtesy of the Historical Society of Washington, D.C.)

purchase provided the basis for the disputes with the local elites that ensued after his return to Batopilas.

In addition to Shepherd, Robinson, Fargo, Blanchard, and Ashbel Barney, the initial board of directors included his personal friends Stevens and George W. Quintard, who was closely associated with the Morgan Bank and a director of the Colonial Trust, Leather Manufacturers, Eleventh Ward Banks, Erie Railroad, and of Manhattan Life Insurance and the German-American Realty Companies. The board also included Henry Havemeyer, of the American Sugar Company and a director of the Colonial Bank of New York. The new board members represented the

additional capital and expertise needed to direct enlarged mining operations. Stevens's and Quintard's positions in the transportation industry
helped in arranging the transport of silver bullion to San Francisco, New
York, and Asia. Railroad magnate George Pullman, who also helped in
this regard, provided access to railroad technology including rails and
cars, while Quintard manufactured rails and equipment at his Morgan
Steel Works on the East River opposite Manhattan. Horace Porter, a civil
engineer and vice president of the Pullman Company, and Blanchard, as
a major figure in the building materials industry, provided additional
expertise to the construction of the tunnels, railroads, and aqueducts to be
developed at the mining complex.

Among Alexander's directors with railroad backgrounds, Pullman had
gained fame as a capitalist and leading innovator in the industry, especially for the creation of palace sleeping cars for passenger trains. His notorious strikebreaking tactics employed against his workers in the United
States, however, would later seriously damage Pullman's reputation. His
interest in Mexican mining paralleled that of fellow Chicagoan, Potter
Palmer. Robinson, who remained a director, also had railroad expertise.
In 1890, he obtained a patent in New York City for a new ore-carrying
freight car.

Porter, the son of two-time Pennsylvania governor David Rittenhouse
Porter, "a grand uncle in law of Abraham Lincoln," and a captain in the
Union Army during the U.S. Civil War, had served as General Grant's
aide-de-camp. During Grant's tenure as president of the United States
(1869–77), Porter filled the position of presidential chief of staff. Grant
and his son Jesse Root Grant were longtime friends of both Shepherd and
Porter and held a great interest in the Mexican Southern Railroad, which
they planned to construct across the Isthmus of Tehuantepec. The former
president's son also held an abiding interest in Mexican mining.

In 1879–1881, as a vice president of the Pullman Company, Porter
could have been acting on his own at Batopilas, but the Grants probably
had considerable influence in his decision to take part. Porter later became a general and received the Congressional Medal of Honor for
gallantry in the Cuban campaign of the Spanish American War. President William McKinley then appointed him U.S. ambassador to France
(1897–1905). In Paris, he befriended the Musy family, which included
a president of Switzerland and, in Mexico, Luis Musy, the principal

photographer at Batopilas during the 1880s and 1890s. The Porter and Musy families later intermarried.

Blanchard's products included terne (an alloy of lead and tin) and aluminum. He was a partner of William Frishmuth the head of the Frishmuth Foundry in Philadelphia. They jointly held three patents for the improvement of aluminum through an alloy that included silicates identical to those found at Batopilas. Blanchard had the capacity to have produced the tin, terne, or aluminum roofing placed on the new and enlarged buildings at the Hacienda San Miguel during the 1880s and 1890s. Frishmuth was the sole aluminum manufacturer in the United States for a fifteen-year period during the last third of the nineteenth century. He enjoyed several ties to Shepherd. His foundry fabricated the aluminum cap for the Washington Monument, which was under construction throughout Shepherd's tenure in Washington. Frishmuth worked with architect Adolf Cluss, who designed Shepherd's Row, two Smithsonian Institution buildings, and Eastern Market among other structures in Washington. Both Frishmuth and Cluss were of German birth, participated in the 1848 student uprisings there, found refuge in the United States, and lived in Philadelphia. Clearly, Cluss or one of his followers offered the design for Shepherd's Castle at San Miguel, which resembled the Smithsonian. J. D. Smith, the president of the New York Stock Exchange, facilitated access to public investors, and the company was duly registered on the Exchange. Meanwhile, Shepherd also maintained close ties with Wells Fargo, continuing its role as "our banker" for the BMC.[10]

Alexander, whose segregationist racial politics coincided with the values of the Washington, D.C., Maryland and the Southern United States elites at the time, immediately recognized the Hacienda San Miguel as a site for a lordly way of life, separate from the "Chinese" (Asians), Africans, Mexicans, and "Indians." His later lifestyle reflected that proclivity. Shepherd and his family lived across the river from the Mexicans in a "foreign colony" he created. His children ventured to the other side for recreation and special events. Later, he would send his sons to the University of the South at Sewanee, Tennessee, to complete their educations. In addition, Alexander noted that the site was a virtual fortress, offering a high level of security from potential robbers. That and social concerns led him to choose separate living from the town. Shepherd was no exception in this

The Shepherd family and friends at the Hacienda San Miguel. (Courtesy of the Library of Congress)

regard; American managers and owners of large mines in Mexico invariably established segregated facilities.

After deciding to purchase the mines, Shepherd chose to return to the United States by way of Chihuahua and Texas and report his findings to his partners. He realized that the political tranquility offered by President Díaz, the new and draconian military dictator of Mexico supported by the United States government and the financial titans of New York City, would allow him to exceed Robinson's sensational mining successes even if the surface deposits had been exhausted. After having suffered the clipper ships with their ups, downs, and rolling to and from Panama, he decided the overland trip through Chihuahua and Texas was safer and more comfortable. Travel by sea from New York to Panama, the malarial trek across the Isthmus of Panama, and the sail north against the Japanese Current of the Pacific Ocean proved to be a greater test than the threat of Apache raiders led by Victorio, the Comanche, and bandit gangs in Chihuahua and west Texas.

In 1880, after the company named its first board of directors, comprising Shepherd, Robinson, Quintard, Porter, Pullman, Blanchard, and Stevens, Shepherd led his family and an entourage of seventeen to Batopilas. The group included Stevens and Colonel James Morris Morgan, an engineer. Morgan's brother, Captain Philip Hicky Morgan, served in Mexico City from 1880 to 1885 as the U.S. envoy extraordinary and minister plenipotentiary to Mexico and proved to be an invaluable intermediary for Shepherd with Porfirio Díaz and the Mexican government. After Morgan's term in office, Enrique (Henry) Clay Creel, the son-in-law of Governor and General Luis Terrazas and the son of the U.S. consul in Chihuahua and former New York banker Reuben Creel and Paz Cuilty of the state oligarchy, filled that role. The Morgans were related to Charles Morgan, the original owner of the Morgan Iron Works in Manhattan, which Quintard had purchased. Seventeen American employees made up the rest of the party including "Doctor Ross," a surgeon intended to provide care for the family and also for injured miners, a mining engineer, a metallurgist, a teacher for the Shepherd children, and a bookkeeper. They rode in "luxury" in a "Private Car," as far as San Antonio.

During the last leg of the railroad portion of the journey, from Houston to San Antonio, they rode on the newly completed Sunset Line, which gained its sobriquet because the workers faced due west during its construction across Texas. At San Antonio, Shepherd bought some "wild mules" and then hired cowboys to break them for use in carrying his entourage overland by carriage. Riding horses and carriages, they set out for Fort Conchos, Fort Davis, and then Presidio del Norte on the border. The trip consumed three weeks. The Mexican customs officials at Ojinaga–Presidio del Norte received them with suspicion, and the travelers spent two to three days "fussing" with them before gaining entry. At that point, a squad of mounted private guards escorted them from Presidio to Chihuahua City.

At Chihuahua City, Alexander purchased a number of "mountain mules," capable of carrying their considerable supply of household and industrial goods into the Sierra Madre. Meanwhile, the Terrazas family and other state elites warmly welcomed and entertained them for several days. Two days after departing the city, they entered the Sierra Madre. Their initial contact with the Tarahumara occurred when some members of the party visited a cave dwelling, probably near Carichi. The Raramuri living space inside the cave measured eight feet in diameter, and featured an iron skillet used over an open fire near the entrance, a metate (stone for grinding corn), and two goats. Following the main trail taken by Robinson twenty years earlier, they reached the rim of the Barranca del Cobre four days later.

The precipices, flora, and wildness that characterized the barrancas stunned the family. James Morgan noted the speed of the river. They heard the wolves at night, listened to tales about the grizzlies, a few of which still roamed the backcountry, and of the "hostile" Yaqui Indians, some of whom lived to the northwest, in the western reaches of the mountains. The genocidal hunt for Yaqui scalps was still going on in the Sierra Madre.

Shepherd's wife and seven children gladly settled into the well-guarded "perfect paradise" represented by the Hacienda San Miguel. Alexander Jr., who would later run the mines, was eight years old at the time. His brother Grant was only five. The hacienda had been cleaned up and an L-shaped building suitable for residential living prepared. It included an enclosed garden and large front porch. Morgan wrote of how impressed he was with the wealth of silver and the grandeur of the canyons. Given his sense of social hierarchy and connections with the New York elites, he chose to identify "Mr. Fargo," not Robinson, as the seller of the mining and hacienda complex.

The Shepherds and their employees were heavily armed in "a fortress guarded as carefully as for a European monarch." Their armory included "rifles, pistols, and other implements of an offensive and defensive nature." In addition, perhaps to emulate Hernán Cortés, the conqueror of the Aztec Empire more than three and one-half centuries earlier, Alexander prominently displayed a pair of dangerous mastiffs as his companions. They also served as watchdogs. Their reportedly violent dispositions frightened natives and visitors alike. Given the weapons the Americans brought with them, the small private army they inherited and enlarged upon, and the proximity of Mexican soldiers, the only notable crime committed against the BMC occurred away from the hacienda. A Yaqui miner robbed and killed Charlie Mayhew, a mine supervisor, when he ventured out to a mining site with payroll monies in the early 1880s.[11]

The use of force by the company, however, extended beyond law enforcement to the suppression of labor unrest and public demonstrations, problems that surfaced soon after the arrival of Shepherd and his associates. Only intimidation by the Mexican army and higher authority dissipated that resistance, but the friction between American owners, labor, and town authorities recurred from time to time over the next thirty years.

Shepherd quickly established himself as the strongest force in the region by developing friendships with a mix of power players, including General Díaz and the state oligarchy, especially the conqueror of the French and famous Indian fighter Luis Terrazas and his son-in-law Enrique Creel. In 1881, Alexander visited Don Porfirio, as Díaz was called by his friends and some critics, in Mexico City. It was at that point that Díaz became the padrino to at least one of Shepherd's children. They enjoyed mutual close friends in Ulysses S. Grant, the Morgan brothers, and Creel. Díaz then served temporarily as minister of economic development (*fomento*), a position in which his responsibilities included the personal approval of mining concessions. He returned to the presidency in 1884.

In the beginning, Shepherd almost immediately renamed the original San Miguel Tunnel as the Porfirio Díaz Tunnel and transferred the rubric "San Miguel" to the former San Antonio Tunnel across the river and upstream from the hacienda. In 1884 he restarted Robinson's project to deepen and improve the Díaz Tunnel. He planned for it to intersect from below all of the silver veins that extended downward through the mountain. In December 1881, the tunnel reached 1,350 feet (410 meters) into the mountain and already intersected twelve veins of silver. Under construction from 1884 until 1907, the deepened tunnel eventually reached 9,050 feet. Divided in two sections, labeled A and B, it featured 8,000 feet of narrow-gauge railroad track for the movement of ore. Shepherd liked to call it "the longest in the world," a claim contested by the owners of a similar construction in Brazil.

And almost immediately, in 1880, Alexander succeeded in the purchase of Yaqui Indians from human traffickers and had them brought to the mines at Batopilas. One account holds that, to minimize security concerns and keep them close to the worksites, he placed them in the San Miguel Tunnel (former San Antonio Tunnel) a half mile north of the Hacienda San Miguel across and upstream from the Díaz Tunnel. Although the exact status of the Yaquis remains unclear, one should remember that many thousands of them had been arrested and deported from Sonora for resisting the dissolution of their pueblo homelands by the

government and the acquisition of those properties by private landholders, most notably famed imperialist demagogue Charles Conant and the
Richardson Construction Company of Los Angeles, California.

Shepherd also immediately established ties with the state elites, which
he strengthened during the next twenty years. His friend Enrique Creel
married Angela Terrazas, a daughter of the governor. Enrique, as the son
of the American consul and Paz Cuilty, a sister-in-law of Governor Terrazas, was marrying a distant cousin. The marriage, like that of the Robinson and Terrazas families, underscored the cohesion of wealth and political power in the state. The marriages benefited the Terrazas family by
further developing the close ties of the family with the American elites in
the state and providing dual citizenship for the offspring of these unions.
A descendant, Santiago Creel, became the secretary of foreign relations
of Mexico under the administration of President Vicente Fox, the grandson of an American hacendado who immigrated to Guanajuato in the
wake of the Mexican Revolution. As Enrique increasingly assumed a
leadership role in the Chihuahua oligarchy, including partnership with
the MacManus family as owners of the Chihuahua mint, he and Alexander expanded their business and political relationships.

The Shepherd, MacManus, and Creel families frequently visited each
other during Alexander's visits to the state capital. The three men entered
the ill-fated Kansas City, Mexico, and Orient Railroad syndicate together.
Shepherd opened a large account in Creel's bank in addition to sending
about half of his ingots to the mint; Creel ensured social tranquillity at the
mines of Batopilas and nearby Urique by dispatching troops to provide
security and pursue reported bandits. Creel's importance became apparent when he replaced the local officials at Batopilas after they demanded
that Shepherd build a clean-water aqueduct to bypass the effluent from
the smelter at the Hacienda San Miguel. The community leaders had
decided that excessive levels of cyanide and mercury in the drinking
water were making their townspeople ill and even killing them, and
something had to be done about it.

Frank MacManus used his ties with the Chihuahua oligarchy to become one of Mexico's largest land speculators. His firms, the Compañía
Gómez del Campo, MacManus, Asunsolo y Socios, and the Compañía
Deslindadora de Terrenos Baldíos, sold vast tracts of rich farmland, falsely
declared sterile and unoccupied by the federal government, to rich Amer-

ican buyers and the Terrazas and Creel families. These properties surrounded the large tracts held by Shepherd on the south, east, and north.[12]

By 1880, when Shepherd joined the alliance of the Terrazas family with Díaz, many of the local elites in western Chihuahua already resented their loss of political independence to the oligarchy of central Chihuahua. Within a few years, the local elites in the western part of the state added water pollution and land theft to their list of grievances against the Americans and then, in the late 1880s, the presence of U.S. colonists, who began to settle to their immediate north.

The local elites in farming and ranching towns like Guerrero and Casas Grandes at first supported the privatization of town communal property, from which they initially benefited, but, by the mid-1890s, the economies of scale created by the larger American-owned farming, ranching, mining, and timber companies left them unable to compete. Many of them faced bankruptcy. At that point, they adopted a more critical and eventually hostile view of the powerful and wealthy newcomers. Instead of bringing the great benefits to the state economy that the western chihuahuenses anticipated on a scale grander than that of the disappointed batopilenses, the Americans, as usual, only helped increase the wealth of a well-positioned few. In doing so, they also helped displace and weaken the majority. But, during the 1880s and 1890s, the losers could only mount piecemeal and stopgap forms of opposition because of the overwhelming power represented by the combination of the federal government, state oligarchy, and American capital. During the 1880s and 1890s, a new political and economic order emerged in Batopilas, Chihuahua, and Mexico, characterized by centralized political control over the regional peripheries that had earlier enjoyed virtual autonomy and local hegemony.

The local elites did not give up, however. At first, in the 1880s, local or customs officials at Casas Grandes, Guerrero, Ojinaga, and El Paso del Norte (Ciudad Juárez) blocked shipments of goods or refused to approve the entry papers of American technicians, engineers, and settlers. But these actions, when overruled by the new power elite, only made the process more painful for its opponents, helping to pave the way to the Mexican Revolution. The American interests involved simply appealed over their heads to state and federal officials. During the 1880s and 1890s, Governor Terrazas and the federal ministers of economic development,

Generals Díaz and Carlos Pacheco, responded energetically to the demands of American capitalists. Thereafter, the higher officials of the regime demanded loyalty oaths from the local authorities and ordered them to allow the Americans to go about their work "unmolested."[13]

In Alexander's case, all he had to do was notify the Terrazas group in Chihuahua or U.S. Minister Plenipotentiary Philip Morgan whenever he had a problem, and the issue was settled almost immediately. At first, in the early 1880s, Ramírez, still the jefe político of Batopilas, some local businessmen, and gambusinos saw Shepherd as a wealthy interloper and crude bully. From their perspective, he was interfering in local politics, making unfounded claims for mining properties and real estate that had not been Robinson's to sell, and practicing brutality in his use of forced Yaqui labor. In addition, Shepherd had acquired concessions of acreage from the minister of economic development and was asserting those claims as well. Meanwhile, the gambusinos' efforts to oppose the imposition of a wage system of compensation had come to nothing.[14]

Ramírez and other Batopilas elites openly joined the miners in disputing Alexander's assertions of ownership over a number of the mines and surrounding properties. Not long after Shepherd's arrival, Ramírez ordered the local police to arrest Alexander because he sent men to work some of the mines that he and other Batopilas elites considered their properties. Ramírez and his allies were perhaps hoping to negotiate a compromise, but the American quickly protested to the authorities in Chihuahua and Mexico City. Generals Terrazas and Díaz now regularly consulted with the U.S. minister plenipotentiary in Mexico City. They ordered Alexander's immediate release and then sent a detachment of federal troops to Batopilas, where the commander even interrogated Ramírez.

The episode removed any doubts the jefe político may have had regarding Shepherd's importance, and he backed down. In ordering the troops in, Terrazas and Díaz had effectively legitimated Alexander's mining claims, use of private guards, and credit and scrip currency practices. The government's actions cowed the local authorities and businessmen into silence. Although the gambusinos continued to hold public protest meetings and threatened to strike, their coalition with the town elites had been broken. Isolated from their erstwhile allies and intimidated by the army, the gambusinos had been greatly weakened, and Shepherd was now able to carry forward his plan to replace them with wage laborers.

Ramírez tried to explain the episode away to the commander of the troops as a misunderstanding, but the disagreements ran deep. Shortly afterward, the government appointed Jesús "Jesse" Hernández, one of Shepherd's mine foremen, to replace Ramírez as the jefe político. It would be several years before Ramírez established a "friendship" with the Shepherd family. Hernández had served as one of Robinson's two principal mining superintendents during the 1860s and 1870s. He continued his work as a mine supervisor and Batopilas political leader for years thereafter. The local elites, including Ramírez, his sons, and Town Councilman Ramón Orozco, who was an immediate relative of the already alienated elite Orozco family of Guerrero, grudgingly accommodated Boss Shepherd. Orozco, a merchant, was important in Batopilas. The relationship that evolved between Shepherd, now sometimes derisively known as the Patrón Grande, and Ramón Orozco is unclear. In 1910, Pascual Orozco, a visiting relative from the western Chihuahua town of Guerrero, seized control of the main plaza at Batopilas and, from there, assumed the military leadership of the Mexican Revolution.[15]

The American, Mexican, and Chihuahua financial elites wanted to extract as much wealth as possible from Mexico's mines. The United States was industrializing at an unprecedented rate and needed precious metals for wealth and coinage. The great mineral companies were already becoming international firms, by expanding first into Mexico and then into Central and South America. Their principal owners sat as directors on the boards of major banks, insurance companies, and railroads reaching from the Atlantic to the Pacific Coast. The Batopilas Mining Company was one of their most significant mineral operations.[16]

The mining magnates saw opportunity in Robinson's growing despair, despite the more than $1 million per year that the mines had produced between 1861 and 1879. The hardships, tragedy, and incessant threats posed by rebels and bandits that Robinson had endured gave them the advantage. In 1879, Shepherd learned that, although the most obvious surface deposits of native silver had been taken out, there were still enough for bandit-rebels to obtain $100,000 in silver during the two-month-long occupation of the mines in 1872, and gambusinos were still making a living chipping raw silver by hand from fissure veins. Shepherd assumed local responsibility for managing the mines because of the uncounted riches and the remoteness of the place, deep in the Sierra Madre and far from the prying eyes of Congress.

The Batopilas Mining Company

In 1879, the original buyers Shepherd, Pullman, Porter, and Blanchard paid $600,000 to Robinson for an 80 percent share of the Batopilas mining complex. Alexander and his mining engineers convinced them that, if he applied high technology and a rationalized economy of scale to the mines, they would pay well. That project entailed an increase in the volume of silver ore production that would exceed costs, the recruitment of specialists in the U.S. economic leadership, the introduction of capitalist-labor relationships, that is, taking advantage of the lower wages that prevailed in Mexico versus the United States, the end of gambusino contracts, and the use of forced Native American laborers under American overseers.

The directors anticipated that the lower labor costs of mining in Batopilas would contrast favorably with the expensive labor used in the silver bonanzas in the western United States. In pursuing the BMC's goals, Shepherd and his assistants worked within a complex mind-set and sense of superiority that eulogized their work as a civilizing mission, rejected the notion that the Yaquis, Apaches, and other "savages" were fully human, dismissed outside criticism, and rejected what they considered the utopian dreams of those batopilense workers and small businessmen who believed in municipal self-government, political diversity, and a prosperous new world that would benefit a broad base of the citizenry, not just the "entrepreneurs."

To fulfill their grandiose plans, the original directors recruited an elite upper management team for the BMC. One of the new board members, U.S. Senator Jerome B. Chaffee of Colorado, provided the business know-how, capital, and political connections in Washington for dealings with the U.S. Department of State and the Mexican government. Chaffee, one of the nation's most successful mining impresarios, had developed the Bob-Tail Lode and tunnel in Colorado before organizing the famous Little Pittsburgh Consolidated Mining Company. The Bob-Tail tunnel was the longest in Colorado for many years. The senator's political influence included a long-term membership on the National Committee of the Republican Party and intimate friendship with former President Grant and Matías Romero, the Mexican emissary to the United States, who, in turn, was close to President Díaz. Chaffee's daughter married Ulysses S. Grant Jr. Shepherd underscored Chaffee's importance in Batopilas when he dubbed the mines the Comstock of Mexico. Chaffee's wife was Miriam Comstock, a daughter of the Nevada tycoon.

Another director, Andros Boynton Stone, had been a full partner in the Chicago engineering firm of Stone and Boomer since the 1850s. The company designed canals, bridges, and aqueducts. Those projects included the Michigan and Illinois Canal, which linked the Great Lakes with the Gulf of Mexico via the Mississippi River system. The firm built the first bridge across the Mississippi River and constructed bridges for twenty-four railroads in Illinois, Missouri, and Wisconsin. Stone expanded his operations during the 1860s to include the production of Bessemer steel for boilers, steel rails and beams, and plate and sheet metal. As president of the American Sheet and Boiler Plate Company and the Cleveland Rolling Mill Company, he was positioned to provide the engineering knowledge and materials needed for the construction of aqueducts, canals, bridges, boilers, and tanks at Batopilas.[17]

Benjamin P. Cheney was the third important addition to the BMC board. Besides enjoying business ties to Stone, he provided banking, railroad, and political connections through his close ties to the Morgan Bank, presidency of the Northern Pacific Railroad, directorship with the Atchison, Topeka, and Santa Fe Railroad, and close ties to Yale University. The Northern Pacific and the Santa Fe both enjoyed connections with the Asian silver market through the Pacific Mail Steamship Company. In the 1880s, the Santa Fe was building a line from north to south across Chihuahua under the rubric of the Mexican Central. It would carry silver ingots from Chihuahua City to the United States. In addition to all these relationships, Shepherd maintained the company's older ties. Besides continuing Wells Fargo's role as "our banker," he shared the title of vice president of the BMC with Robinson. But, in reality, Robinson was out of the picture. Until the mid-1890s, when he died, he continued to live in Talbot County, Maryland, and to visit New York on business. Shepherd, in contrast, relished the role of Boss or Patrón Grande at Batopilas.

Meanwhile, the company retained influential Mexicans to represent its interests with the governments in Chihuahua City and Mexico City on a daily basis, not depending on consular or ministerial intervention. Alexander recruited Creel, who was still a young man, as a shareholder and director. The choice was apt because Creel became the Mexican minister of foreign relations. In 1880, the new directors, using Robinson's original mining concession, for which they had paid the $600,000, applied to the Mexican government for ownership approval. General Díaz, who had temporarily assumed the position of minister of economic development in the administration of President Manuel González, met with Shepherd in Mexico City. Díaz not only approved the transfer of the concession but also encouraged Alexander to apply for a more extensive land grant, which led to the conflict with Ramírez and the other batopilenses. Both Díaz and González strongly favored the sale of economic concessions to financially powerful Americans. After Díaz returned to the presidency in 1884, he held the office and maintained his policies until the revolutionaries toppled him from power in 1911. Díaz liked strong male personalities, and he was very impressed with Shepherd. Díaz referred to him as one of the only two Americans in Mexico on whom he could rely without hesitation. The other was railroad tycoon Collis P. Huntington, who bought Mexico's richest iron deposit, just east of Durango City, Durango, some 280 miles southeast of Batopilas. He constructed a line from Eagle Pass, Texas, to his mines without a government subsidy.

In 1880, while Shepherd was still attempting to consolidate his authority over Batopilas, the local citizenry quickly realized that this was not the beginning of utopia. Besides physically separating himself from them, Alexander seemed to emulate Cortés with the two mastiffs that threatened anyone who approached without his permission. His assertion of ownership over all of the mines in the San Pedro and San Miguel complexes and adjacent lands engendered serious opposition. The Batopilas merchants, gambusinos, and the jefe político, Ramírez, correctly saw Shepherd as a threat to municipal autonomy, free trade and the free working of the mines, but they did not know of his connections with General Díaz through General Grant. Compounding the problems, Alexander's enlarged operations led to an influx of new but impoverished workers to the area. The recruits gave Shepherd cheap labor, but the squalid conditions that resulted gave the town leaders yet another concern. By 1882, the population had quadrupled, and crime had come to their streets.[18]

The gambusinos, in addition to the Batopilas elites, believed that Shepherd was entitled only to the Hacienda San Miguel and to the specific mines that had been worked by Robinson. In 1880, the miners held a series of public meetings to express complaints about being denied their traditional rights to firewood and water (granted under Mexican usufruct), longer and more rigid workdays, the end of gambusino rights, pay in devalued scrip money instead of silver pesos, the higher prices in the company store in contrast to the Robinson era, low wages, and the more dangerous working conditions brought about by the removal of the silver pillars that supported the roofs of the mine tunnels.

The local elites chimed in, complaining about the misuse of scrip money, namely, Shepherd's practice of forcing them to accept discounted values when they redeemed it at the business office in the Hacienda San Miguel. They saw the new system as an injustice depriving them of income and independence, and took note of the wealth contained in the shipments of silver ingots by the Conducta to the mint at Chihuahua City and to Mazatlán, and the ostentatious way of life so quickly adopted by the newly arrived owners and foreign retainers vis-à-vis themselves. They watched as James Morgan took command of the Conducta and escorted vast amounts of silver to Mazatlán and Chihuahua City. The flow of wealth constituted a bonanza "beyond the dreams of avarice" and beyond the control of the Mexicans.

Morgan described the American-batopilense conflict as he and other Americans saw it:

The governor had brought with him a large amount of paper money which he had had printed in New York. He at once opened a store at the hacienda and told the miners that he intended to pay them with this paper money and that they could buy what they wanted at the store with it, and the miners greedily accepted his offer. Then to their amazement he ordered them to knock down those rich columns containing Heaven only knows how much native silver to the ton.

Naturally there were storekeepers and others who became envious, and they reported to the Government at the City of Mexico how the Governor had defied the law both in the matter of the columns and in the issuing of paper money without the consent of authorities.

The row got him into communication with the President Don Porfirio Díaz, and soon this extraordinary Washington man had authority to do pretty much as he pleased in the Batopilas district, and even the mighty jefe político, or sheriff, was courting his favor.[19]

With the bad feelings that prevailed between Alexander and the Batopilas elites, he initially got no cooperation from them with regard to the miners. So he once again turned to higher authority, this time to settle the labor dispute. He enlisted the armed force of the government, rather than using his own men, who were still being trained at that time and might not as yet have been reliable. After several more weeks of unrest, the federal authorities sent a sizable unit of cavalry troops equipped with at least one machine gun and a mountain artillery piece.

The commander of the troops met with Shepherd and immediately informed Mayor Ramírez that everyone in town was "invited" to spend Easter Sunday at Satevo, the site of the Jesuit mission four miles downstream established in 1702. There they would enjoy food and drink provided by Shepherd and be "entertained." During the hike to Satevo, however, the mounted troops began to crowd the civilians, frightening them and herding them toward their destination. In the course of their "command attendance" at the Satevo festivities, the miners, local elites, and their families were treated to a display of military maneuvers. The cavalry troops charged in formation and individually, lancing imaginary enemies. Meanwhile, the machine gun sprayed bullets in selected spots, and the cannon made a great deal of noise firing shells into cliffs and sending up clouds of dirt and smoke over the surrounding terrain. The awed spectators then returned to Batopilas, where they were treated to free drinks in the plaza. One unhappy observer noted that there was no further talk about strikes or unrest among the miners or batopilenses for five years, until labor organizers from outside arrived in 1887. After detailing the intimidation, the observer put it ironically: "Everyone had a great time, . . . and at nightfall they went home happy."[20]

During a trip out of the canyon Morgan noted the continuing animosity:

> There is no race on earth that the Mexicans, high or low, hate as they do the Americans, and Don Ramón [Ramírez] (the merchant in Batopilas) did not hanker after our company and made no secret of the fact. But to avoid incurring the displeasure of the all-powerful Governor Shepherd

he, with rather bad grace, consented to allow the two Gringos to ride along the same trail in sight of his Highness's mules.[21]

Once his control had been established, Boss Shepherd set up a transitional regime in the company's management. At first, he retained Morris and Hernandez, Robinson's former administrators, as mine supervisors. They knew the personnel and the mines. Then, after one year, he replaced Morris and Hernández as the principal mining superintendents but retained them in other capacities. Morris, married to a batopilense woman and father of four children, two boys and two girls, stayed on as a low-level mine supervisor, a private storekeeper, and respected member of the community. Hernández stayed on as a mining foreman, but, more important, Shepherd saw to it that he replaced Ramírez as jefe político. That act legitimized Alexander's control over law enforcement. The company positions held by Morris and Hernández and the political power gained by Hernández laid the basis for the Boss to extend his political influence over a wide area of southwestern Chihuahua.

By 1885, Shepherd, having consolidated his political and police power over the canyon region, no longer had to consider the demands of the gambusinos. He set out to further rationalize production at the mines by hiring Godfrey Garner, an English mining engineer and graduate of the University of Edinburgh. Shepherd chose Gardiner for three reasons: to forestall having to hire a Mexican for the job, as suggested by the government in Mexico City; to prioritize the mines to be worked; and to professionalize all aspects of the operation. Gardiner enjoyed great success in his endeavors, working for Shepherd until 1890,when he accepted a job offered him by Enrique Creel at the La Gloria Mining Company in nearby Cerro Colorado.

In sum, Alexander's manner of operating the BMC stood in stark contrast to his predecessor's. Robinson had worked in anonymity for nearly two decades in the sierra. His lack of interest in the Tarahumaras and other locals and in the rebel occupations of the mines had not alienated the wider public, nor had he felt the need to replace the local authorities with his own functionaries. Indeed, he had made friends with some of the locals and even accepted the responsibilities of a padrino in Batopilas. In contrast, Shepherd established control during his first years in Batopilas by replacing the locals with Americans and other foreign experts in all the key company positions. By no later than the end of his third year, he had even replaced the civil authorities with his own employees. His imperious manner of operating separated him and the Americans from the intimate relationships that Robinson had established.

In the late 1880s, when Alexander finally realized that he needed the "others" in the area and established intimate contacts with Ramírez and a few local elites, it was on the basis of what his son Grant approvingly called a feudal relationship. Alexander had passed his attitudes on to his sons. His arrangements with the authorities included a detachment of federal troops whose commander coordinated his efforts with Shepherd and the close support of the state government. It took a few years for Alexander to reestablish a working relationship with the merchants of Batopilas, but that came because it was in their mutual interest. It even included an on-and-off friendship with the Ramírez clan. In the broader context, Shepherd extended the "feudal" system to include the workers and wider citizenry. Visitors to the Hacienda San Miguel had to satisfy an armed guard in a two-story heavy stone tower at the gate before gaining entry. An aide, backed by one of the mastiffs, would intercede when visitors approached Alexander's office.

The sense of live and let live, the toleration of different traditions and objectives, had ended in Batopilas. As Alexander secured new investors and gained control of an area covering 132,779 acres, including ranch and timberlands as well as the mining concessions, he abolished the practice of gambusino mining in the region. Then, through increased vigilance, he further rationalized labor costs by reducing the amount of time workers took to do jobs. Because gambusino and casual work practices had signified character, independence, and manliness, these two steps evoked a continuous, simmering resentment in Batopilas toward the Patrón Grande. He had disrupted popular cultural practices and values.

After the 1880 enlargement of their holdings, Shepherd's chief mining engineer, Walter Brodie, had set out not just to discipline labor but to expand the scale of operations. Directors Quintard and Stevens both agreed to the project before returning to New York. They understood that, if the San Pedro mining complex on the Batopilas side of the river was ever going to realize its potential, the San Miguel Tunnel had to be greatly extended through the base of the mountain in order to intersect the fabled Roncesvalles, Pastrana, Todos Santos, and San Pedro veins. The vertical depth of the shafts to these veins made them too expensive to work from the surface. The mines already abandoned were impossible to work economically by digging from above because they required the laborious lifting of 70-pound loads of nonpaying earth from far below the surface while the men cut through the earth searching for continuations of the veins.

The Mexican owners saw the veins as too expensive to exploit or as "dried out." In contrast, the newcomers considered them to be still fabulously rich in the interior of the mountain. After acquiring control of most of the veins through the initial deal made with Robinson, the new owners then claimed the inactive mines associated with the Pastrana and Cata veins and long claimed by the Lebrun and Ramírez. Shepherd and his associates acquired them through denunciation or outright purchase for very little cash.

Shepherd, Quintard, Stevens, and Brodie understood, as Robinson had before them, that if they tunneled through the mountain known as Cerro de Todos Santos and installed rails on which ore cars could roll, they could reap a bonanza by intersecting the veins from below. The rails could be obtained at cost through the several railroad directors who sat on the BMC board. By December 1881, the railroad into the newly christened Porfirio Díaz Tunnel and its mule-drawn ore cars had reached 1,350 feet into the mountain and already encountered a rich vein. Workers then constructed a preliminary processing plant at the mouth of the Porfirio Díaz Tunnel to process crude ore. Director Stone, as a leading canal and bridge builder, undoubtedly played a role in the design of the enlarged aqueduct that they then built. It followed the same three-mile route downstream from La Junta to the mouth of the tunnel as Robinson's had, but it was wider and deeper. They extended the tracks from the Díaz Tunnel railroad across the river over a new bridge and joined them to the same-gauge tracks that ran one-half mile from the San Miguel mine to the hacienda.

Using the new aqueduct for the power they needed, they installed motorized equipment for what they christened the "San Antonio processing plant" located in front of the tunnel. In addition, they constructed dikes to further protect the Hacienda San Miguel and the plant there. By 1883, the company had produced 1,250,000 pounds of refined silver from the veins in Cerro de Todos Santos. Workers had scooped tons of raw ore from steep, sometimes vertical, tunnels deep inside the mountain, and sent it down to the railcars waiting below in the Porfirio Díaz Tunnel. After shuttling it outside to the San Antonio processing plant with its new-fangled turbine in front of the Díaz Tunnel, they had crushed the ore and separated most of it before carting it across the river for refining at the smelter in the Hacienda San Miguel. The company quickly realized fabulous, largely unreported profits through the enormous quantities of ore it processed and its higher rate of silver retention.[22]

Shepherd had salaried crews work 12-hour shifts, twenty-four hours a day, extending not only the Porfirio Díaz Tunnel but also other deep but still profitable shafts, such as the one to the Veta Grande vein. This effort engaged hundreds of men. Meanwhile, across the river, the miners con-tinued excavating the new San Miguel Tunnel, a mile upstream from the hacienda, which intersected the rich Carmen, San Antonio, and Veta Grande veins from below. The several experts Alexander brought with him quickly proved their worth. The chemist measured the value of raw ores. Mining engineer Brodie originally planned the projects and offered Shepherd solid advice on the structure of the soil and of the potential of the deposits, as did engineer Garner, who joined them in 1885. Two bookkeepers kept a careful record of profits and losses, while an unknown third person maintained a secret set of books.

The "white" foreigners lived with the Shepherd family in the segre-gated seclusion of Hacienda San Miguel and received salaries far in excess of the approximately 25-centavo base daily wage Shepherd offered the barreteros in Batopilas. Meanwhile, Shepherd and his family en-larged and improved the already beautiful Hacienda San Miguel. The hacienda's high walls, which ran along the river and then to the moun-tains behind it, provided protection from bandit raids; its isolation sepa-rated the family from the poverty, beggars, crime, day laborers, Yaquis, Tarahumaras, other Native Americans, and prostitutes in the town. Alex-ander, like his white, Southern, and wealthy American counterparts, be-lieved in racial segregation. He insisted that the "white" employees live in houses constructed on the 13-acre grounds of the Hacienda San Miguel. In fact, none of the skilled administrative and technical personnel were Mexicans, and he had replaced the local authorities with his employees.

In the mid-1880s, however, the federal government imposed a law that required Shepherd to host a series of Mexican student observers from the National School of Mines so they might gain "on the ground experience" from the foreign operators. This requirement did not, however, greatly inconvenience the Patrón Grande. Having to compromise occasionally was something Alexander could accept. In 1866, in Nashville, Tennessee, Charles Todd Quintard, the brother of Shepherd's most active partner and the second Episcopal bishop of Tennessee, sponsored the creation of Fisk University for African Americans in the vicinity of the far more richly endowed University of the South near Sewanee. The brother served as a regent at Sewanee, which admitted whites only. Yet the family members took great pride in Charles' good deed and failed to note the pathetic conditions that prevailed at Fisk.

Consistent with the values of Southern elite paternalism, Alexander sent his sons to Sewanee for bachelor's degrees while offering his "girls" far more limited educations by means of well-born private female tutors brought to Batopilas from the United States. One of them, "Miss Griswold," was a relative of Bessemer patent holder James Griswold, who had worked with George Quintard at the Quintard's steel mill in New York as part of the Union's construction of fifty-four *Monitor*-class ironclad warships during the Civil War.[23]

The Yaqui Indians of Sonora, with whom Boss Shepherd dealt, suffered an even grimmer fate than the kidnapped urban petty criminals and poor in central Mexico. In the minds of Díaz, the Mexican elites, and Alexander, they combined a number of negative images—criminal, working class, illiterate, prisoner, and "Indian"—to constitute a Mexican "other." In the case of the Yaquis, contractors hauled thousands of them, charged with rebellion, to the Pacific port of Salina Cruz in southern Mexico, from which they were marched overland to the Valle Nacional or to the Yucatán Peninsula to serve fatal sentences in the malarial henequen plantations. In contrast, the contractors offered most mestizo workers from central Mexico a luckier fate, sending them to the chicle and hardwood plantations in Campeche run by Phoebe and later William Randolph Hearst, Victor DuPont Jr., the head of Marathon Oil and the Old Colony Trust Bank of Philadelphia, and by other energy and oil magnates in New York.

In Batopilas, Shepherd achieved his low labor costs by arranging with enganchadores having government connections to bring in free Yaqui workers and, allegedly, a lesser number of prisoners. The Patrón Grande reportedly treated the prisoners terribly, while the free Yaqui also offered him a tremendous bargaining advantage vis-à-vis mestizo workers because they were so vulnerable. They lived in constant danger of arrest by the army in the surrounding areas of Sonora, northern Sinaloa, and northwestern Chihuahua. The bounty declared by Chihuahua's governor, Luis Terrazas, during the 1870s on the head of every Apache paralleled awards offered in neighboring states; the authorities still could not distinguish between the scalp of an Apache, Yaqui, Raramuri, or Mayo. The army officers and their men, under orders, committed mass murders of Indians. A former soldier, who became a police officer, described what he saw:

> My name is Genovevo Uribe. I was born in Chihuahua. I am 31 years of age. They took me in the military draft when I was an adolescent. I served for eight years in the 25th infantry battalion in the campaign against the Yaqui Indians. I witnessed more than four hundred executions of Indians . . . some were hung from trees, others executed by firing squads, some by pistol shots in the back of the head, and others cut down from behind.[24]

Given the threat to their lives, hundreds of Yaqui free laborers found their way to the mines at Batopilas, Urique, and other sites in the Sierra Tarahumara. At Batopilas, these free laborers at least did not have to remain in the tunnels after completing their shift. The Chihuahua elite's atrocities against Native Americans did not abate until the end of the century and then only because of the declining threat presented by Comanche and Apache raiding parties. Discrimination, however, remained strong, and an "Indio" could never feel safe in a society in which the elites stressed their "whiteness." Boss Shepherd took advantage of the situation.

The batopilenses suddenly found themselves, not in Las Hadas, but instead caught up in a mining boomtown with the likelihood of also becoming a forced labor camp. Earlier, artisan-like individual labor practices had actually been reinforced by Robinson's technological innovations, which included sledgehammers and enlarged, cement-reinforced arrastras. Now, however, a factorylike environment emerged as motorized equipment moved tons of earth at once while the workers stood in clouds of silica dust. The individual fulfillment through independence, education and family life long sought after by Mexican Liberals had been replaced by men working prolonged shifts in a place increasingly characterized by extreme inequality, drunkenness, saloons, prostitutes, and brothels.

Seeing this, the Tarahumaras employed their traditional strategy for survival. Most of them returned to the vastness of the mountains, to settlements sometimes sheltered from outside attack by priests, or to their isolated caves. In so doing, they not only survived; they also preserved their way of life, which included giving to the collective good of their communities rather than taking from their fellows, as they perceived the actions of the Chabochis (outsiders). Most of them refused to accept the disciplined regimen in the mines at Batopilas, Urique, or La Bufa. That rejection opened more opportunities to Mayo and Yaqui job seekers. These hounded and hunted men found working in Batopilas a form of refuge. The town was legally incorporated as a pueblo, with its own small police force and a private "army" controlled by Shepherd.

Alexander's labor practices regarding Yaqui prisoners paralleled those of Díaz in the Valle Nacional and the Yucatán Peninsula, including the payment of labor contractors for bringing them to Batopilas. Shepherd also used Yaqui and Mayo free workers willing to work in the mines in order to flee the "Indian hunters" and the probable prisoners. As previously noted, Alexander allegedly held the Yaqui prisoners at night in the renamed San Miguel Tunnel, located on the east side of the river north of the Hacienda San Miguel. The prisoners gained access to the sun at dawn, when the work shifts began. Those who marched to work on projects across the river or in other areas of the canyon could also expect daylight for a few more hours during their time spent going to and returning from their work sites.

Those sent to the hacienda to work in the refining process or construction projects could expect daylight most of the time. The dusty and humid air in the tunnel, however, quickly led to lung infections and death among those incarcerated there. Death began to claim them one by one after about six months. Smelter workers, some free and some prisoners, suffered from cyanide poisoning because that catalyst was used in separating the ore. Many smelter workers died quickly; those working inside the mines suffered from silica and lead poisoning and perished after more prolonged illnesses.

Shepherd's labor strategies also included extending credit at the company store to keep unskilled and skilled laborers at their jobs. The weekly 50 percent deduction from the workers' earnings was supposed to accurately represent the cost of food and clothing obtained at the tienda de raya and of transportation to Batopilas. That the charge was universal, however, indicates that it was a running account controlled by the Patrón Grande. The plantation owners in Yucatán, Campeche, and the Valle Nacional made identical charges for credit at the company store and for the considerably larger transportation costs imposed by the enganchadores, ostensibly for train and ship travel. The debt peons learned later, when isolated and under guard on the plantations, that their wages were too low to allow them to pay their debts and that they could not leave until their obligations had been met. Most of the debtors, however, had little or no command of arithmetic and could not effectively contest the debts charged to them.

At Batopilas, Alexander deducted 50 percent of their weekly pay because he had a cooperative arrangement with the cantina operators and merchants in town, who gained the other 50 percent in the course of the weekend debauchery. Since the company store was the only choice for many of their needs, the free Yaqui, Mayo, and Raramuri workers found themselves to be virtual prisoners because they could not pay their debts.[25]

Shepherd's approach to industrial and private life in Batopilas coincided with the moral preachments of his contemporaries and the terrible personal setbacks he had endured. Alexander hoped the silver bonanza would finance his return to high status in the United States. At the same time, unrestrained by the critics he faced in Washington, he endeavored to create what he considered an ideal way of life for himself and his family in the wilderness.

As a "man of destiny" like Cecil Rhodes and other contemporaries in the "South Seas," "Darkest Africa," and the "Mysterious Orient," Alexander sought to create his own version of the Southern aristocratic plantation house and lifestyle among the Mexicans and Indians, who, in his eyes, were obviously backward and inferior. As a patron or benefactor, he provided leadership, discipline, and employment in return for profits and a lordly way of life. As the paternalist leader, he consciously created a stable and hierarchical social order and believed that the Mexicans and

Indians in and around Batopilas would not respect him if they were overindulged.

Shepherd, Nahum Capen, who was the editor of the *Boston Globe*, General Phillip Sheridan, and other American leaders of the time assumed an inherent inequality between the average citizens of Mexico and the U.S. elites that extended well beyond Native Americans. For Alexander, social stratification was the natural order of things. The organic unity of Batopilas was based on the production of wealth to be consumed at the higher level of existence represented by the metropolitan areas of the United States. Isolation had served to exaggerate and highlight patriarchal ideas and practices in the American South before the Civil War, and so it was in Batopilas. In Alexander's mind, his business and the library, garden and Protestant chapel at the Hacienda San Miguel separated him from the masses and placed him within the idealized role of patriarch. Consistent with elite U.S. Episcopalian slave owners of the mid-nineteenth century, Shepherd held democracy, Batopilas workers, and the local elites in contempt.[26]

The psychological roots of Alexander's outlook and behavior are found in the still-vibrant beliefs of the mid-nineteenth-century Episcopalian slaveholders of Maryland. In 1842, Episcopalian leader Thomas Bacon explained that God had "laid the foundation of justice and equity between man and man by making each in his several stations. The honor and obedience owed rulers should be reciprocated by the protection of a subject's rights and liberties. It was the duty of slaveholders to feed, clothe, shelter and to expect fidelity and honest labor from their slaves."[27] All of Shepherd's practices regarding the mutual duties and responsibilities of supervisors and inferiors were consistent with the deeply held beliefs of conservative Episcopal worshippers in the nineteenth century. He demanded strict obedience to rules, in the mines and in the household. At the mines, Alexander, also consistent with American practices toward slaves and workers in the first moments of the Industrial Revolution, imposed direct discipline and supervision over his workers.

In Batopilas, the application of this paternalist outlook justified the construction of a castle with fortified walls, a watchtower, and a moat provided by the river. Shepherd's adoption of the term *Patrón Grande* fit his self-image of Boss. In Washington, at the height of his power, Alexander and his wife consciously set about the creation of a seigniorial way of life. When they moved from their former mansion, which was larger than and situated near the White House, they named their new home Bleak House in commemoration of the one made famous in the Dickens novel.

Dickens created the image of a large aristocratic family, led by a patriarch, in which the eldest son, younger sons and daughters had pre-ordained roles. Taught intense family loyalty, the daughters were socially controlled through the teaching of social conventions. Dickens's characters and Alexander held worldly ideas consistent with the duties and ceremonial life associated with running Washington, D.C., or for the operation of a large rural estate in Mexico. The boys deferred to their father, whom they recognized as the Patrón Grande, but they learned that batopilenses and Mexicans were beneath them. They were duly sent away to Sewanee after home teaching at Shepherd's Castle.

Shepherd's paternalism at home equaled that portrayed by Dickens. In his household, he exaggerated the worst aspects of patriarchalism found in contemporary elite American gender relations. He displayed benevo-lence, repression, cruelty, and kindness while grooming his eldest son, Alexander Jr. (Alex), to succeed him in the manner of primogeniture as general manager of the BMC. The younger boys, Grant and Conness, were educated at Sewanee like Alex but were not expected to assume command. The daughters were trained to serve as charming wives to, it was hoped, wealthy American husbands. Only Dora escaped this fate. She married an American supervisor at the mines and moved to Chihuahua, where the couple successfully managed a hotel for many years. The other daughters, led by May, the eldest, lived in Washington, D.C., where they occupied Bleak House with their mother, who chose to spend almost all of her time there, away from her husband.[28]

As a youth, Grant Shepherd unconsciously acted out the class and racial supremacy he learned at home. At nine, he fired a shotgun at a Mexican servant in order to enjoy the pleasure of breaking the olla the man carried and seeing the contents spill all over the hapless victim. Later, when he pulled a gun on a Batopilas policeman, Grant demon-strated his contempt for "lesser people" and the conviction that authority did not rest with them. Despite his obvious culpability, a telegram to the governor from his father forced Grant's release the following day. He had no fear of punishment; rather, his principal concerns while in jail were for his own comfort and convenience.

Grant's contemptuous description of the Batopilas police officers who took him into custody and held him transcended the usual pleadings of defendants. He revealed a profound sense of superiority toward them. He learned these attitudes from events witnessed during his youth while growing up in the segregated and unequal system his father established and from day-to-day family conversations regarding various Mexican "inferiorities," including "dullness of mind." The Patrón Grande and his heirs believed that, by virtue of birth, they were superior to the local Mexicans. Policemen and servants should accept, not question, their power.[29]

Grant described his father's conscious effort to create a feudal Bleak House type of regime at home and in the society that surrounded him. He recounted racially segregated employment practices, the use of scrip money rather than a free-market economy to control the barreteros, a company store where half of labor's earnings were consumed in necessities and deducted from wages, separate residency, a private army, the use of company supervisors as the mayor and other officers in the ostensibly independent town, and the treatment of Yaqui Indian forced laborers as property rather than humans. In return, the servants and lower laborers, as Thomas Bacon intoned and Grant believed, owed Shepherd respect as "their great arbiter and protector."

Shepherd's children quickly understood that they enjoyed privileged status vis-à-vis their Mexican neighbors. As a youngster, Grant, the second of three sons, displayed his sense of superiority in obvious ways. Besides firing the double-barreled shotgun from several yards away at the clay water jug that one of the "loyal and dedicated" servants was carrying on his head to the house from the well, Grant joined his brother Alex in amusements such as siccing their mastiffs on members of the local feline population and watching them and other fighting dogs occasionally catch up with and tear the cats to pieces. In one of their favorite pastimes, they tied lit cigarettes and cigars to the tails of dogs and cats and enjoyed watching their panicky and agonized reactions.

Grant and his brothers each carried a gun stuck into their belts. As teenagers, they began imbibing tequila and other hard liquors and visiting the cantinas in Batopilas. They often stayed all night, away from their father's direct supervision, returning in the mornings to the hacienda or to the mines, where they worked as foremen. They made several friends in the bars, which were frequented by prostitutes serving the mining camp.

Alexander's Maryland experience with slaves served him well in his struggle with the gambusinos. Mid-nineteenth-century slaveholding ideology went beyond economic concerns with the cost of labor. It taught that slaves or serfs should not be allowed to grow their own small and separate crops because that indulgence bred the theft of labor time and money and led to the creation of independent wealth, thought, power, and insubordination. A properly working and understood patriarchal capitalist economy, in contrast, would provide profitability and stability. The resulting social harmony would transcend worker resentments and, in Batopilas and Mexico, the ever-present threat of economic nationalism.[30]

After he had consolidated his position at Batopilas, Shepherd also demonstrated a necessary racial and sexual flexibility. He tolerated limited miscegenation among his employees despite his segregation of the mining company elites from day-to-day social interactions in town. This toleration also corresponded with that of mid-nineteenth century Maryland slaveholders. As a result, an African American employee at the Hacienda San Miguel married an "Indian woman," and one American supervisor chose a mestizo bride from the town.

In the years that followed, the contracts approved by the Mexican government demonstrated the power that Shepherd exercised in the immediate area of Batopilas and the Copper Canyon region. Justo Sierra, a noted scholar and future minister of culture in the Díaz government, and Governor Enrique Creel represented the company in its negotiations at Mexico City for the next two decades. In 1884 and 1886, Sierra, acting for Shepherd, requested and Ministers of Economic Development, Generals Díaz and Pacheco, approved mining, water, timber, and land concessions that provided a further material definition of the American's power.

Díaz and Pacheco finalized land titles for Shepherd's claim to ownership in perpetuity of the properties north of Batopilas extending from the river up the canyon sides in the Arroyo de las Minas, where the San Pedro mines were located, and for three miles into the highlands southwest of Batopilas. The concessions surrounded Batopilas on the three sides not occupied by Shepherd's Hacienda San Miguel, which faced the town from across the river. The concessions downstream from town to the Arroyo de los Tachos surrounded the Descubridora mine, which Shepherd already owned. Díaz gave Shepherd and the company the lands under the pretext that it was a single tract of *terrenos baldíos* (unused and unoccupied property) and therefore owned by the government. In fact, the batopilenses had long used the properties for roads, trails, firewood, construction materials, freelance mining, farming, and the grazing of goats and other animals.

The government also ceded important water rights to Alexander. The initial concession gave him the power to build the dam at La Junta and ownership of the strip of land for the aqueduct that extended from the dam to the Díaz Tunnel at the northern edge of Batopilas. There he piped water across the river to the Hacienda San Miguel. Shepherd had already begun the construction of the San Antonio reduction plant at the mouth of the Díaz Tunnel. The government also exempted him and the BMC from all taxes for twenty years with the exception of the *timbre* (minting fee), imposed at the state mint in Chihuahua City. The ownership of nine square miles of land to the southwest of Batopilas that lay alongside the old Camino Real to Mazatlán laid the basis for undetected, or at least unreported, silver exports. James Morgan commanded the mule trains that carried the undeclared silver to the Sea of Cortez for shipment out of Mexico. "Sometimes I carried the silver to Mazatlán on the Pacific Coast. . . . We usually traveled about twenty miles a day. The mules [each carried] from two to three hundred pounds on their backs [at a value of $2,000 to $3,000 per animal]."[31] The government also paid the company 2,500 pesos yearly for the next ten years for advertising its products in mining journals. Díaz later renewed the company's tax exemption for another twenty-year period.

Over the next two decades the number of largely American skilled employees at the BMC slowly grew from six to eighteen. They remained in segregated housing, vastly superior to that of the Mexican employees, and dined with Shepherd on holidays and special occasions. Otherwise, the company offered them a dining room on the ground floor of the castle. The highest wage earners among them enjoyed salaries some twenty times the average of twenty-five centavos per day paid to the rank-and-file Tarahumara, Yaqui, Mayo, and Mexican barreteros. The low salaries of the Mexican miners had nothing to do with the value produced by their labor. The imbalance of political power that prevailed was the principal determinant in defining the bargaining strength of the workers.

This bargaining strength diminished dramatically when Shepherd used his connections with powerful regional and national elites, Terrazas, Creel, and Díaz to consolidate his position at Batopilas. Indeed, it was through these connections that Alexander obtained Yaqui forced laborers. Despite the increased per-worker production of wealth at Batopilas after 1880, the barreteros' wages remained pitifully low relative to the per-worker value produced.

The extreme imbalance of political power at Batopilas and other mining centers exceeded the effect of market forces in determining wages, a condition found throughout the American experience in Mexico. Miner earnings, or labor costs, did not exceed 6 percent of the BMC's gross income and may have been as low as 3.75 percent. Exact numbers are impossible to ascertain because the workforce fluctuated between 500 and 1,200, the company's confidential pay records are available for only a few years, and those records contradict the salary figures that Shepherd submitted to the government. The "official" figures, published by Engineer Manuel Fernández Leal, the secretary of economic development in the cabinet of General Díaz, showed that, between 1892 and 1896, the Batopilas mineworkers earned an average of $1.50 per day or approximately $390 per year. The miners produced a total of $3,070,463 worth of silver during those four years or $4,094 per worker yearly. According to the data Shepherd gave Leal, the laborers would have received more than 10 percent of the value they produced in wages. In contrast, Alexander's personal books suggest the much lower wage of $75 yearly and a return to the common workers of less than 2 percent of the value produced.

Wages in the adjacent states of Sinaloa and Sonora were far lower than claims made by Shepherd to the government. This was also true when worker earnings are compared to the amount of wealth created. During the late 1860s in Sinaloa the highly capitalized Sinaloa Mining Company headed by New York capitalist Frederick Weidner and his Knickerbocker Bank associates paid their miners a base rate of twenty-five centavos daily during a bonanza in which the owners gained hundreds of thousands of dollars for a 22.4 percent net annual return.[32]

Meanwhile, Alexander and his family enjoyed an elegant, L-shaped one-story hacienda residence building facing east and north, surrounded by a beautiful garden. Bougainvillea, jacaranda, jasmine, fruit trees, and other flowering plants extended out from the house on the three sides; the fourth came within a few yards of the mountain that rose steeply behind the hacienda complex to the east. To the west the 30-foot-high wall with its small parapets and rifle slots protected the family from intruders or onlookers. They imported much of the household furniture from the eastern United States and Europe including a piano, cabinets and armoires. Immediately northwest of the residence, they installed a tennis court. There, too, large and brilliant bougainvillea climbed the walls, which, along with the jasmine and jacaranda trees in the garden provided color and aroma. The orchard that surrounded the place consisted of avocado, guava, orange, poinsettia, and *obelisco* trees. The last reach a height of forty feet while attaching their trunks to buildings and walls in the manner of vines.

To combine elegance with tropical beauty, Shepherd had the two-story edifice, which included the company offices and formed the northern wall of the garden enclosure, enlarged to a "castle" of three stories. The building, clearly designed by Adolph Cluss or one of his disciples, was expanded by German artisans brought from outside Mexico to install Italian marble and German stone mosaics and to create the remarkable structure thereafter known as Shepherd's Castle. The artisans turned the castle into a late-nineteenth-century Gothic Revival edifice, the type that was then the rage of British and European nobility and the Anglican-Episcopalian elites of England, Washington, and the U.S. East Coast. They built the roof in a standing seam pattern with terne or aluminum. Terne was pliable and slow to rust, whereas aluminum did not rust at all, but was prone to pitting after prolonged exposure to the elements. If aluminum was used, Blanchard and Frishmuth undoubtedly provided it. They finished the roof with a crenellated trim and the rest of the building with Italian marble floors and with detailed brickwork lining for the windows, doors, and porches. A "great tiled swimming pool, as large as the public bath of a city . . . occup[ied] the basement." Alexander then furnished the building with imported desks, lamps, and rugs.[33]

As Shepherd imported new technology, he brought in American chemists, mechanics, and mining engineers, while continuing to employ American bookkeepers and an American doctor. A handful of British technicians joined them. In late 1882, the BMC exceeded 500 workers and, by the middle of the decade, the number had swelled to over 800 in the mines with a handful of other employees in the way stations between Batopilas, Mazatlán, and Chihuahua City. Meanwhile, the population of the town swelled from less than 1,500 to over 6,000. The new people included a contingent of Mexican miners and their families, diverse shopkeepers and merchants, a few hundred Yaqui, Mayo, and Tarahumara Indians, and Chinese launderers as well as "African" and itinerant workers.

A bizarre lifestyle emerged in Batopilas, which resulted from the working conditions and from how the wealth produced at the mines was used. On Saturday afternoon, the miners and workers stood in front of the superintendent's office waiting for their pay. In a practice known as *raya*, each worker received his pay in company scrip after the deduction of his weekly purchases at the tienda de raya. The bills were notably dirty, but the workers knew that they were redeemable. They not only covered necessities at the store but also were accepted by the cantina operators, food vendors, and prostitutes, who all treated them as cash.

The manner in which Shepherd dispensed and the workers received their pay reflected a serious though not incapacitating psychological problem on Alexander's part, as well as the generalized class and caste relationships that developed in Batopilas. Shepherd alternated between hyperactive periods and debilitating depressions, during which he retreated for days at a time to a small building at the southern end of the estate, where he slept with his mastiffs. During these depressive episodes, he sometimes exploded in rages; on other occasions, he insisted on personally dispensing the salaries to the miners individually. All of this tied in with his disgrace and isolation from Washington, D.C.

Alexander required the employees to form a long line that began some thirty feet from the pay window located at the southeast corner of the castle. Each worker waited his turn and then approached the window with his sombrero extended in front of him and high enough for Shepherd to place the coins in it. The employee waited while Alexander, sitting behind the wall on the north side of the window, in the shadows and completely obscured from the employee's view, calculated the amount of wages due. Then, without a word, the Patrón Grande extended his arm and dropped the amount received into the hat. The worker then said, "Gracias," bowed, and stepped away.

After the men received their pay, most of them went to the river to bathe. They entered the water to wash the dried sweat and mud from their bodies, which were gray, colored by the silica and lead that came out in puffs of dust from the rocks as they chopped at them in the mines. Many of them swam, while others floated in the comfortably cool water for a time, enjoying a respite from the week of hard work, all of this in stark contrast to the family's time in the tiled pool. At sunset, as the canyon walls took on rich and deep hues of red and then purple while the sky slowly darkened, a freshening breeze sprang up and continued into the early evening. Then the shadows covered the town, extended across the river, and up the canyon walls above the Hacienda San Miguel.

"Concluding their country style and rustic bathing," the miners went "home" or to their living quarters and dressed in clean clothing for the evening. They put on freshly washed and pressed white shirts, white linen or cotton pants with wide legs, red neckerchiefs, and white "ten-gallon" and even wider straw hats. The clean clothes felt good to men who had worked twelve-hour shifts wearing only pants or breechcloths while coated with lard for five weekdays plus six hours on Saturday. The wives prepared their husbands' clothes; other women, including prostitutes, performed the same task, for a fee, on behalf of the numerous single men. While they were washing and smoothing their partners' clothes, the women looked forward with anticipation to the pleasures of Saturday night, a pastime in which they, too, would forget for a while the daily toil that characterized their lives.

The miners' white attire was not typical for the people in the Sierra Madre or the barrancas. Rather it appears to have been, at least in part, an escape from their darkly lighted experience in the mines, where they wore virtually no clothing other than pants and huaraches or, in the case of the Yaqui, Mayo and Tarahumara workers, breechcloths because of the extreme heat. The workers covered their bodies with lard in order to escape at least some of the damaging effects of the thousands of rock chips that struck them daily and the silica and lead-filled dust that colored them with a gray coating in the performance of their labors. The candles in their hats or on the walls and floors of the tunnels and the moments spent depositing ore at the entrance gave them their only relief from the prolonged darkness. There was probably a high incidence of blindness.

As a result, miners from around the world often wore white during their times of celebration and leisure. Although most of them donned huaraches for the Saturday night festivities, and a few were barefoot, some status-conscious mechanics put on cheap shoes. That gesture signified their self-esteem and the desire to emulate the more sophisticated outside cultures represented in Batopilas. These social actions are often born out of the overlapping narratives that result from the adoption of new practices and beliefs alongside the old. Meanwhile, some of the miners stayed home, others stopped to have a "bite to eat," with their women, but most of them were single and at any rate eager to "hit the streets" and celebrate.

The men, many of them without women in this boomtown, began to fill the long, straight road toward the Plaza del Taste in the center of Batopilas. They came in groups of two to four, and sometimes more, calling excited and humorous greetings to each other while using a mix of vulgar Spanish and local epithets. When they reached the first taverns, they would have a drink of mescal, stay for a while, and then move onward down the street toward the plaza, stopping at the next cantina that struck their fancy. Batopilas lacked the social stability of the more established mining towns such as Parral, located in south central Chihuahua, in more agreeable climates and not isolated in the wilderness. The transients did not overwhelm those places because of their larger stable populations. In Batopilas, the population more than tripled between 1880 and 1883, and most of the newcomers were single men. Many of them were being paid regular salaries for the first time in their lives, while performing highly dangerous work. Their life expectancy, given accidents, silicosis, typhoid fever, dysentery, and alcoholism, was between thirty-five and forty-five years.

As the revelry in Batopilas continued, some of the men became extremely intoxicated, before ever reaching the center of town. The casualties fell by the wayside, lying in the street in languid stupors. Some of them looked like corpses to shocked visitors. In many cases, friends picked up the unconscious celebrants and dropped them inside or in front of their houses and living quarters. In the other cases, the police hauled the bodies away and threw them in the unfinished schoolhouse, which was used as a drunk tank and jail. The Yaqui, Mayo, Tarahumara, and single men, some having neither eaten nor bathed because they lacked female support, were notably vulnerable to the effects of the mescal. They tended to fall earlier in the march, but the others would soon catch up to them in their levels of inebriation. In this manner, the early casualties were put out of action until Monday morning and protected from further self-inflicted damage. On Monday morning, after they paid fines using their company scrip, the police released them so they could be back at work on time in the mines.

The participants filled the small Plaza del Taste, exchanging joyful greetings and playful insults. The plaza, characterized by its riverfront, tropical trees, and gazebo, was named for the tropical taste trees that dominated the garden in its center, but it had changed since Robinson first saw it more than twenty years earlier. The wealthier families had withdrawn a block or more west around the cathedral and two blocks south, around the main plaza.

By mid-evening, a few of the miners were singing at the top of their voices. The songs, usually plaintive wailing presentations about unrequited love, evoked whistles, catcalls, and cowboy-like yells from the companions of the extemporaneous performers. Sometimes an entire group, with their arms around each other's shoulders, would move forward singing and weaving in an unpredictable and unintended dance-like movement. Meanwhile, someone wailed a song laced with ironic protest about life in general or the hardships of miners. As night fell in the plaza, small instrumental bands and more than one pair of marimba players began their serenades. The music sprang forward to overwhelm passersby and listeners. In a few cantinas, cacophonic brass bands, accompanied by the rat-a-tat-tat of young and old sometimes inebriated men beating on dirty and worn-out drums, seemingly competed with each other to see who could make the most noise.

When it was dark, candles lit the houses and bars. The partiers filled the plaza. The storeowners kept their establishments open, selling clothing and sundry items. They earned as much on Saturday night as they did for the rest of the week. A strange mix of copper coins, "Shepherd bills," scrip from the Miners Bank of Chihuahua City, and a lesser amount of scrip money from the Santa Eulalia mines near the state capital all passed as acceptable currency. The irony was that, here in the heart of one of the most productive silver mining areas in the world, none of that metal made its way into local use. Meanwhile, in Mazatlán, Mexican government bills and silver pesos provided the basis for exchange. Prosperity in Batopilas depended on the exportation of the metal to the United States via Chihuahua and Mazatlán.

The groups of workers seemed to divide themselves on the basis of their occupations. Machine operators, barreteros, and smelter workers passed each other in the streets with smiles on their faces. Most of them were glassy eyed by 9 p.m. Playfully shoving each other after well-told jokes within their respective groups, they passed others in the street exchanging greetings and whispering observations and, more usually, good natured jokes about each other with their hands playfully cupped sideways, next to their mouths, and directed to their companions' ears in pretended secrecy. Occasionally, these actions resulted in quarrels between those who felt insulted and those who pled no wrongdoing. At that point, small crowds gathered to watch, while the friends of the antagonists regularly intervened between them, offering coherent and incoherent explanations, real and imagined, that usually satisfied the participants and spurred them on to the next cantina.

The crowd in the Plaza del Taste mixed and remixed, with women of all ages joining in. Some of the women merged with the groups of men, while others formed their own momentary clusters. Some of them were domestic employees of the company and could share workplace gossip and cordialities with their male counterparts. Others were batopilenses, young single women and their married sisters. Meanwhile, the single men hoped to find a female companion to enrich the evening. Some of them were already attracted to a particular woman, and the females certainly had their favorites. Quick glances and lingering smiles sometimes gained a salute from the male as he bowed and doffed his sombrero in an awkward but gallant sweeping gesture of salute.

Ancianas (old women) sat with each other to watch the action and catch up on the news that was important to them. Those conversations included the whereabouts of children, births, deaths, rumors, and insights regarding the motives behind recent actions taken by others. If a batopilense wanted to know what was going on in town, it was best to ask one of the ancianas in the Plaza del Taste, but they would not tell an outsider anything. At the other end of the life cycle the men treated the teenaged girls in the crowd, if beyond the initial stages of puberty, like adults. The girls often had already established monogamous relationships by the age of fourteen. Unmarried cohabitation was common, as was early teenage pregnancy.

Many of the younger and most of the middle-aged women in the plaza had a domestic relationship with one of the drunken men and many of them entered the cantinas to share drinks with similar couples. They, too, became intoxicated and often bellicose and noisy, but, using a discretion born of experience, they usually did not separate themselves from the crowd. After darkness fell, a woman who had been drinking walked alone at her peril.

The constant intermingling continued. As the hour grew late and the alcohol took greater effect, the noise grew louder. Jubilant laughter filled the square along with the ever-present music. Couples began to fight over broken promises and imagined slights. Sometimes relationships ended during these altercations, and, dangerously, new romances sometimes emerged in front of the enraged former partners. While sexual liaisons took place during the passions of the evening, usually the domestic situation of prospective partners was taken into consideration, if not that evening, then the next day. The brief fights between rival suitors, however, took place later in the night, and were usually limited, to fisticuffs. Murders and killings in self-defense, however, occurred from time to time.

A few of the Americans from the Hacienda San Miguel joined the celebrants. During the early 1880s, before Alexander's sons were old enough for drunken sprees on Main Street and in the Plaza del Taste, the American participants included the administrators, chemists, and mining engineers, but they attended the better places. The crew supervisors, the two nurses, and the live-in tutor employed for the education of the Shepherd children also celebrated, but they, too, exercised discretion. Alexander avoided the hubbub in the center of the plaza, although he sometimes visited members of the business community and observed the action with a mixture of awe and disgust. The visitors from the Hacienda San Miguel arrived on horseback and in small carriages. Some of the local businessmen, most of whom welcomed the weekend bashes, hosted the Americans in their homes, exchanging stories and pleasantries. The Shepherd men often carried pistols in their belts, befitting their special status and power.[34]

By 1883, some of the fifteen to eighteen American employees working at Batopilas could be found each weekend in the Plaza del Taste enjoying the music, drinks, and food. The male professionals and supervisors found sexual relationships with batopilense women, but, with rare exceptions like Achilles Morris, who married a mestizo woman, these attractions did not lead to formal living arrangements. The American elites in Batopilas consorted with Mexican women in a manner consistent with cultural practices in segregated and unequal localities in the Southern United States. During the 1880s, the town's complement of light-skinned and blond illegitimate children testified to the frequency of these relationships. Some years passed before even the lower-status African American cook married a batopilense woman.

Shepherd and the local businessmen expressed their disapproval of the drunken excesses that took place on the weekends. They noted that a number of the Native American and mestizo workers had fallen into misery and degradation. Alexander, however, encouraged the debauchery by continuing to pay his employees late on Saturday afternoon and to redeem the scrip when presented by the operators of illicit businesses. A defender of his practices might note that human wrecks are visible in any society at any time. Critics in the community, however, saw the workers as hapless victims of Shepherd's exploitation, the unremitting harsh conditions, and their own ignorance:

> In this scandalous bacchanal the workers find relaxation, they enjoy themselves, they get drunk, they laugh, they lose themselves in the game, and sometimes they cut each other or kill. That is how they escape from the onerous and dangerous work that faces them the rest of the week. What a present they live in, agitated and turbulent! What a dark and foreboding future for our working class! . . . Virtually none of them has even a small savings with which to prevent the misery and indigence that awaits them in case of illness or injury or old age, if they are able to reach it. . . . The workers, deprived of well being, including the most rudimentary levels of education, only serve as motors of bone and flesh for the tasks not performed by the steam engines or water wheels. . . . The authorities and persons of influence, anyone with honor, should help the workers establish mutual aid savings banks . . . in order to help them through their illnesses and to help them leave a patrimony for their children.[35]

Some of the better-educated batopilenses saw Alexander's and the other Americans' behavior as offensive. But they coupled complaints about the corrupting influence of outsiders with criticism of their own neighbors who did not behave properly during the weekend bashes or who did not belong there in the first place:

> Sometimes single and small girls mixed with these groups, holding the hands of their mamas; while employees of the American Company carried on animated conversations in loud voices, using the idiom of Washington, and certain that only a few of those present could understand them. Infirm and ill old people also joined in along with naked, dirty, lard-covered, idiotic, and semi-savage Tarahumara, arrogant Negroes who strutted about like Czars of Russia with their enormous boots clanking on the cobblestone streets, and disciples of Venus Aphrodite in search of productive pleasures.[36]

In 1887, Alexander legally formalized in yet another way the expanded property concessions given him by Díaz and Pacheco. He incorporated the Batopilas Consolidated Mining Company (BCMC), which included what had earlier been 350 separate workings and ten companies owned by the BMC. The asserted purchases, however, were of individual operations claimed by Mexican miners whose ownership was rejected by the Mexican government for various reasons, usually related to an asserted failure to pay taxes. The creation of the BCMC made business and political sense because the separate mines required individual reports to the government and justifications when the concessions were being renewed before federal authorities. Without Díaz, Pacheco, and the Patrón Grande's prestige to back up the company in the future, some of the more contested claims might become vulnerable. Hence, in 1902, following Alexander's death, the directors announced a second reincorporation that merged even more, previously overlooked, mines with the BCMC. The maneuvering underscored continuing political insecurity vis-à-vis local and nationalist critics despite all the trappings of power.[37]

Meanwhile, Shepherd presented little evidence of the mine and smelter purchases to the upset and doubting directors in New York. He also failed to note most of them in the company record books. In sum, he claimed that, between 1887 and 1902, he had made cash outlays totaling $1,950,000 for mine purchases and $2,700,000 for improvements. The credibility of those assertions is tested next.

CHAPTER 4

The Patrón Grande, Community, and Corrupt Practices

Its go, go, go. If you don't feel good and slack off, that's no excuse.
. . . There are no paid holidays, no vacation, no sick days.
—William Gelenites

This dust accumulated in his breathing-organs, then closed
together like cement . . . he would never see his thirtieth birthday
—B. L. Coombes

DURING THE LATE 1890S, labor unrest in Mexico shook the compla-
cency of the Díaz regime. It developed at the same time as the struggles
between capitalists and workers, resulting from mine labor organizing,
swept across the American West. The turmoil reached Batopilas despite
its isolation. The Patrón Grande beat back the challenge, however, and
maintained his control over local politics and law enforcement. He not
only defined the terms of employment in the mines; he tolerated no input
from the local authorities or workers.

It was in that context that, in 1898, radical labor "instigators," representing what Grant Shepherd called a renegade union came to Batopilas
from "who knows where" and initiated an organizing drive in the face of
the combined opposition of Boss Shepherd and the local authorities.
Alexander and his managers took no overt action, even though some
10 percent of the men not only sympathized with the union but also
walked off the job. The "agitators," however, quickly learned who controlled events in the remoteness of the barrancas.

One can only hope that, after realizing the power of Boss Shepherd
and confronting threats from the police and the fear of the workers, and

lacking the outside support and protection available in less isolated communities, the labor organizers fled the scene. They later attributed their failure to organize Batopilas to the subjugated and debased conditions of the workers.[1]

The company's official position was that it gave the workers humane treatment and a good salary. Using that argument, the deputy chief (*subjefe*) of police in Batopilas reminded "newly arrived" and therefore uninitiated workers who might listen to the "agitators" that they were entitled to all the hospital care they needed, good salaries, and emergency and long-term loans at no interest. The deputy chief and his men informed the laborers that, if they persisted in their challenge, the Patrón Grande could not continue to pay "lazy, good for nothings" for not working. The policemen also made it clear that if the "instigators really wanted to improve conditions, the best thing they could do was leave the place and its people in peace." The organizers "disappeared" in the dead of night. In his memoirs, Grant never mentioned the Yaqui forced labor, silicosis, arsenic poisoning, or what happened to the organizers or men who went on strike.[2]

In addition to the reported tunnel imprisonment of the Yaqui prisoner-laborers and the resultant lung disease, an independent observer would have pointed out other shortcomings in Shepherd's treatment of the miners. The Mexican government required hospital services of the mining companies under federal mining laws, but the doctors at the hospital provided only the limited service of setting the broken bones of the many men who incurred severe internal injuries. The company ignored the fact that virtually all of the miners suffered from silicosis. Furthermore, Alexander maintained an emergency loan policy whereby he rendered financial aid to the workers at his own discretion rather than through a mutualist fund. That policy gave him power over the miners at the most critical junctures of their lives, at the moments of illness, injury, disability, and death.

By extending his workers credit for tools and other expenses, Shepherd was able to hold them in place through debt peonage. The Patrón Grande deducted 50 percent from their weekly wages for payment of debts charged to the miners by enganchadores for their transportation to Batopilas. Alexander assumed the collection of these debts and then applied a 50 percent deduction against the remainder to cover debts charged to them at the tienda de raya. The mostly illiterate workers had little or no control over the amounts charged them. The condition of debt

The ruins of the Batopilas Consolidated Mining Company hospital, located north of the Porfirio Díaz Tunnel, as seen from the east. (Courtesy of the Historical Society of Washington, D.C.)

peonage resulted from Mexican law, which enabled creditors to use government officers to detain debtors and even pursue and bring them back to work until their obligations had been met. After the imposition of fines, the workers owed more than ever.[3]

For the workers, the day shift in the mines began before sunrise and ended in the early evening. The night shift began in the early evening and ended at dawn. The miners worked in two 12-hour shifts on weekdays and one six-hour shift on Saturday. Most of them arrived wearing huaraches, loose-fitting shirts, and pants made of strong fabric. The Yaqui, Mayo, and Tarahumara barreteros only wore waistcloths. Having already coated themselves with lard for protection from flying chips, silica-laden dust, arsenic, lead, sulfur, and zinc, they made the sign of the cross as they passed the nichos containing crucifixes and a likeness of San Miguel or San Antonio in the mine entrances. Other men, working surface diggings

The entrance to the Porfirio Díaz Tunnel, sometimes called the "world's longest mine tunnel." (Courtesy of the Historical Society of Washington, D.C.)

or conducting exploration, made their own religious arrangements and prayed to a wider range of saints, including San Antonio, the protector of miners; Santa María del Carmen, the protectress of Batopilas; and San Pedro, for whom the town was named.

The Porfirio Díaz Tunnel intersected rich veins of silver, beginning with the Aurora, followed by the San Miguel, Roncesvalles, Camuchin, Todos Santos, and the Descubridora. These veins, originally worked as outcroppings on the surface, had been followed downward until the task of bringing out the ore in a vertical climb was economically unfeasible. The tamenes, carrying bags of ore weighing up to seventy-five pounds on their backs and supported by straps wrapped round their foreheads, could move the load upward on ladders and across platforms for a distance of some 700 feet, six times a day. The men needed to rest after each arduous hike out of the hole. The tunnels changed all that by facilitating the extraction of ore from below, saving time and effort.

Excavated earth, a power plant, and a drainage tunnel below the mouth of the Porfirio Díaz complex, as seen from the northwest. (Courtesy of the Historical Society of Washington, D.C.)

As they dug the tunnels, the men searched for the intersecting veins on the sides and roof of the shaft. When they encountered crystallized rocks, they tested them for mineral content. If the formation looked promising, they dug narrow tunnels at an angle to the main shaft until they determined whether it was what they were looking for. In the meantime, the main crew continued digging, pushing the tunnel ever deeper under the mountain. When they found the great veins of silver, the men followed them upward from the tunnel.

They drove their picks and drills into the fractures around the ore-bearing granite and quartz. Each blow released small puffs of dust made up of the silica, lead, zinc, sulfur, and smaller quantities of lead and arsenic, all of which occur naturally in the earth of the region around Batopilas. During every phase of the excavation, the miners, breathing heavily, got full doses of the material. The richest veins, though they

The mill at the entrance to the Descubridora mine. Tunnels replaced vertical access to the ores in the late nineteenth century. (Courtesy of The Bancroft Library, University of California, Berkeley)

normally no longer carried much native silver, still carried ore that approached 75 percent in purity. During their best moments, the miners "hit" *gallos* (sheets of silver) between three inches and ten feet in thickness that filled the fissures between the rocks. The extreme heat, created by pressure in the earth that developed during ancient earth movements, had formed the gallos.

In order to reach the pay dirt beyond the harder rock masses, the miners frequently used dynamite to break through and clear out working room. As the men scraped the ore from the stope (mine face), they sent it plummeting downward to the tunnel through chutes, or they dragged it more slowly down slopes. The clouds of poisonous dust that resulted easily defeated the handkerchiefs employed by the barreteros to protect their lungs, throats, and eyes. In this manner, gravity helped move the ore

Hacienda San Miguel, as seen from above Batopilas in the 1880s. (Photograph by Luis Musy; courtesy of the Library of Congress)

to the mules and carts waiting below. The animals hauled the mineral in full carts out of the tunnel to crushers located below the entrance. In contrast to the Robinson era, this method of ore extraction freed the men working in the Porfirio Díaz and San Miguel Tunnel complexes from one of the most onerous aspects of the mining experience.

The water-powered rock crushers used at the tunnel entrances re- duced the pieces of ore to smaller sizes, which were then loaded on horse- drawn ore cars and carried to the Hacienda San Miguel for smelting and storage. After the mid-1880s, workers also hauled virtually all of the ore from the smaller mines to the smelter on mule carts, where it joined the large quantities coming from the tunnels. At the south end of the Ha- cienda San Miguel, crews of skilled workers applied the full weight of modern technology in order to convert the ore into silver ingots.

The ore from the tunnels and other mines was handled separately because of differing compositions. The dam at La Junta and the aqueduct provided the running water needed to generate the electrical power used

The company office building known as Shepherd's Castle in the Hacienda San Miguel in the 1880s. (Photograph by Luis Musy; courtesy of the Library of Congress)

by the rock crushers at the San Antonio plant. Then, at the south end of San Miguel, a work crew shoveled the ore from the cars into a large pile or, by the late 1880s, onto a conveyor belt that moved it to steam-driven rock crushers, which ground it into 30-mesh particles. The steam-driven equipment had replaced Robinson's mule-powered arrastras. Because the smelting process was often backed up by the great quantities of ore being processed, men shoveled the ore from the rock crushers into storage bins. A crew then shoveled the ore from the storage bins onto a belt, which carried it to another set of crushers known as Huntington mills. The Huntington crushers reduced the ore to powder, and the workers added a salty alkaline water solution mixed with mercury, creating slop. The grains in the ore now measured between 80 and 100 mesh.

Moving buckets dipped into the slop and carried it to agitating tanks, where the valuable metal was further separated from the rest of the material. Workers then drained the excess material into the river. After the

Hacienda San Miguel, probably in the 1890s, showing the family residence to the left of Shepherd's Castle. (Courtesy of The Bancroft Library, University of California, Berkeley)

men added cyanide in order to maximize the separation of the silver particles from the remaining impurities, the silver-laden slop rested for over a day. The cyanide, like the mercury, still came from Batopilillas, conveniently situated 100 miles to the north in the Sierra Madre. The silver, bound to the mercury and cyanide, settled to the bottom. Finally, after another phase of agitation that removed almost all of the mercury and cyanide, the expert workers in charge of the operation examined the color and density of the mixture.[4]

At each stage of the process, the men flushed the impure top layers away from the heavier metal, leaving a concentration of silver higher than the 92.5 percent that qualified it as sterling. The mill at the hacienda had fifty smelting furnaces that poured forth molten silver and lead, which the men blended at a ratio of 92.5 percent to 7.5 percent, into molds for the

Ore after arriving at the Hacienda San Miguel. Note the rails and the mules used for hauling. (Courtesy of The Bancroft Library, University of California, Berkeley)

77-pound ingots. The larger part of the mercury and cyanide was used over again and again. The men once again dumped the waste, laden with poisonous materials, into the river about one-half mile upstream from Batopilas, where the citizenry depended upon the river as their principal source of supply for a variety of purposes including irrigation and drinking water.

The Patrón Grande assigned overseers to supervise the mining, the transportation of ore to the Hacienda San Miguel, the smelting process, and to prevent theft. As the workers left the mine, a specialist checked them one by one for gold and silver contraband. The Native American workers who attempted to steal gold dust had one advantage over their mestizo and foreign counterparts. They could place flakes of gold on their fingertips and then run them through their greasy shoulder-length hair,

Swampers working in the storage facility where the refined ore awaited smelt-ing. (Courtesy of the Historical Society of Washington, D.C.)

depositing them in an almost invisible way. A "culprit" was usually caught only because of a splurge in spending. The mestizos, lacking the long hair, resorted to body cavities or the hollowed-out soles of their huaraches, or they placed particles inside their clothing by various means. The Shepherds believed that they even resorted to bags in their stomachs, attached to their teeth by strings. Periodic distractions and lapses in vigilance at the mining entrance allowed miners to slip out with small quantities of silver and gold. Sometimes they stored it near the entrance, waiting for that occasion when the inspector was distracted.

Alexander Sr. conducted an unrelenting struggle against theft. Inspectors recorded each load of ore, the mine from which it came, the number of ingots produced at the forge, and their storage. The stages of refining and smelting, however, were too complex and prolonged for one individual to view the process in its entirety. Overseers sought to overcome the remaining loopholes in security at the Hacienda San Miguel by searching the laborers thoroughly at the end of each work shift. Once the ingots

Smelter workers and the smelting furnaces, which turned the ore into ingots. (Courtesy of the Historical Society of Washington, D.C.)

reached the storage silos located near the southwestern edge of the complex, they were placed under armed guard. At that point, Shepherd took
over. The Patrón Grande controlled the final accounting for the silver
produced and stored, and his figures had to be accepted on faith by the
New York directors.[5]

Alexander's actions in Batopilas bring to mind the accountability problems that plagued large American companies as they reached out to areas
inaccessible to all but the most intrepid pioneers. How could the BCMC
directors, in New York, maintain control and audit expenditures and
income with a strong operating partner in such a remote place? Although
the company owned one of the richest silver mines in world history and
little of its profits ever reached the miners, even less took the form of
dividends in New York. The largest dividend ever paid by Shepherd,
$2,000,000 in 1884, was intended to create a sensation among Wall Street
investors at the moment the company placed its stock on the New York

Stock Exchange. In the years that followed, the dividends disappeared, while Shepherd created palatial surroundings on his 13-acre estate at San Miguel, maintained the Bleak House mansion in Washington, D.C., imported select European wines to Batopilas from New York in order to maintain a large exclusive and frequently used wine cellar, and amassed an expensive rare gun collection. He even brought in the genteel young Griswold woman as a tutor for his children.

Although Boss Shepherd only returned to Washington twice during his more than twenty years in Batopilas, his wife took periodic and extended trips to the U.S. capital, where she entertained and took part in the social life. When they were old enough, Alexander sent his children off to elite preparatory schools on the East Coast; the boys continued on to Sewanee College in Tennessee, where they gained bachelor's degrees and their already traditional southern elite viewpoints regarding racial and social distinctions were reinforced. Shepherd also built a house in the upper reaches of the Sierra Madre in order for his family to find relief from the heat.

The Patrón Grande spent amounts of cash for his personal and family activities far in excess of his salary of $15,000 yearly plus dividends on his investment. After 1887, the company paid no dividends while he was alive. He explained to the New York directors that, although the improvements and enlargement of mining operations consumed short-term income, they guaranteed future profits because of the almost limitless supply of silver that the company owned. Alexander's lifestyle and that of his family, however, raise the same questions that plagued him when he was in charge of public works contracts in Washington. How could his salary and the meager returns reported to the Batopilas Consolidated Mining Company have supported his personal expenditures?

Shepherd died at 7:45 a.m. on September 12, 1902, of peritonitis, the inflammation of the membrane that lines the abdomen, "brought on by appendicitis." His companions could not get him out of the barrancas quickly enough to save him, and the doctors at the hospital he had installed at Batopilas lacked the medical skills and technology to perform extractive surgeries on the torso. There has been speculation in Batopilas that the symptoms of arsenic poisoning are so similar to appendicitis that a vengeful batopilense working in the kitchen might have poisoned the

Patrón Grande with a principal ingredient of the toxic waste he had been dumping in the river for two decades.[6]

At the time of Boss Shepherd's death, the directors had not seen a dividend in fifteen years. The production records of the Batopilas mines, however, contain anomalies that suggest he had diverted company income for his own use. That situation corresponded to the practices of his associates at the Banco Minero de Chihuahua, where he maintained an account for Batopilas Consolidated. His friend Enrique Clay Creel, who served as governor of the state, and Enrique's son Juan controlled the Banco Minero. During the U.S. financial crisis of 1907, trade between Chihuahua and its market to the north suffered greatly. Many banks in Texas closed as a result, and the Banco Minero teetered on the brink of collapse. The total of its deposits fell by one-third. In the midst of the trouble, Juan took over as president of the bank and attempted to refinance it with French capital. Those negotiations, however, proceeded slowly because the bank did not have the value initially claimed by the directors. Then, on March 2, 1908, the Banco Minero officials announced that unidentified bandits had robbed them of $295,000 pesos (at that time, a peso equaled forty cents). Suspicions immediately arose because of longstanding rumors that the Creel brothers had been diverting bank funds.

The Chihuahua state authorities, heavily influenced by the Terrazas-Creel oligarchy, invited Antonio Villavicencio, a notoriously corrupt police detective from Mexico City, to investigate the case. The issue of diverting funds would be obscured by an investigation of the "burglary." Detective Villavicencio had been indicted, convicted, fired, and imprisoned in the national capital for malfeasance in his duties. After his "investigation" of the bank "robbery," Villavicencio and his aides ordered the arrest and imprisonment of several working-class suspects, who had no criminal backgrounds. Despite the lack of solid evidence, the state authorities acted on Villavicencio's charges. They convicted the accused and kept them in prison for three years despite successful appeals, outside of Chihuahua, that established that the defendants had not been allowed proper representation and that there was important exculpatory evidence.

Witnesses finally revealed that Villavicencio had tortured the suspects during interrogation. But it was not until 1911, after the revolutionaries had thrown the Díaz and Terrazas-Creel regimes out of national and state office, that the prisoners were released. At that point, Abraham González, the new revolutionary governor of the state, prepared charges against Enrique and Juan Creel for embezzlement in the case of the missing bank funds and for misuse of the justice system in a cover-up that resulted in the conviction of innocent citizens. Only the intervention of revolutionary President Francisco Madero with Governor González saved the Creels: "In the special case of Don Enrique Creel I ask that you take into consideration that he has been the Ambassador of Mexico to the United States and that he has also served as Secretary of State, for which in this case we should exercise caution, that is, we should proceed only if there is absolutely conclusive evidence."[7] Juan, in turn, also benefited from his father's prestige.

During Shepherd's reign in Batopilas, endemic official and private sector corruption characterized Chihuahua, Sonora, and Sinaloa. Alexander maintained business and political contacts in all these states. From the 1860s until the revolutionary decade after 1910, customs officials at Mazatlán looked the other way in return for payoffs as silver passed through duty free and unregulated. The metal also left Mexico via unidentified points along the northern coast of Sinaloa, and even via the capital city of Chihuahua. Contraband was a major component of foreign export and import trade. Some Batopilas silver also went through Álamos and Guaymas in Sonora, the same state that provided Alexander with his Yaqui forced labor. During the 1880s and 1890s, Chihuahua became a central part of a nexus of contraband, and smuggling grew ever more blatant. Boss Shepherd joined in along with his *compañeros*, the Creels, who ran the Banco Minero, and dominated state law enforcement and government.[8]

The numbers tell the story. The value of silver in pesos officially sent out by Shepherd through the Chihuahua mint and other official smelters from 1880 through 1897 was as follows:

1880 to 1882	1,611,209
1883	720,864
1884	1,053,863
1885 to 1886	1,004,090
1887	511,054
1893	1,182,508

1894	572,152
1895	711,586
1896	413,752
1897	564,059

In 1902, after Alexander's death, the few remaining mines in the region that had been operated separately from BCMC management were brought under centralized control. That step finally provided the directors with clear records of expenditures and simplified contract renewals, their defenses against lawsuits brought by Mexicans, and accounting matters. Under Shepherd Sr., a multiplicity of business entities had the same owners and operators, but he prepared the data and could assign production amounts to any mine without outside auditing. Without such oversight, the Patrón Grande could manipulate output and expense data in his reports. Although the exact years do not match, during the late 1880s and 1890s, the Todos Santos mine alone produced silver in amounts that equaled those Shepherd recorded for the entire BCMC. Walter Brodie provides us with the production totals at Todos Santos:

1888	395,685
1889	475,798
1890	375,174
1891	336,903
1892	627,423
1898	537,033
1899	590,451
1900	1,141,317
1901	1,511,207
1902	1,140,060[9]

From 1888 to 1902, a peso generally equaled $1. Todos Santos was a principal mine across the river from the Hacienda San Miguel, accessed by the Porfirio Díaz Tunnel.

In some of those years, other mines among the eleven principal lodes outproduced Todos Santos. At the Chihuahua mint, originally created by the Mexican government to control silver production but now controlled by the Creel family, officials accepted the output figures offered to them by Shepherd at face value. Meanwhile, the directors in New York complained about expenditures that absorbed all of the growth in BCMC income. Their attempts to obtain detailed and objective accountings failed until after the Patrón Grande's death.

Until 1902, Shepherd continued to send unauthorized shipments of silver west on the Camino Real from Batopilas to Mazatlán and Altata, and lesser amounts through Guaymas and unnamed sites on the Sinaloa coastline. The proceeds from the unauthorized shipments never reached the BCMC's coffers in New York. Ultimately, Shepherd was the only person to see the final ore and ingot production and expense figures, which the company bookkeeper in New York, mint officials, and directors had to accept on faith.

No one overtly questioned the use of the mule trains that went west on the Camino Real over La Cumbre ridge southwest of Batopilas and on past El Rodeo to Fuerte and the Pacific Coast. The New York directors evinced no awareness of this practice, although they must have known that the route was used for imports and that Robinson had sold ingots exported via that route in Asia. The Patrón Grande had exercised unquestioned power over BCMC affairs and the lower civil authorities in the region. Shepherd's claim that increased expenditures absorbed the greater values produced at the mines was partly true, but ultimately lame.

For example, the original San Miguel Tunnel, renamed in honor of Porfirio Díaz, had already intersected the Veta Grande (Mother Lode) before his arrival and was producing on a grand scale. It provided revenue while Shepherd greatly expanded the workforce, as much as tenfold, and put up to 800 miners at work in two shifts twenty-four hours per day in the renamed Díaz and San Miguel Tunnels. He followed up that action by naming the new processing plant outside the Díaz Tunnel "San Antonio." By the mid-1880s, the miners were reaching the deeper subterranean extensions of surface veins that had produced fabulous bonanzas in the past, including the Pastrana, Carmen, San Antonio, Roncesvalles, San Pedro, and Todos Santos.

At the San Miguel Tunnel complex, one and a half miles upstream from the Hacienda San Miguel, Robinson's men had already accessed the Veta Grande. By working upward from the tunnel, that vein produced a 200,000-ounce bonanza of pure silver during the 1870s. The Veta Grande continued below the tunnel as well. The San Miguel Tunnel also intersected the San Antonio and Carmen veins from below. The San Antonio surface diggings had produced 10 million pesos in silver between 1786 and 1800, while, between 1790 and 1820, the Carmen yielded 30 million pesos, or 1 million pesos per year, by means of primitive technology. These figures are even more impressive when it is remembered that the primitive technology of Spanish arrastras, hammers, and mercury used in the refining process lost up to 50 percent of the silver content in the ore.

How rich were the other veins intersected by the tunnels? Between 1730 and 1750, miners using primitive equipment worked the surface diggings at the Pastrana vein. The barreteros dug downward into the earth, while the tamenes brought most of the ore out by carrying it up ladders in bags on their backs that were strapped to their foreheads. Still other workers then broke up the rocks with hammers and pulverized them with large circular milling stones. The miners working the Pastrana vein produced 48 million pesos in silver over the twenty years, or 2.4 million pesos per annum. During Shepherd's era, a peso generally equaled $1. In the mid-1880s, Shepherd's men intersected the Pastrana vein from below, via the Porfirio Díaz Tunnel. They gleefully reported that it was as rich as the surface deposit and went to work on it with jacks and double jacks, four- and eight-pound hammers.

In 1887, Alexander Sr. paid his last dividend, totaling "about $1,000,000" to the New York directors, yet the admitted total value of production that year was only $511,054. That action reveals the great discretionary powers he enjoyed. He had decided to withhold funds for contingencies or to fulfill other plans and then changed his mind and surprised the directors with a dividend larger than income. Only a saint could withstand the temptations of such autonomous power and the obvious opportunity for personal gain, and Boss Shepherd, aka the Patrón Grande, was no saint.

In the succeeding five years, Alexander's reported earnings from silver extracted at Batopilas exceeded those of 1887, and, in 1893, they leaped up to $1,182,508. Yet he reported no net profits, even though he paid his workforce a maximum of only 5 to 10 percent of the value produced at the mines. During the rest of the 1890s, earnings exceeded the 1887 figure by an average of almost 30 percent before more than doubling to $1,141,317 in 1900. In 1901 and 1902, they rose even higher, to $1,511,207 and $1,140,060, respectively. Still Shepherd reported that his expenses exceeded income.

He made the claim despite the continuing work on ancient tailings that, deposited in large mounds in front of the tunnels, were already broken up and remained rich in silver from veins like the Todos Santos, Pastrana, Carmen, and San Antonio.

While the directors realized few benefits from the wealth being produced, the miners fared worse. Pay for peons remained at $75 per annum, while a *barrenador* (borer), *tanatero* (ore hauler), or *barretero puntista* (pick worker) made 350 pesos per year (1.50 pesos per day) before the 50 percent tienda de raya deduction. Calculating an average of 700 laborers working every day except Sunday and producing a total value of $1,000,000, the workforce realized significantly less than 10 percent of the value produced. Only the supervisors who lived in the Hacienda San Miguel complex and Alexander seemed to be doing well. The supervisors earned $1,500 annually, while Shepherd's ultimate income is unknown.[10]

Notably, the asserted costs for mining at Batopilas plummeted sharply immediately after Shepherd's death, when the New York directors took a more active role in the auditing of daily operations. As declared production expenses fell after outside observers from the board reviewed the books, Alexander Jr. continued rendering operating and production reports. But now these submissions offered detailed explanations for costs. In 1902, before the Patrón Grande's death, the costs for refining ore ran $4.64 per ton, but, in 1906, the expenses for these same operations had fallen to $2.44 per ton. In 1902, the charges for hauling the ore out of the barrancas were set at $36 per ton, but, in 1906, they had dropped to $23, with crews of equal skills doing the work.[11]

In Shepherd's defense, one should point out that he accomplished a great deal. The Hacienda San Miguel now featured a 100-ton stamp mill, the Díaz Tunnel ran more than 8,000 feet under the Cerro de Todos Santos, and the San Miguel Tunnel ran 1,350 feet under the Cerro de San Antonio. The miners still referred to the mill in front of the San Miguel Tunnel as the Hacienda San Antonio. It reportedly cost $500,000 to develop. Although it is unclear when the stamping mill for high-grade ores at the Hacienda San Miguel became fully operative, the other power-driven technology was already in place before Alexander's death. At the San Miguel smelter, the roasting and lixiviation plant for the roasting, washing, and percolation of solubles in order to create concentrates, the canals, and all other facilities were also operational as a result of his leadership.

Despite his wild exaggerations of costs, Shepherd's numbers do not come close to accounting for the vast wealth produced, and all of it with cheap labor. The entire 13-acre Hacienda San Miguel processing plants, housing, and general offices cost little more than $500,000.[12] Robinson, still a member of the board in the 1880s, knew about the easy access and egress to and from Mazatlán, Altata, and other points on the Sinaloa coastline that Shepherd used for shipments, and he knew that silver could be moved through those places. It took no imagination for him to add Chihuahua City to the list, but he was not active in the leadership of the mines and died a decade after the last dividends were paid. His death ended the directors' ability to analyze BCMC with the acuity needed to protect their interests.

One can only imagine the reaction of the New York directors after 1902, when they finally saw the precise data regarding production and costs. By then, the older major veins had been worked upward from the tunnels, but Batopilas continued to thrive, and the company prospered for another ten years because of new bonanzas, found largely in digging downward from the tunnels. In 1907, the company paid its last dividends to investors, 12½ cents on stock carrying a par value of $20.

From the mid-1880s until the 1910 revolution, the American managers of the Batopilas mines continued to perfect the production process. That meant the increased application of imported technology and the rationalization of labor, that is, higher per-worker productivity and reduced costs. When the Patrón Grande died, his oldest and most reliable son, Alexander Jr., took over at the site as the assistant manager in charge of daily operations and reported on a frequent basis to general manager Walter Brodie in New York. Brodie, an astute mining engineer, had helped Shepherd Sr. get operations started in Batopilas from 1879 through much of the 1880s.

From 1902 onward, the on-site supervisor shared information on a continuous basis with the board of directors, which, by 1910, had added noted financiers Dudley Evans, president and director of Wells Fargo Bank and director of the Mercantile Trust Company; Alphonse W. Zimmerman, director of Wells Fargo; Nicolas F. Palmer, director of the Mechanics

National Bank, Manhattan Life and Atlantic Mutual Insurance Companies, and the Quintard Iron Works; George W. Quintard; Edgar W. Jorgensen, director of the Indestructible Fibre Company; George W. Field, director of the U.S. Express Realty Company; Gates W. McGarrah, president of the Mechanics National and director of the Astor and Bankers Trust Companies and of the Manhattan Life Insurance Company; Francis D. Merchant, director of the Mutual Life Insurance Company of New York; Edward L. Stevens, director of Metropolitan Life and the Trust Company of America; Louis H. Scott, director of the New York Cement-Stone Company; and Henry E. Howland, director of the Lawyers Title Insurance Company, who came from a family noted in the nineteenth century as the nation's leading importer of gold and silver from Latin America.

The BCMC directors approved major projects and handled most dealings with Mexico's national authorities. They also monitored the instructions given Manuel Prieto, the company's lawyer in Mexico City, by the Chihuahua management.

Quintard, Alexander Jr.'s brother-in-law, took over as the chief financial officer. There is no sign that Quintard, who in the 1880s had been the protégé of Shepherd Sr. in Batopilas, ever forwarded suspicions regarding his mentor's handling of monies to the New York directors. The payment of dividends, however, began again immediately following the Patrón Grande's death despite a 27 percent decline in production at the Todos Santos mine from the previous year.

Alexander appointed Grant Shepherd, his younger, hard-drinking, more erratic, but tough and intelligent brother, as a mine foreman. Grant supervised mestizo, Yaqui, Mayo, and Tarahumara miners at various sites including the Porfirio Díaz Tunnel complex. The less than 150-man workforce in the mines and smelters at that point included a five to one ratio of mestizos to indigenous miners. Enganchado peons were still working the mines, but there is no evidence of Yaqui prisoners after 1902.

The receipts for Yaqui prisoners no longer appeared in the company books. The practice may have been hidden in a manner similar to Boss Shepherd's bookkeeping strategy regarding costs and earnings. Perhaps the horrendous conditions and the death rate among those workers were considered immoral, or the introduction of high technology including power drills made them uneconomical. Meanwhile, the total complement of Americans employed by the BCMC in Batopilas held at eighteen. Grant also managed explorations, as teams of men penetrated hard rock in search of new bonanzas with dynamite, pickaxes, and power drills. The men dug upward and horizontally from inside the mountain, following the silver-laden fissures and solid rock into pockets of frequently unstable and dangerous earth.

Grant's crews epitomized the international character of the miners. They included the foreman Guillermo "El Francés" (the Frenchman), named by virtue of his claimed descent from a Gaul who visited Batopilas long enough to father a child, experienced former gambusinos of both mestizo and Yaqui parentage, and indigenous common laborers, often no more than boys, who carried away loose earth from the stopes in bags to waiting ore carts or dumped it at the mine entrance.

When Alexander Jr. and Grant took over from their father, the mining output was steady, and many of the merchants of Batopilas took pride in themselves and the town. Some of them dressed in imported finery. Virtually all of them worked with the company in a symbiotic relationship in which they took the scrip money in exchange for their goods and then cashed it in at the BCMC office at the Hacienda San Miguel.

At the same time, however, worker unrest continued to simmer just beneath the surface. The periodic unrest of the 1880s and 1890s had been suppressed. In the first case, shortly after Boss Shepherd's arrival, a display of force by the army had ended the combined resistance of the local officials and workers to his extension of authority from the mines to the region. In the second instance, during the 1890s, the now more compliant local police and town officials threatened the labor organizers until they fled in fear for their lives or were possibly killed.

In the early twentieth century, the pace of the work had intensified in response to capital investments, the use of high technology, the declining value of the silver on the world market, the lower grade of ore, and the rising costs associated with its extraction. Two of the mines that intersected the Porfirio Díaz Tunnel, the Todos Santos and Roncevalles, grossed $718,700 against $211,750 in expenses. The Roncevalles vein varied from one to ten feet in width as it coursed through the earth. But, across the river, the San Miguel Tunnel complex only grossed $288,090 against costs of $299,180. The high expenses resulted from the continued need for tunnel and smelter repairs.

Throughout the decade, the directors and managers strove to reduce costs. The miners worked the same long hours, but now there was more danger from silica, cave-ins, accidents, and cyanide because they were digging and processing more ore and using more dynamite and power drills. In 1909, only 800 miners excavated 10,976 feet of tunnels and mine shafts. Power drills had replaced double jacks, and the workforce was some 400 men less than it had been twenty-five years earlier. During the first six months of that year, the men produced 770 ingots of silver with a net weight of 729,792 troy ounces. By the end of the year, work had dropped off because of political violence and growing uncertainty in the region.

Of the 654 men still working, the San Miguel and Todos Santos mines engaged 188 and 163, respectively. The other most active sites were the Camuchin with 113 miners and the Animus with 27. Another 27 men worked on maintaining the San Miguel Tunnel, while 136 found employment at the hacienda refining 26 million pounds of already reduced ore. With wages constant and utopia denied, the resentments among some workers and dissident local elites continued to build. In 1910, some eighty anguished miners gathered in the center of Batopilas and joined revolutionary leader Pascual Orozco when he called upon them to join the Mexican Revolution, led by Francisco Madero against President Díaz.

Batopilas had become a divided place. A few of the leading merchants and political officials liked the Shepherds, but most found it only expedient to cooperate with them. The overwhelming economic and political power of the family and its cohort of American supporters who lived in the Hacienda San Miguel across the river from the town had deprived the local Mexican elites of their autonomy and of their authority when it conflicted with the interests of the foreigners. Finally, the owners had never produced the prosperity that they promised when they introduced full-scale capitalism and high technology. Indeed, the gambusinos lost their position of independence, while the mine workers who replaced them earned an income barely sufficient for survival.

The arrest of Grant Shepherd for drawing a gun from his holster and pointing it at a policeman underscored the divisions between the town and the company and among the Batopilas leaders themselves. Many batopilenses resented the air of superiority assumed by the Shepherd "boys" and the foreign employees with the exception of the African American who married a local mestizo woman and raised a family. When the police arrested Grant, they held him in the jail overnight, but allowed his friends to provide him with food, a mattress, and other comforts. They yielded the following day, when the governor of Chihuahua ordered him released. Grant and the arresting officers and town authorities had made their mutual contempt obvious. The frictions between some of the Batopilas elites and the BCMC would be important when revolutionary unrest surfaced in 1910.[13]

There were even deeper divisions among the batopilenses. Occupying the bottom rung of the social structure, the miners led lives that stood in stark contrast to those of the Batopilas elites, who enjoyed the advantages of safe work, an adequate diet, ample rest, clean clothes, and relatively safe well water, although the cyanide in the river water used for drinking and cooking must have affected everyone to some degree.

Throughout the era of American ownership, the more regimented mine workers faced many dangers besides the dynamite used to blast sections of rock loose. In addition to deadly premature and delayed explosions, the miners, unlike free-roving gambusinos, were required to work in specific areas of the mines. They lived in dread of cave-ins and bell-shaped stones. The only warning came from rats as they scurried away or from the creaking of timber supports. Cave-ins and bell-shaped stones could occur anywhere, and they killed. The widest part of the bell-shaped stone pointed downward and was exposed on the ceiling of the shaft or tunnel. It looked exactly like the countless large embedded boulders in the roofs of the tunnels, which usually extended in several directions, supported by the surrounding rocks. The bell-shaped stones, however, were triangular in shape. They tapered into a point at the top. Smooth on their upward sides, they fell suddenly, bringing down the surrounding earth with them. The larger stones crushed many men, while the smaller ones caused countless injuries and filled the shafts with dust.

The work environment made prevention of accidents difficult. Potential bell-shaped stones in the middle of tunnels or shafts could not be supported with posts because the vertical beams would block the movement of the mules, carts, and machinery. Miners also bumped into them in the darkness. Nearer the working face or stope of the mine, the use of support posts in the middle of the area was impractical because they blocked the digging work. The American doctor at the company hospital

treated countless miners whose bones had been broken by those treacherous rocks, while the larger cave-ins inevitably killed many men. The
hospital professionals, varying from one to two doctors and two nurses,
provided bone-setting services but were unable to stop many forms of
internal bleeding or to rectify more serious bodily harm. The bell-shaped
stones were one of the many reasons for the miners to pray for protection from the saints who stood in their nichos and guarded the tunnel
entrances.[14]

Other problems resulted from prolonged work in the dark. The miners' candles went out often, from drafts, bumps, and depletions of oxygen.
In those situations, the men, entirely in the blackness and covered with
lard and sweat, felt their way around, frequently unsure of where they
were. Exhausted, stumbling, and falling, they breathed heavily, inhaling
the thick silica-laden dust. Silica is the common name for silicon dioxide.
It occurs naturally in quartz, many rocks, and in the sand that surrounds
Batopilas.

In the late nineteenth and early twentieth centuries, the miners suffered even greater exposure to the silica and to lead and other poisons in
the dust because of the increased amounts of ore moved and the pace of
their labors. They had always inhaled the puffs of *polvo* whenever they
sank their picks into the fissures surrounding the veins of silver. Now they
were engulfed by it whenever they shoveled ore downward from higher
levels to the railcars waiting to be filled with ore at the stope. In 1902, the
Patrón Grande had ordered a 20-horsepower gasoline locomotive from
the "Weber people of Kansas City." That event and the power drills raised
exposure to silica to a new level.

The engine pulled three empty cars up a 1 to 2 percent grade, 8,000
feet into the Porfirio Díaz Tunnel on 24-inch light rails. The men at the
stope worked in a cloud of dust, as ore poured down chutes from shafts
being worked above them into large piles, which they shoveled into the
railroad cars. Unprecedented quantities of earth were now moved daily.
Each car held 3,000 pounds of ore for the return trip to the face of
the tunnel.[15]

The laborers outside also inhaled the silica as they unloaded the railcars at the tunnel entrance and worked with the rock crushers. Those who
shoveled the sand at La Junta and mixed it with cement and concrete for
the buildings, aqueducts, and dams were also exposed to high concentra-

tions. The strongest of the workers could inhale that dust for more than a decade without any visible effect. But, sooner or later, the greatest injury of all, silicosis, caught up with them. It derived from the development of hard fibrous nodules caused by the silica in the dust, which adhered to the lung tissue. In addition to the immediate life-threatening dangers they faced, the men lived in fear of silicosis. Many a miner saw his best friend succumb in the manner described by B. L. Coombes: "This dust accumulated in his breathing-organs, then closed together like cement . . . he would never see his thirtieth birthday."[16]

When the miners fell ill, it was already too late. They had inhaled large amounts of silica for years, until the fibrous tissue cells became a mass. At that point, they multiplied on their own, gradually supplanting the normal lung tissue over large areas and preventing the transfer of oxygen to the blood. The condition remains incurable today. In the beginning, it causes shortness of breath. Coughing and wheezing characterize the intermediate phase. In its final stages, silicosis encourages the development of tuberculosis and other related diseases accompany it. The Yaqui prisoners held in the San Miguel Tunnel by the Patrón Grande in the 1880s contracted tuberculosis, or "consumption," after about six months from a combination of dust, heat, and humidity. The silica did not have the time needed to do its deadly work.

When the Batopilas victims reached the final stages of the silicosis, they died slow, agonizing deaths as invalids in the BCMC hospital, in their living places in town, or, in the case of the Tarahumaras, back in their mountain abodes, where their relatives trembled before the power of the evil spirits. Decades later, the U.S. Department of Labor tersely described the effects of the still incurable disease: "Miners develop silicosis when they are overexposed to dust containing silica. Respirable particles of silica embed in the lungs causing scar tissue to form, reducing the lungs' ability to extract oxygen from the air."[17] In the mines at Batopilas, the recommended steps of ventilation and dust suppression for the prevention of silicosis were either unheard of or ignored by management.

The miners feared the many dangers in their work, and they died from them, but many of the Yaquis from Sonora and Mayos from Sinaloa and Sonora, the mestizos, and the Tarahumaras from the barrancas voluntarily joined them because they needed employment. A few Raramuris deemed the jobs essential for their survival as the wild game disappeared.

The lumber mills in the Sierra Madre, such as the U.S.-owned Chihuahua Lumber Company at San Juanito, located on the high elevations in
the Copper Canyon area, offered only a limited number of jobs, largely
for experienced mestizos. For the Tarahumaras, that alternative did not
exist. Employers did not want inexperienced workers with language and
motivational problems, and the overwhelming majority of Tarahumaras
did not want to leave their homelands anyway.

Farmwork offered the Raramuri a possible alternative, but that, too,
would force them to leave their neighbors and beloved homeland in the
sierra to find an uncertain fate. Disease and malnutrition made life hard
and short in the Barranca del Cobre, inside the mines or out, no matter
what the occupation. Epidemic disease and intestinal infections ravaged
the population, regardless of occupation. The average life expectancy for
those who farmed or eked out other livings in the canyons was about
thirty-five years, but if they survived childhood, it was about the same as
the miners, around forty-five years. For the Tarahumara, at least, they died
among their relatives and the revered spirits of their ancestors.[18]

In Batopilas, whether as wives, daughters, or prostitutes, women played
essential roles not only in the survival of the mine workers but also in the
society and economy at large. The importance of socially constructed
female roles made it a simple matter to find new husbands or lovers in the
event of death or estrangement. Some women joined their male counterparts in running boardinghouses and even applied rudimentary mathematics in keeping track of credits, debts, and payments. Many of them
worked as seamstresses at home.

In 1908, Soledad Orozco earned 1.50 pesos by producing six hand-
made bedsheets for the company in about one month. Other women
worked as self-employed laundresses in competition with several Chinese
families whose adults and children participated in patriarchal small businesses. The opportunity for laundry work existed because the wives and
lovers of miners joined higher-status women in a search for relative clean-
liness. Because of the dust blown through the barrancas, elite and middle-
status women needed washed clothes almost as badly as the miners' companions in order to have clean beds.

Working-class women of mestizo descent and some Tarahumaras
worked as laundresses for the miners and townspeople. They used strong
soaps and pounded the clothes on stones in the river, with its high con-

centration of arsenic, cyanide, mercury, and lead. In the short term, the process left them with rough and toughened hands, and, in the longer range, countless maladies resulted. The women worked for their husbands, lovers, sons, brothers, and neighbors. Sun-dried on the rocks at streamside, the muslin and linen clothing of their men quickly took on a worn look, with tattered edges.

The Chinese laundresses served a higher echelon of local society and introduced a better-quality product, clean and well-pressed clothing. The Chinese laundrymen and -women found most of their business came from those who wished to appear somewhat "above" the laborers. They worked largely for the BCMC, the mining professionals and gang foremen, and for the shopkeepers and officials in town.

During 1908 and 1909, however, the company paid labor contractors Cristina Villalobos and Nu Wong, representing two ethnicities, two pesos or eighty cents per week for each woman retained as a *planchera* (washing and ironing woman). Between five and nine women worked five days a week cleaning and ironing linens in their homes for the staff residing at the Hacienda San Miguel and for the guests the company maintained at the humble Batopilas Hotel. Villalobos and Wong probably kept in excess of 50 percent of the proceeds, leaving each working-class woman with a weekly salary of about forty cents, or twenty-one dollars per year. That situation compounded the ethnic rivalry between mestizo and Asian launderers with the class relationships between Wong and the workers. It also demonstrated the social fluidity of mining town culture as new entrepreneurs, in this case Chinese, began to play significant economic roles alongside the traditional merchant capitalists.[19]

Working-class mestizo and Asian women also made livings by selling merchandise in stores, sewing fabrics for the local retailers, working as domestics, or by selling food heated on braziers in the street, all this in addition to their duties in the home. The work of mothering was especially grueling. Most children died of dysentery and stomach disorders during the first two years, and many of the remainder succumbed to childhood diseases before they were ten. During the week, the working-class women rose from bed early in the morning to grind corn for several hours in order to prepare the tortillas needed for the meals of the day. They performed the work on a metate (stone grinder) while on their knees. On weekends, women street vendors sold meats, tortillas, fritters, tamales, and corn sticks to the revelers in the Plaza del Taste and on the main street leading into town from the mines upriver. A few of the Tarahumara women joined their mestiza counterparts as maids, but they had to be taught Mexican household arts.

Prostitutes constituted a small percentage of the approximately 1,500 women in Batopilas. The majority of them came from the cities of Mazatlán and Culiacán in Sinaloa, some from Guaymas and Álamos in Sonora, and others from the small settlements scattered along the Sea of Cortez coastline. A few of them were chihuahuenses. The more desirable among them resided at the brothel run by María Gómez and satisfied the needs of the local elites and foreigners, with the exception of men of African descent. In California, the pimps brought prostitutes from Mexico and China on indentured contracts, often in effect for six months. In Batopilas, the same situation probably prevailed. At any rate, no more than a dozen prostitutes experienced the high status achieved through residency in the Gómez house.

The less desirable among them, whether soliciting from domiciles or hustling in the street, settled for workingmen, usually miners or small shopkeepers. This group of women provided the crucially important nurturing that the single laborers would otherwise lack. The middle-level prostitutes, those who fraternized on a longer-term basis with the mestizo miners, usually performed the laundry tasks and cooked for three or four special partners. They joined the other women at the entrances to the mines to provide home-cooked corn tortillas, black beans, rice, and sometimes goat meat and gravy to the exhausted men. Sometimes they gained a degree of legitimacy in working-class society by marrying one of their partners.

Batopilas was undoubtedly like other mining camps of the American West and Latin America, where the miners who enjoyed domestic relationships with females were healthier and lived longer than those men who lacked them. Among the advantages were a more regular diet, including hot food brought to the mines, daily emotional support, and a place to seek refuge during illness and times of distress. As they helped maintain the well-being of the miners, the women unintentionally contributed to the dynamics of silver mining.[20]

At any point in time, several women served as midwives and herbalists; several others served in professional capacities. During the 1890s and

1900s, at least two formally trained Americans worked as nurses in the company hospital, while, over the years, several literate mestiza women worked as teachers at the Nicolás Bravo primary school. Between 1900 and 1909, Sophia and Laura Ontiveros Balderrama took employment as nurses in the hospital. They were the daughters of the merchant, mine owner, and at one point Batopilas mayor Jesús Ontiveros. In 1911, they married the American doctors Hugh Max Helm and Jerome Triolo, who had arrived there in 1909. Both of the men were from El Paso. By the time the sisters married, their parents had already died, and they, like other women in Batopilas and their male counterparts, were assuming greater agency and redefining their identities. At the same time, the better-educated Americans associated with the BCMC were beginning to see their Mexican counterparts in a more favorable light: as people struggling to achieve a better life.[21]

The Shepherd children, however, remained apart. They enjoyed private American women tutors, before departing for private preparatory schools in the United States and, for the boys, Sewanee.

Meanwhile, the Mexican schoolteachers and women who ran small shops joined the laundresses and boardinghouse operators as cultural intermediaries between those of lower status in the community and the Batopilas elite. They frequently interacted with the women on both extremes of the social order. While the elite and working-class women did not directly socialize, both sides interacted with the professionals and shopkeepers. They transmitted the news of events such as births, marriages, illness, arrivals, and departures and provided interpretations of romances and scandals.

In the male community, professionals, supervisors, and shopkeepers played much the same role because of their periodic access to the Shepherds, other foreigners, town elites, and workers. Visitors, including mule skinners, brought the news of the outside world to Batopilas, while posters announced local events.

Women of all social categories suffered abuse in Batopilas, but those who lived with the miners endured chronic drunkenness and the concomitant beatings, neglect, and vile language. Meanwhile, the miners' children suffered all of those ordeals and other dangers. They could not resist the exploration of abandoned mine shafts with their pits, dangerous bell-shaped stones, periodic cave-ins, and forgotten water wells, from which they could not be extricated once they fell in. They also splashed and played in the tainted river water in order to have fun and escape the oppressive summer heat. Crowded in a narrow ravine with a river to the east and mountains on the west, most of the women and children lived next to or within earshot of cantinas. They saw the sometimes larger-than-life figures of provocative prostitutes, painted and gaudy in their dress, and they heard the obscenities. Neighbors and sometimes the more affluent batopilenses took in orphans as household servants until they reached their early teens. At that point, they were on their own.[22]

The mines caused the development of at least some support industries beyond local laundry workers, cantinas, merchants, and prostitutes. The company, in order to avoid the five-peso-per-bag fee imposed on exports by the government assayers, shipped its sulfur by-products hundreds of miles to a refinery at Monterrey, Nuevo León, creating some employment there. The Patrón Grande, after exhausting the timber resources around Batopilas, ordered the lumber used in the construction of a new bridge across the river between the Hacienda San Miguel and Batopilas from a sawmill at Urique in the adjacent barranca to the northwest. However, the iron beams for the bridge were not produced in Chihuahua. They had to be imported from the United States to Bocoyna, then the railhead of the Kansas City, Mexico, and Orient Railroad. Located forty-five miles northeast of Batopilas, Bocoyna served as the warehousing center for the region. Arrieros then led mule teams into the canyons to deliver merchandise at Batopilas and other sites.

During the 1890s and first years of the twentieth century, the Shepherds and their financial backers in New York invested heavily in new technology. These innovations were prompted not just by the logic of capitalism, in which cost savings lead to higher profitability, but also by the continual decline in the value of silver on the open market. As the per-ounce value of silver decreased, the need to reduce costs while producing it increased. The highest priorities were to find the richest deposits and reduce manual labor to a minimum. Labor shortages in the rough and remote barrancas required several strategies, including labor recruitment and control and the introduction of technology.

By 1906, the machinery at the reduction plant in the Hacienda San Miguel included an impressive array of machines: a steam engine; a 100-ton stamp mill that smashed 850 pounds of ore per stamp; six Bartlett concentrating tables, where the removal of other materials began, an amalgamation plant capable of handling twenty tons of silver ore, mercury, and cyanide at a time; and roasting and lixiviation plants, each capable of processing eight tons daily. The Bartlett tables consisted of three levels. Ore was placed on the top shelf and water applied to separate "heads" (metal) from "tailings" (waste). The tailings were treated over again at levels two and three.[23]

By the middle of the first decade of the century, the difficult work and minimal salaries had caused shortages of skilled labor in Batopilas. The town shrank to less than 4,000 from its peak of 6,500 only twenty years before. Now Shepherd Jr. paid bounties to labor recruiters in order to secure unskilled workers from other parts of the barrancas and their skilled counterparts from farther away. Stonemasons (jacklegs) were in greatest demand. They enjoyed opportunities in the growing cities, and skilled men had to be recruited. Ramón Fierro collected premiums for his success in bringing them there. His strategies and the nature of the promises made to lure stonemasons from the more enjoyable climes of the Pacific Coast and the cities of Chihuahua are not known, but the hardships of Batopilas were well known and the shortages continued.

Unfortunately for the Chihuahua economy, rather than support the creation of a regional steel mill, the Patrón Grande and other American mine owners consistently turned to the United States for construction and processed materials, including replacement parts as well as technologically advanced machines. Boss Shepherd bought iron bars and rails from the Colorado Iron Works of Denver, and his son continued the practice. They also imported dynamite from the firms of Krakauer, Zork, and Moye of San Antonio and the Shelton Payne Arms Company of Saint Louis, both through outlets in El Paso.

The American miners in the Sierra Madre recognized the transitional nature of their specific enterprises, and few planned to enter other ventures in Chihuahua once the bonanzas played out. Alexander Jr. imported industrial goods rather than investing in the construction of an in-state manufacturing support network that would have stabilized the economy. The shipments were quite large, comprising four railcar loads per year, each containing 600 cases. In 1906, with social unrest growing in the countryside, he added weapons to the lists, ordering new rifles called Protectoras de Mina, from the two companies.[24]

In contrast to the acquisition of technology, the Shepherds ordered raw materials from local as well as foreign sources. They obtained salt from the Sinaloa seaside from contractors in Fuerte, on the basis of a long-term contract, and corn, beans, and wheat from producers in Chihuahua, Sinaloa, and Sonora. For adequate year-round supplies of the beans and wheat, however, they turned to farmers in Texas, California, and the upper Midwest of the United States. As a result of these strategies, the major impact of the mine companies, in addition to stimulating local employment in the diggings and in the provisioning of raw materials, came in stimulating the growth of the transportation industry. The ports of Mazatlán, Altata, Topolobampo, the trading centers of Álamos, Fuerte, Guerrero, and Chihuahua City, and mule train operations all grew in response to the flow of imported products for the producers and consumers at Batopilas and the other mining sites in the Copper Canyon complex.[25]

In the Patrón Grande's case, however, he struggled to control local resources and supplies. The early confrontation with the gambusinos and town leaders had ended with his victory, but the establishment of a far-reaching monopoly over the region had one dramatic exception. The lumber industry remained decentered because of the rugged physical geography of the Sierra Tarahumara and the independent-mindedness of the foresters.

In most of the Sierra Madre, the foresters foraged in the mountains in order to supply the timber used in the construction of the tunnels and buildings. To do this, they required at least some financial resources in order to buy the cutting tools and mules for transportation and to pay their employees. Boss Shepherd quickly realized that he could drive down the costs of these essential products by owning the surrounding countryside. The acreage that he purchased in the beginning and amplified in the course of the 1880s provided the raw materials needed for greater BCMC self-sufficiency. The company attempted to realize that potential by using transportation technology to reduce labor costs.

Long before Robinson arrived in the 1860s, the mine operators at Batopilas had paid tree cutters like Julián and Juan José Torres on the basis of the number and quality of the white pines they delivered. In the first decade of the twentieth century, a load of pine slid down mountainsides, hauled by mule to a cart at the base of the barranca, and then brought to the Hacienda San Miguel could bring five pesos. The men incurred considerable expense during their endeavor. The work required a minimum of two men with mules to move the timber because of the uneven terrain in the mountains. They then loaded it on the carts and hauled it to the hacienda. The transit also required two men to provide protection from robbers and the few remaining wolves and cougars.

Beginning in 1906, Shepherd Jr. attempted to bypass the often illiterate, yet independent and well-paid foresters for the cutting and trimming of trees and the recutting of them to size as planks and beams for construction and as firewood. The company needed massive quantities of pine planks and beams for the construction of buildings and tunnels, as well as of firewood, largely cedar, in much smaller pieces. Alexander Jr. was willing to pay twenty pesos per cord for the firewood (*leña*). The planks and beams could come in lengths reaching twelve feet and more, whereas the firewood had to measure exactly two feet in length, although its widths could vary. He asked Guillermo Schultz to help him find 200 to 400 mules to do the hauling.

The batopilenses competed intensely for firewood in the vicinity of town, and during the 1880s and 1890s, many of them had resented the Patrón Grande for claiming that his mining claims and property titles entitled him to the firewood found on the land as well. In Mexican usufruct, the great landowners allowed the peasants and workers to forage for leña since it was necessary for survival. Exclusive rights to firewood did not automatically derive from property ownership; in fact, the sharing of essential resources such as firewood and water was understood. In the first decade of the twentieth century, Alexander Jr. entered into a dispute with one of his tenants on BCMC-owned land. Macario Torres, the renter, refused to recognize Shepherd's claims of absolute ownership over the leña. Alexander Jr., after repeated threats, attempted to evict Torres, by at first ordering him off the land. Torres refused to leave as per his reading of the terms of his lease agreement. Shepherd then exercised his influence over the local authorities. Carlos Bernal, the jefe político of Batopilas, delayed taking action for months but eventually supported the American in contradiction to widespread practices.

Meanwhile, foresters like Julián and Juan were providing a desperately sought-after product. They disappeared into the mountains for a week at a time and returned when they had accumulated all the wood their mules

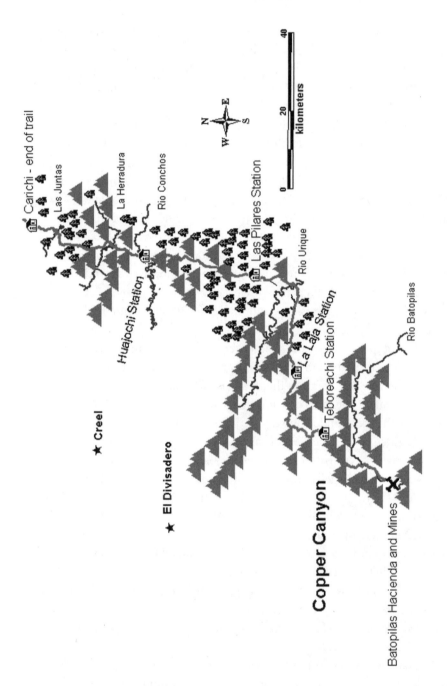

The Conducta trail, which required a five-day trip. (Courtesy of Jerry Brown, Bear Creek Survey Service, Durango, Colorado)

could carry, or when they deemed their shipment to be enough. Shepherd Jr. decided to pay their prices for the time being, but he believed it was essential to bypass the self-managed timbermen because they were an expensive and unpredictable source of supply. Shepherd figured out the solution; it was a revolutionary idea. He would install "a tramway between four to six miles long to bring wood down to here from the mountains" using salaried workers.[26]

In pursuit of this goal, Shepherd contracted with A. Lescher and Sons to provide wire rope and with the Medart Patent Pulley Company (both of Saint Louis) and other U.S. firms to ship the additional parts needed for the tram. He quickly ran into problems, however, due to the ruggedness of the terrain, the softness of the soil, and the special nature of the task, which required adaptations in the way of towers, belts, bolts, wire, and slings. All of them had to be individually made, and the parts shipped frequently did not meet specifications. Near the end of 1908, the tramway had still not been inaugurated. Shepherd did succeed, however, in connecting the small San Antonio mill with the complex at Hacienda San Miguel by means of an aerial tram, which provided for the transportation of ore less than one mile.

In another major effort to reduce operating costs, Shepherd and W. R. Kaufman combined to design and bankroll an easier and faster road out of the barrancas toward Chihuahua City. The old Conducta trail followed the Río Batopilas the short distance northeast to La Junta and continued in that direction along the tributary stream for another nine miles to the Teboreachi Station. After another three miles north over rugged terrain, the Conducta turned east for twelve miles before reaching the La Laja Station. From that point, it covered another nine miles east, crossed the Río Urique and the eastern reaches of the Barranca de Urique, and proceeded six miles due north to the station at Las Pilares. The next day's journey took the Conducta twenty-five miles due north to the Huajochi Station near the headwaters of the Río Conchos. It was then another thirty-seven miles of rugged trail north to the Raramuri-mestizo town of Carichi. From there, it was a mere seventy-five miles east by train to the mint at Chihuahua City.

The new route reduced by two days the time needed by the Conducta and mule skinners (arrieros) to reach the San Antonio de Arenales Station of the Kansas City, Mexico, and Orient Railroad, located at what is now

The Conducta at the mint in Chihuahua City. (Courtesy of the Historical Society of Washington, D.C.)

the city of Cuauhtemoc, some fifty miles north of Carichi. That was a crucial advancement because the freighters took sixteen to twenty days and charged $80 per ton to carry goods between the station and Batopilas. It also reduced the time needed to transport lumber from the sawmills at Madera, located to the north of the Sierra Tarahumara, to the Hacienda San Miguel by one day. By 1908, the railroad had reached the timber camp at San Juanito and the miners made a new adjustment. They brought the Conducta northwest from Las Pilares to Cortoraba (Creel) over easier terrain. From there, it was an easy haul via Bocoyna to the railhead at San Juanito.

In 1908, Julián and Juan Torres were still carrying out their independent timber harvesting and selling their product to the BCMC. In November, they brought in a total of five cartloads, three owned by Julián and two by Juan. Julián received fifteen pesos for his efforts, and Juan grossed ten. From that total, they had to pay out at least half for the feeding and maintenance of their animals, tool replacements, and personal sustenance. That left them, however, with a tidy sum in comparison with the miners' income, and the company burdened with an unpleasant expense it could not avoid.

Moreover, in contrast to the miners, laundresses, ironing workers, seamstresses, smelter workers, and other company employees, the timbermen exercised considerable independence. Like the former gambusinos, they controlled their workday and methods. They decided where and when to work, how long, and how hard, in accordance with their wishes. The company officials, who insisted on conformity in work practices from their employees, were forced to accept the timber delivered by Juan and Julian on their own schedule and pay them a negotiated sum because they needed the lumber.[27]

In 1906, the old disputes over water contamination broke out again. Led by Ignacio and Leonardo Ramírez, sons of merchant Guadalupe Ramírez, who originally sold some of the mines to Robinson, some *ayuntamiento* (town council) members challenged Shepherd Jr. by demanding that the company guarantee delivery and maintenance service to the three-inch pipe that drained water off to Batopilas from the pipe leading to the Hacienda San Miguel. They pointed out the obvious, that, when the pipe went dry, batopilenses were forced to consume water polluted by the effluent from the smelters at San Miguel and San Antonio. Alexander Jr., like his father, refused to guarantee the delivery of water or to maintain the pipe, claiming that his responsibility was to the owners in New York and that he could not jeopardize the company's profitability by providing an extraneous service. An old dispute was now being argued on both sides by a second generation.

In response to the challenge, Shepherd Jr. exploited the differences among the batopilenses and between them and the state elites, as his father had done, in order to avoid providing the water and pipe maintenance service. First, he denounced the idea of three ornamental public fountains as a frivolous expense that would affect the company's operations and employment. Then he suggested to the workers that the ayuntamiento should provide individual house water service to the several hundred permanent homes in Batopilas and charge each family three pesos a month. That income, he declared, would enable the town to establish its own water service and to maintain the pipe. The ayuntamiento, however, already provided individual service to thirty-five elite families, the only ones who could afford it. The other 4,400 people obtained drinking water from nineteen public faucets and carried it away in clay jugs (*jarros*).

Finally, after having failed to crack the batopilenses' unity, Shepherd Jr. turned to the state authorities. The Patrón Grande had done this in 1880 and 1892 during the mining claims disputes with the Ramírez heirs, and again in the 1880s and 1890s, with the labor unrest, and finally, in the 1901 water dispute, when public demonstrators accused the BCMC of poisoning the townspeople with arsenic. Shepherd Jr., in order to put the confrontation behind him, called on Governor Enrique Creel for a decision. Creel recommended that the company allow the three-inch pipe to continue drawing from the aqueduct when water reached its level and that no service support or cleaning of wastewater in the river was required or justified. Like Shepherd, the governor declared the fountains a frivolous expense.[28]

Older disputes that transcended local issues reappeared in the last decade before the outbreak of the Mexican Revolution. Following Boss Shepherd's death, Ignacio and Leonardo Ramírez once again tested the BCMC's claims to the Pastrana and Cata mines. This time, however, their suit reflected the rise of nationalist sentiment. Having lost twice before because of the Patrón Grande's close ties to the Chihuahua oligarchy and President Díaz and their interventions on his behalf, the Ramírez brothers demanded their rights as "Mexican Citizens" and implied fraud on the part of the highest authorities in the nation. They chose to seek relief in the recesses of the mid-level bureaucracy at the Ministry of Economic Development in Mexico City and in the lower federal courts. In those places, it was possible to find patriotic individuals sensitive to their plight. The Ramírezes knew that the company was potentially vulnerable because it had not been able to produce titles to the Pastrana mine during their litigation of 1892. They believed that they had lost then only because of the now-deceased Patrón Grande's high-level political connections in Chihuahua and Mexico City.

As council members on the ayuntamiento of Batopilas, Ignacio and Leonardo also knew that the Shepherds, both Sr. and Jr., had intermittently tried since 1895 to get the mayor to "authenticate" titles to the mine. The mayor continued to refuse and revealed their efforts to the Ramírez brothers. Acting on the belief that they had lost in 1892 solely because of the Patrón Grande's political connections, they sued again as soon as the old man was dead. This time, they included the testimony of the previous owner, Jorge Lebrun of Álamos. Lebrun correctly claimed the original sell-buy contract between himself and Robinson did not include the Pastrana and that they had operated on that basis until Shepherd entered the scene. The resolution of the problem now rested on the definitions of vague property lines, including one measured from a rock, political influence, and the strength of arguments relying on the locals' traditional definitions of who owned what.

In 1902, following his father's death, Shepherd Jr. responded to the challenge by again attempting to obtain authentication for the Pastrana claim from the *presidente municipal* and the ayuntamiento of Batopilas by presenting numerous local tax receipts. This was a mistake because the Ramírezes were sitting members of the ayuntamiento. Not only were they able to block the move; they were also made aware of the company's strategy and legal position. Alexander Jr. then tried to finesse the officials at the Department of Economic Development. Using Manuel Prieto, his prominent Chihuahua lawyer, he asked for "authentication" of the Pastrana claim by presenting tax receipts for the ill-defined property.

The Department of Economic Development officials noted the discrepancies and lack of legal title and refused to act for several years. They demanded presentation of the original bill of sale or title. Shepherd Jr. lacked both documents. In the meantime, he continued to exercise de facto control of the mine. It was not until the end of 1906, after communicating with the governor of Chihuahua and high officials in Mexico City and sending them titles to all of the properties surrounding the Pastrana and elaborate survey reports done by mining engineers under- and aboveground, that Shepherd Jr., Brodie, and Prieto were able to satisfy the higher-ups in Mexico City that the property was theirs. The officials overruled the claims made by Lebrun and the Ramírez brothers.

The Ramírez heirs were too smart to force the issue for the moment; after all, the company controlled the bulk of armed force at the site and still enjoyed the support of high officialdom. Perhaps they felt that time was on their side. They had already joined with a popular coalition of batopilenses in the ongoing disputes over safe drinking water and firewood. The locals had lost both these cases as well, in the courts and with the government officials. Meanwhile, the Ramírez brothers gained repeated election to the council. They enjoyed strong electoral support in their continuing struggle with the Americans. In a manifestation of national and regional pride, a broad base of popular resentment emerged in Batopilas during the late 1890s and the first decade of the twentieth century.[29]

The BCMC continued, however, to exercise a powerful influence on the life and social hierarchy of Batopilas. Beyond the water contract and the buying of supplies from local merchants, its payroll fueled the economy, while the wide range of salaries and job quality it offered maintained local caste, gender, and class relations. The company continued to hire Americans and British citizens as supervisors and engineers. Alexander Jr. paid them according to who they were and his assessment of their importance to the company's success. For example, he paid himself $1,500 yearly as superintendent and $15,000 as a shareholder. He paid each of his supervisors $1,500, including Grant.

The family and its American and British employees lived well. During summertime, their wives and children took vacations at a cabin that the Patrón Grande had ordered built at a higher altitude, in Yerbabuena. They lived there for weeks at a time for several decades. The recruitment of professionals to the Sierra Tarahumara, however, was often difficult. The resident mining engineer normally earned $1,200 per year but, at one point in 1906, when Shepherd Jr. could not fill the position, he offered a candidate for the position, who was living in Oregon, twice that ($200 per month) if only he would come immediately. The prospective employee rejected the offer.

A few months later, feeling a bit more confident, Alexander Jr. recruited an engineer living in Denver for the normal salary of $100 per month. Mining engineers commanded high salaries because they possessed the ability to precisely map directions underground. That enabled the burrowing miners working in the tunnels to intersect the veins that had become nonpaying when worked from the surface. The schoolteacher and his assistant and the American assayers and smelter mechanics earned unspecified, but more modest amounts.

At the other end of the social spectrum came the laundry workers, comprising Chinese women working for the American males and mestizo and Raramuri women cleaning the clothes of the miners. On the next rung above the laundresses came the seamstresses, whose salary may have been equivalent, but they seemingly had more freedom from discipline and could set their own pace. Moving up the salary scale, the peon laborers in the mines earned a reported $75 annually before the Revolution, but the peso was devalued by 50 percent in 1905, and the wage was also subject to the 50 percent deduction for their accounts at the tienda de raya. They suffered a sizable decline in real wages in 1905 as the BCMC reduced labor costs in the midst of the declining value of silver in the markets.

The company paid workers more when at least some skills were involved. In February and March 1911, the machine or hoist operator and a peon, actually an assistant, in charge of the important duty of removing the floodwater (*desagüe*) from the Santo Domingo mine in order to keep it operating, received daily wages of 3 and 2 pesos, or $1.50 and $1.00, respectively. Those earnings greatly exceeded the centavo amounts per day paid to laundresses and ironers, or even the income of the foresters. Then, in May, underscoring the special knowledge required for the work, Shepherd Jr. increased the daily pay of the peons working on the floodwater by 12.5 percent to 2.25 pesos, more than double the rate then being paid to barreteros.[30]

Between 1860 and 1910, the people of Batopilas experienced continuing tension between their dreams and the economic realities brought to bear by American capitalists closely tied to the global marketplace. The traditional gambusino practices had caused a low level of productivity and earnings but provided a considerable degree of personal freedom and choice to the miners. The modern capitalists altered the traditional employer-employee relationships in the mines by introducing disciplined work routines, standardized wages, and high technology. In doing this, they disrupted the cultural traditions and economic system. Despite that high price, the increased productivity achieved by the workers failed to bring about a more comfortable living for them or Batopilas because of the imbalance of power that evolved between capital, town, and labor.

The greater volumes of ore processed at the Hacienda San Miguel created an unprecedented level of environmental degradation that went beyond the poisoned drinking water for the townspeople. The surrounding countryside was stripped of trees, including ancient groves, which led to serious flooding. Meanwhile, public unrest continued to focus on the pollution of drinking water; it was significant because it involved collective actions in the form of strikes by the miners and demonstrations by workers, townspeople, and local elites. The BCMC leaders overcame the resistance by using company guards and, in extreme cases, by calling on the state and national governments for armed intervention.

The Revolution

By 1910, Batopilas had reached the end of another phase in its periodic economic and political exposures to the outside world. After 1910, the Mexican Revolution and the declining value of silver on the world market would combine to disrupt production and ultimately close the mines. The townspeople's dream of realizing unheard-of wealth had died away in the early 1880s, and the degraded boomtown of those years had evolved into a quieter, more viable place. Meanwhile, family life survived, and the mines continued to provide a steady, if smaller, number of laborers with work while supporting a steady, if more modest, economy.

Trouble, however, was brewing in Mexico and Batopilas. In 1906, striking workers at the American-owned Cananea copper mine, some 330 miles to the northwest of Batopilas, seized control and dynamited some of the shafts. Then, in 1907, the textile workers in the region around Río Blanco, Veracruz, rose up and seized the town. In both cases, General Díaz used the Mexican army to restore order, with a heavy loss of life in the Rio Blanco episode. Then, in a political error, the army transported the bodies of the slaughtered workers to the port of Veracruz in open railcars in order to intimidate the public. The action had the opposite effect.

Workers, local elites, and campesinos in cities and pueblos across the nation demanded a higher degree of political participation than offered by the dictatorship and the foreign businessmen who controlled 90 percent of Mexico's incorporated capital. In Batopilas and other places in western Chihuahua, significant minorities of the populace were willing to risk the overthrow of what they considered the tyranny of General Díaz. Meanwhile, the majority of the people were unwilling to actively support the regime. Many of them supported the vehement demands of defeated presidential candidate Francisco Madero for electoral democracy and its implications for wider civil liberties and greater social equality.

The social conditions and political alienation at Batopilas paralleled those of the nation. "The celebration of Don Porfirio's birthday lasted one month, costing the Mexican people more than twenty million dollars in gold," writes Victor Villaseñor. "No Indians were allowed in Mexico City during the celebration. No mestizos or dark-skinned people. . . . This then was the straw that broke the burro's back. And the poor, hungry people of Mexico rose up in arms by the tens of thousands, breaking Don Porfirio's thirty-year reign and the Revolution of 1910 began."[31]

In late 1910, Pascual Orozco, the most important battlefield leader in the overthrow of President Díaz, announced his decision to join the Revolution in the Batopilas civic plaza. Some eighty disaffected mining company employees and other men joined him. Orozco, a prominent mule skinner with at least seven mule teams that carried supplies to the miners in the Sierra Madre of Chihuahua, was visiting his cousin Ramon Orozco, who lived in a large patioed home immediately southwest of the civic plaza.

Pascual encountered Joaquín Chávez, who he believed had stolen some calves from him, and shot him and two of his men to death in the plaza. When the Batopilas police attempted to arrest Orozco, he killed three of them as well. Supported by Apolonio Rodríguez, a blacksmith, iron foundry worker, and proclaimed *maderista*; Bríjido Torres, a mule skinner; Ignacio Félix, a timekeeper who worked for Rodríguez; Rafael Becerra, a small mine operator and ex-gambusino; and Blas Opinel, a merchant, Orozco called for the people to gather in the plaza. He announced that he was joining the Madero revolution and appealed to them for support. It was at that point that eighty workmen, mostly miners, joined him.

The widespread dissatisfaction at Batopilas provided a significant number of recruits. The poorly armed men, anticipating Shepherd's response and carrying rifles, pistols, and dynamite, went up into the barranca above La Junta and set up an ambush. A few days later, they wiped out a larger army force sent to suppress the uprising after Shepherd Jr. had telegraphed the authorities, warning them about the incident. The rebels took the soldiers' weapons and moved northward in the sierra. Within a few weeks, they had recruited hundreds of adherents from the other mining centers and controlled the small towns of the Sierra Madre from the area around Madera in the north to Satevo, south of Batopilas: "Other parties sprang up against the government far removed from the lines of the few existing railroads. These bands of the discontented soon learned that they could dominate the situation by teaming up and crippling the railroad, and dominating the small towns."[32]

Between 1880 and 1910, the BCMC had officially delivered silver valued at 23,400,000 pesos to the outside world. After 1910, the shipments slowed because of the danger presented by revolutionary forces in the Copper Canyon region. Elsewhere, the picture was spotty. In 1911, while the silver mines of Chihuahua still shipped ingots valued at 18,038,673 pesos to the mint in the state capital, Mexican revolutionaries in the northwest of the state began warning American farming colonists to abandon their properties and leave the state.

Along the northern Chihuahua frontier, in May and June of 1911, armed men launched the first of countless invasions of the 1,256,000-acre T. O. Riverside and 2,512,000-acre Palomas Ranches, owned, respectively, by members of the Swift packing house family and Edwin Marshall, the first treasurer of the Texas Oil Company. Those estates dominated the Mexican border region of the state, extending from the eastern edge of Arizona to the twin cities of Ojinaga, Chihuahua, and Presidio, Texas.

Then, in 1913, while the American colonists were fleeing to El Paso in fear of revolutionaries, men under the command of General Francisco Villa held up a train carrying a silver shipment from Batopilas at the San Andrés Station. They confiscated 122 ingots, valued at 163,200 pesos. Villa later returned the silver in exchange for 20,000 pesos in cash.

The high point of former mule skinner Villa's power in Chihuahua came in 1914. At that time, he supported the creation of the National Mutualist Confederation of Miners. The union claimed to represent the workers of Batopilas and other mining operations in the region. Its program began with the banner "All for One and One for All" and called for a child labor law, mutualist savings accounts, cooperatives instead of company stores for the workers at all large enterprises, sanitary toilet facilities in the workplace, public education, and disability and retirement benefits for all workers. These were the expressed goals put forward by the locally popular writer José Sánchez Pareja in Batopilas thirty years earlier.

In 1915, the forces supporting Venustiano Carranza for the presidency of the nation decisively defeated Villa's men in central Mexico. Their victory came in no small part as the result of American arms provided them by U.S. authorities at the port of Veracruz. The *carrancista* authorities, however, were far more nationalistic than Díaz. They also demonstrated a degree of social strategy, responding to continued popular and nationalist unrest by carrying out a selective land and labor reform program in Chihuahua and wherever else in Mexico the quelling of revolutionary turmoil required it. Then, with the U.S. government distracted by war in Europe, the carrancistas also canceled eight contracts for oil field development held by the largest American and British companies in the states of Campeche, Chiapas, San Luis Potosí, Tabasco, Tamaulipas, Veracruz, and Yucatán; and reissued them to Mexicans.

In Chihuahua and other border and coastal areas, they cancelled American titles to land totaling tens of millions of acres. Among the enterprises and individuals affected were the Southern Pacific Railroad, Standard Oil, American Smelting and Refining, Otis Chandler of the Los Angeles Times, and General Otis Lindsey who, associated with the Morgan Bank, was "forming a corporation exploiting immense territories in northern Baja California." The days of unchallenged company power in the Barranca de Batopilas were over.[33]

Despite their defeat in central Mexico during the spring of 1915, the *villistas* retained their power over much of Chihuahua and Batopilas. On August 28, forces led by villista Generals Julio Acosta and Julián Granados won a strategic victory over their Constitutionalist rivals, commanded by General Luis Herrera. That outcome forced the American mining companies and haciendas to accept the union and continued villista control of the Sierra Madre. For the American elites in Chihuahua, the nadir came in 1916, when villista guerillas wreaked havoc with their enterprises, while General John J. Pershing's Punitive Expedition supposedly looked for them where they were not—in the valley floor east of the Sierra Madre. In 1915–1916, mining was suspended at Batopilas and most other mines in the state. A total of only 1,512,246 pesos in silver arrived for processing at the mint that year.[34]

Between 1917 and 1923, over 15,000,000 acres of land in Chihuahua, formerly held by the state oligarchy and Americans, was given to the citizenry of the pueblos. Early on, Assistant Secretary of Development, Colonization, and Industry A. Ríos summed up the attitude of the carrancistas toward American mining companies: "These enterprises, in their entirety, are a threat to the principles of the revolution and [the owners] will ceaselessly continue their efforts by any means whatsoever until they get what they want."[35]

Under pressure from the Carranza government, the mining company operators in the Sierra Tarahumara dramatically increased wages. Instead of weak pesos, the new pay scales offered $1 daily wages for unskilled workers and $1.25 for skilled workers, despite the latter's "plentiful presence." In this manner, the government won over many workers and townspeople in western Chihuahua. The villistas, however, continued to fight, dividing the populace and creating bitter new enemies.[36]

In 1919, after the villista threat was greatly reduced, the town leaders in Batopilas joined with company management in denouncing "the shameful unprecedented crimes committed by Francisco Villa against the honorable people and their interests [which have caused them] to organize and arm themselves in Social Defense groups in order to fight this bandit without quarter [because] he has raped the women of pueblos like Satevo and . . . Namiquipa because their husbands did not wish to serve him as accomplices."[37] In a scornful tone, they noted that the villistas in their region were nothing more than lowly Apaches and Yaquis.

While the mines in other parts of the state recovered during 1918 and 1919, the level of violence in the region around Batopilas did not subside until 1920. By then, the will of the owners was broken, and the value of silver had fallen so much that it was no longer feasible to extract it. The Batopilas mines officially closed in 1921. An estimated 50 percent of the silver reserves present in the sixteenth century still rest inside the mountains. They will remain there until the world market places a much higher value on that commodity or another one. Then Batopilas, like the Phoenix, will rise from obscurity and again become a focal point of outsiders from Mexico and the United States.

Conclusion

And the gold they so badly want only brings them anguish
through the fear that they might lose it and for that
reason they can never find peace.

—Tarahumara wisdom

IN THE END, THE OPPRESSIVE nature of the American mining company's interactions with a cross section of Mexican society, rural and town, indigenous and mestizo, in Copper Canyon and Batopilas led to its undoing. After their entry into the American economy, the miners, batopilenses, and other people of the canyons experienced the termination of gambusino practices, the destruction of their environment through massive deforestation and water poisoning, forced labor, unequal pay, the suppression of unions and the "disappearance" of labor organizers, racial segregation, and political dictatorship through the creation of a company town and the intervention of the Mexican army. This reflected a dynamic that occurred in Mexico at large, the Caribbean islands, and Central America. Those abuses changed the consciousness of many batopilenses, motivating their participation in the Mexican Revolution of 1910.

It did not start out so badly. Robinson transported native silver to Mazatlán and then on both to Wells Fargo and the U.S. Mint in San Francisco and to Asia. He utilized traditional mule skinners (arrieros) with their mules and the modern Pacific Mail Steamship Company, run by New York financier William Aspinwall and supported for two generations by the chairmen of the National City and Morgan Banks, which carried silver and other products to Asia, including points as far removed as Cochin, India.

But Robinson's strategies anticipated later American corporate policies in Mexico and the Third World. Those included the export of native silver, a raw material, which allowed him to bypass the development and employment of skilled locals in refining, smelting, and minting. Robinson's behavior also anticipated that of the American oil, sugar, coffee, and henequen companies when he avoided the payment of federal taxes by bribing local and port officials at Mazatlán. The greater abuses, however, came with Boss Shepherd's "rationalization" of labor as part of a modernized system of production.

Initially, the ruggedness of the terrain engendered cultural isolation and placed the Americans and transient miners in contact with a centuries-old way of life in Batopilas and a surrounding indigenous culture with even more ancient roots. The remote nature of the area provided a zone of refuge for the Raramuri, but it also facilitated the extreme abuse of the Yaquis, other laborers, and townspeople by the powerful mine owners. In contrast to the frictions caused by Shepherd's practices, the people of Batopilas had adapted to and lived alongside indigenous culture with minimal conflicts for over two centuries.

The purity and enormous size of the silver deposits greatly influenced the evolution of the mines and the community. Most silver is mined as a secondary deposit found in a mix with the principal one, not in the almost pure form that Robinson encountered. The high silver content in the ore made it unnecessary to import high technology and capital from 1861 to 1879. In the latter year, Shepherd's arrival signaled the end of the free gambusino and almost casual mestizo and Raramuri work practices. He imposed a strict wage labor system. Then, during the 1880s, the steamships that stopped in Mazatlán, Altata, Topolobampo, and Guaymas, followed by the railroad, which reached the mountains above Batopilas in the first decade of the twentieth century, further integrated the region into the U.S. economy.

The highly capitalized production methods used after 1879 quickly created an alienated day laboring class. Workers encountered the loss of discretionary powers, greater wage differentials between miners and supervisors, a steady reduction of employment brought about by labor-saving power drills and equipment, the loss of skills due to a narrowing of tasks, and the lack of contact with the finished product. They also encountered increased illness, especially a severe increase of silicosis brought on by the use of power drills. Earlier, the gambusinos had practiced workers' self-management, making the tools, selecting the area to be worked, mining by hand at their own pace, transporting the ore to the smelter, and performing the refining tasks.

From 1879 onward, the expansion of the industrial wage system and the capitalist conviction that time represented money meant more intense supervision and faster, harder, and more tedious work. Along with speedups and the narrower range of mining skills employed, Shepherd's use of carefully selected, largely foreign superintendents to mediate capitalist-worker relations truncated the influence of the miners and made them more dependent on him. His force of armed men and the puppet municipal government reinforced the workers' consciousness of dependency.

In this manner, the Patrón Grande anticipated the strategies of modern corporations like American Metals, Phelps Dodge, Anaconda, and American Smelting and Refining in the Third World. He created monopolies over the economy, politics, and culture of Batopilas. First, he personally replaced the small independent owner-miners and later the gambusinos with BCMC employees. Next, he placed the shopkeepers and other businesspeople in town in a state of dependency through the use of company scrip. Finally, he assumed direct political power by replacing the independent jefe político with an employee, while rejecting the authority of the local police. He created a company town and reinforced his position by developing a close relationship with state and national politicians and army officers. He imposed a dictatorial regime in the canyons.

But the Patrón Grande went even further. In the absence of an effective nation-state that could have balanced the relationship between capital, labor, and the people in general, Shepherd imposed racial segregation, debt peonage, and forced labor, while he clear-cut the delicate primeval forests in the barrancas. These practices reshaped the culture of the batopilenses: their pastimes, gender relations, savings rates, housing tenure, health conditions, and social security, the environment, and even the definition of childhood through his use of child labor. Although the BCMC provided the minimal level of hospital care required by the government, the pervasive mutualist societies found in more accessible mining towns in Mexico could not develop in Batopilas because the tienda de raya absorbed 50 percent of wages, creating widespread debt peonage.

Contrary to more recent American strategies in the Third World, however, Shepherd did not attempt to impose Protestantism. Because of his enormous and unchallenged power in the economic and political spheres, the Patrón Grande saw no need to challenge religious beliefs and practices. The miners continued to pray to San Antonio, Santa María del Carmen, San Miguel, and San Pedro as they entered the mines, while the citizenry maintained their alternative view of material existence and hardships through the practice of traditional ceremonies and rituals. The missionaries and later the parish priests had long before sanctioned on-going folk practices rooted in pre-Columbian beliefs, which the native people syncretized with Catholic doctrine. As Shepherd's power grew, local and working-class religion remained largely a grassroots practice.

The Tarahumaras, the miners, and the folk of Batopilas expressed deep needs in their choices in worship. Their veneration of saints, whether Antonio, Carmen, Miguel, or Pedro, would have still been recognizable, whether the Protestants were there or not. In the Shepherd era, the saints offered relief as the miners faced cave-ins and bell-shaped stones and died of silicosis and mercury poisoning. When modern science arrived, the batopilenses guardedly adopted the limited medical and pharmaceutical services rendered, but the Tarahumara people of the canyons accepted those advancements only as a last resort, and, even today, many Raramuris regard doctors and nurses with distrust. The tesquino rituals continue to play an important role in their beliefs and lives. Science has caused very few people in either locale to change their minds about the ultimate issues evoked by nature, spirits, or Savior.

When Robinson arrived in Batopilas in the 1860s, the townspeople largely supported the ideas of inclusivity and prosperity promised by Mexico's Liberals, but in the ensuing fifty years, the company moved to impose absolute political control. The importance of the silver industry in the national economy strongly motivated the steps taken on behalf of the Patrón Grande by the collaborating Mexican elites led by Díaz, Pacheco, Terrazas, Creel, and the town official appointed by Shepherd.

Boss Shepherd and the national, state, and local elites believed in a racist meritocracy that held indigenous people in contempt and did not appreciate the depth of their thinking. The belief and the applied strategies derived from it allowed the American capitalists to suppress working-class agency first by contravening the authority of the Batopilas merchants and then by offering them compensation in order to divide them from the workers. While the trade-off led to the impoverishment of the miners, most of the local elites, like their national counterparts, tolerated the oppression of the workers, while enjoying the benefits bestowed upon them by the Patrón Grande.

Nineteenth-century Mexican liberalism had something to do with that result. The Liberals, devout believers in the idea of progress, thought that someday the "indios" could be redeemed by becoming mestizos. However, many also considered the impoverished citizens of native descent who resisted Europeanization to be mentally inferior and comparable to "mulas." Their prejudices coincided with Shepherd's mid-nineteenth-century Maryland Episcopalian-Methodist belief in African American inferiority, social separation, and slavery.

The enormous wealth produced by a small number of people during the 1880s and 1890s was sufficient to have provided the Las Hadas utopia anticipated by some batopilenses, but it would have required more equitable sharing. Like the elites of other centers of great natural wealth in Mexico, Bolivia, Liberia, Peru, South Africa, and elsewhere in the Third World, the American elites and their Mexican counterparts and collaborators at the national, state, and local levels rejected that possibility.

When organized local political resistance resurfaced, it was because intolerable water pollution had affected and antagonized the local elites. The Batopilas elites, however, distinguished between that issue, along with their complaints regarding the ownership of some mining claims, on the one hand, and the workers' demands for more just wages and better working conditions, on the other. They also failed to challenge the deforestation of the barranca carried out by the BMC for decades, which resulted in devastating floods.

By 1910, working-class alienation in Batopilas had reached such an extreme that eighty men, including a timekeeper and a gang foreman, volunteered in the town plaza to follow Pascual Orozco in beginning a democratic revolution against the government. The people in other regions of Mexico and the Third World have taken similar revolutionary actions in support of leaders such as Emiliano Zapata after suffering the abuses of outsiders and local overlords.

The divisions between the workers and local elites in Batopilas continued during the revolutionary period of 1910–1920, when Francisco

Villa, who controlled the state government, empowered the workers by promulgating his support for the National Mutualist Association of Miners. Later, near the end of the Revolution, as Villa lost power in the state, his armed and avid Yaqui Indian supporters, seeking financial resources, periodically raided the mines where their ancestors had been ill treated. Those actions underscored social antagonisms over property between countryside and town people. The Batopilas elites denounced the Yaquis and appealed to the national government for protection.

Following the demise of the BCMC in the early 1920s, the Mexican agrarian reform program divided the company's domain among the people of the canyons. By the late twentieth century, 670,000 acres had been given out to some 2,369 heads of family in the Batopilas region. Nearly all of the allocated terrain, however, is suitable only for the grazing of goats. Only 16,000 acres, dispersed in small patches on the mountains and hilltops and less precipitous slopes, serve as farmland for the rural folk.[1]

Today, the people of the canyons remain culturally diverse, mestizo and Tarahumara, urban and rural. They seek distinct objectives ranging from material wealth to spiritual connectedness with their ancestors. They use the land and commerce both for profit and for subsistence. The rural mestizos have a more commercial orientation, but they join the majority of Raramuris in continuing a cooperativist political economy consistent with ages-old community and religious convictions.

Up to this point in time, the Tarahumaras and other people of the canyons have successfully negotiated the unending challenges presented by the outside world. They accept limited applications of modern medical treatment, commercial timbering, and both legal and illegal crops, while resisting incursions that diminish their sense of independence and self-defined well-being.

During the years after 1920, when nationalistic patriotism and agrarian reform sentiment overtook Batopilas as a result of the Mexican Revolution of 1910, the people temporarily experienced a reduction of their internal differences. But much of that was due to the fact that the local economy sank into depression because lower world prices for silver prevented extraction of the mineral. The agrarian land grants and lack of income in the town created a degree of equality that endured for decades. When the electrical power plant installed by Boss Shepherd failed, all batopilenses were forced to rely upon candles and gas lamps for many years. In recent times, electrical service has finally been restored.

At present, the new bonanzas of tourism and marijuana provide unprecedented levels of income to the rural folk. As a result, the residence occupied by John Robinson has been restored, but Shepherd's Castle continues its slow decay. The ruins stand as a testament to the American who once ran things here, the Mexicans who worked for him, and those who challenged inequity and dictatorial authority. It should be protected as a national monument. For now, however, prosperity is offered by the Sinaloa Cartel. This time, the batopilenses have no expectation of Las Hadas.

Notes

Abbreviations

The following abbreviations are used in the notes and bibliography:

AGN   Archivo General Nacional
BL   Bancroft Library
BCMC   Batopilas Consolidated Mining Company
BMC   Batopilas Mining Company
CIDECH Centro de Información del Estado de Chihuahua
HC   Hart Collection, Houston, Texas
WNRC   Washington National Records Center

The epigraph for this volume is from Sánchez Pareja, "Reseña histórica," 1. Translations of all Spanish-language quotations throughout the volume are mine unless otherwise noted.

Introduction

The epigraph for the introduction is from Sánchez Pareja, "Reseña histórica," 2.

1. For the case of Joaquín Francisco Salcedo, who questioned the divine right of kings, see folios 63–101, folder 4, vol. 1397, Ramo Inquisición.

2. Judge J. R. Robinson, February 13, 1860, New York, to Hiram Rumfield, as cited in Loomis, *Wells Fargo*, 150–151. The distinguished scholar Sylvester Mowry misidentified Robinson in his book *Arizona and Sonora*, 49. Mowry had been in contact with a member of the family of Juan A. Robinson in Guaymas, Sonora, which had mercantile ties over much of northwestern Mexico. Later, Mowry decided that Juan A. Robinson and John Riley Robinson were the same person. In his investigation of Juan Robinson's business empire in California and Sonora, Mowry even located Juan's relative, T. Robinson Bours, in Stockton, California. Decades later, T. Robinson Bours Jr., Juan's son, operated a mercantile business in Álamos that sold supplies to the Batopilas Consolidated Mining Company (BCMC). Nevertheless, John R. (Riley) Robinson and Juan A. Robinson were different people. For the commercial relationship between Bours Jr.'s mercantile business and the BCMC in the late 1890s, see the receipts in BCMC, Letterbooks, vol. 1, HC. Although the 16-volume set of Letterbooks in HC focuses on the period from 1900 to 1916, volume 1 contains loose pages dating from 1880 to 1925, in addition to its bound pages, which date from May 4 to November 5, 1906.

Chapter 1. Robinson's Quest

The epigraph for chapter 1 is from chapter 41 of Herman Melville's *Moby-Dick*.

1. Judge J. R. Robinson, February 13, 1860, New York, to Hiram Rumfield, in Loomis, *Wells Fargo*, 150–151.

2. J. R. Robinson, "Diary," February 14–March 11, 1861.

3. Ibid.

4. Ibid., March 12–31, 1861. For the best description of the terrain between Fort Davis and Presidio, see Joseph Mussey, Fort Davis, to John Hart, Houston, August 3, 2003, HC. Mussey is the director of the Chihuahuan Desert Research Institute (CDRI), Fort Davis, Texas. For the population of Chihuahua in 1857, see "Documentos justificativos correspondientes a la cuarta parte de esta memoria que trata de la industria y medios de fomentarla," in *Memoria de Fomento, 1856–1857*, 1–12. The report lists 1 city, 136 pueblos, 111 haciendas, and 596 "ranchos o rancherías" in the state.

5. J. R. Robinson, "Diary," April 4, 1861.

6. Ibid., April 5–7, 1861.

7. The best source on the Terrazas family and the Chihuahua oligarchy is Wasserman, *Capitalists, Caciques*.

8. J. R. Robinson, "Diary," April 13–14, 1861. The early history of Cusihuirachi is found in Pennington, *Tarahumar* and in "Cusihuirachi," *Enciclopedia*. For a visual overview and short history of the Sierra Tarahumara, see Raat and Janecek, *Mexico's Sierra Tarahumara*.

For more on the flight of the Tarahumara into the Sierra Madre during the late eighteenth century, see folios 57–72, folder 3, vol. 162; folios 106–179, folder 6, vol. 162; folios 81–84, folder 6, vol. 168; and folios 358–446, folder 11, vol. 176, all in Ramo Provincias Internas.

9. For background on Carichi, see "Carichi," *Enciclopedia*. For more on Tarahumara housing and hunting, see Pennington, *Tarahumar*, 90, 100, 135. For accounts of Tarahumara morality and personal behavior, see Merrill, *Raramuri Souls*; Kennedy, *Tarahumara*, 179–204; Zingg, *Behind Mexican Mountains*, 29–48 and 254–260. For more on animals in the Raramuri worldview, see box 3, Batopilas Collection. I refer to this collection in English because it was not yet formally constituted as an official Mexican archive at the time I consulted it (1994).

10. For background on Sisoguichi and Bocoyna, see entries for them in *Enciclopedia*. For more on Tarahumara games, tesquino rituals, alcoholic beverages, and hunting, see Pennington, *Tarahumar*; Nabokov, *Indian Running*, esp. 163–172, 184–187; Kennedy, *Tarahumara*; and Zingg, *Behind Mexican Mountains*, 63–95, 220–260.

11. J. R. Robinson, "Diary," April 23, 1861

12. For the background of the Cuiteco, see "Cuiteco," *Enciclopedia*. For more on Tarahumara housing in the Sierra Madre Occidental, see Lumholtz, *Unknown Mexico*. For more on Raramuri farming, see Graham, *Mobile Farmers*; and Zingg, *Behind Mexican Mountains*, 49–62. The Tarahumara altars and houses were described in detail at the Raramuri Exhibit, Museo Nacional de Antropología e Historia, Mexico City, July 30, 2003. See Batopilas Folder, unnumbered, HC.

13. For an account of the 1676 visit to Cerocahui by Padres Prado and Pecoro, see Rascón Irigoyen, *Cerocahui*, 26. For descriptions of Tarahumara material life, see Kennedy, *Tarahumara*, 39–107; Pennington, *Tarahumar*, 221–227; and Zingg, *Behind Mexican Mountains*, 49–62.

14. J. R. Robinson, "Diary," April 27, 1861.

15. Ibid., April 28–29, 1861.

16. For maps of the trails around Batopilas, see Batopilas maps, Bancroft Library; and Randolph, *Pastrana Mine*, 12, 20. For the flora and fauna of the area, see Carmony and Brown, *Mexican Game Trails*, pt. 3, pp. 169–207.

17. González Reyna, *Riqueza minera*, 106–107, 497.

18. Sanchez Pareja, "Reseña histórica," 59. For the early success stories of the Marquis de Bustamante and others at Batopilas, see Randolph, *Pastrana Mine*. Production figures for the Batopilas mines can be found in various sources. See also *State of Chihuahua*.

19. For the struggle between Mexican Liberals and Conservatives, see Hale, *Liberalism*; and Reyes Heroles, *Liberalismo*. The best description of Batopilas in that era is found in Sanchez Pareja, "Reseña histórica," 2–11.

Chapter 2. The Invention of the Fritter

The epigraph for chapter 2 is from Traven, *Treasure of Sierra Madre*, 54.

1. White, "Robinson," 21.

2. J. R. Robinson, "Diary," May 26, 1861.

3. Ibid., June 13, 1861.

4. Ibid., May 30, 1861. For a discussion of Mexican religious faith and ceremonies at the time, see Zarur and Lovell, *Art and Faith in Mexico*, 359.

5. Sánchez Pareja, "Reseña histórica", 60; and White, "Robinson", 21. On the silver mining techniques used at the time in northwestern Mexico, including Batopilas, see J. A. Robinson, Statement, and the copy forwarded by Pamela White, HC. On the refining of and recovery rate for silver, see Crane, *Gold and Silver*, 469–552. The source of mercury near Batopilillas is described in the March 1844 report of Cástulo Chávez; see Chávez, *Deposición*, 53–54.

6. White, "Robinson", 21.

7. On the lack of tax payments, see Lerdo de Tejada, Mexico City, to Benito Juárez, Mexico City, 1871, Caja Fuerte, Archivo Juárez.

8. This discussion of Robinson's experience at Batopilas is drawn from J. R. Robinson, "Diary," May 3–June 1861; Sánchez Pareja, "Reseña histórica," 60–68; and Randolph, *Pastrana Mine*, 1–12.

9. Sánchez Pareja, "Reseña histórica," 65.

10. Bargallo, *Minería y metalurgia*, 442. On the limited introduction of new technology, tunnels, and the arrastras, see Randolph, *Pastrana Mine*, 8, 22; and Sánchez Pareja, "Reseña histórica," 10, 65, 81.

11. For descriptions of racial animosities between Mexican workers and Chinese

immigrants, see Gómez Izquierdo, *Movimiento antichino*, 1–183; Hu-Dehart, "Chinese in Northern Mexico," "Racism and Anti-Chinese Persecution," and "Comunidad China."

12. Terry, *Mexico*, 31.

13. The ritual descriptions are from Stross, "Tarahumara," 1–10. See also Zingg, *Behind Mexican Mountains*, 215–241; Kennedy, *Tarahumara*, 139–178; Lumholtz, *Unknown Mexico*, 120–224; Merrill, *Raramuri Souls*, 123–126, 145–154, 162–189; and Pennington, *Tarahumar*, 159–194.

14. Randolph, *Pastrana Mine*, 23, 27. See also Sánchez Pareja, "Reseña histórica," 31–34, 63, 66–68, 71, 75.

15. For passing references to "Junior" Almaden, see the Major General Francis Jay Herron Papers, box 1, and the James F. de Loosey Papers, vols. 22, 27.

16. On the mining tunnels and limited introduction of new technology and arrastras at Batopilas, see Sánchez Pareja, "Reseña histórica," 81, 88; Randolph, *Pastrana Mine*, 8, 22; and Bargallo, *Minería y metalurgia*, 42.

17. Sánchez Pareja, "Reseña histórica," 63–65.

18. Ibid., 60–63, 65–68, 82.

19. Ibid., 75–81.

Chapter 3. Confronting the Wilderness

The epigraph for chapter 3 is from Southworth, *Minas de México*, 130.

1. For a detailed examination of the American takeover in Mexico before 1910, see J. Hart, *Empire and Revolution*. For an excellent discussion of the formation of the Chihuahua elite, see Wasserman, *Capitalists, Caciques*. For the Terrazas landholdings, see Wasserman, *Everyday Life and Politics*, 177.

2. See Maury, "Alexander Shepherd," 394–410; BMC, Letterbook, 1879–1880. For the land sales and colonists, see Juan Fernández Leal, *Memoria de Fomento, 1892–1896*, 3, 16, 21–22; Carlos Pacheco, *Memoria de Fomento, 1877–1882*, vol. 1, pp. 3, 5, 49, 81, 244, 292–297, 524–525, and *Memoria de Fomento, 1883–1885*, 236, 238, 246, 255, 292–293; and Olegario Molina, *Memoria de Fomento, 1907–1908*, xix–xxi.

3. For a careful discussion of forced labor recruitment in central Mexico, see Barrera Bassols, *Caso Villavicencio*, 125. On the use of forced labor in Campeche, see J. Hart, *Empire and Revolution*, 227–232, and in Batopilas, see BMC, Letterbook, 1879–1880.

4. See BMC, Letterbook, 1879–1880, and interview of Gil Sandoval, April 12, 2003, HC.

5. See BMC, Letterbook, 1879–1880. On Edward M. McCook, see *New York Times*, September 10, 1909.

6. See Tindall, "Sketch of Shepherd," 49–66; Pletcher, *Rails, Mines*; and Joint Select Committee, *Report*.

7. On Díaz and the Americans, see J. Hart, *Revolutionary Mexico*, 105–128.

8. For reference to the overland route taken by Alexander Shepherd and Lyndon Stevens, see G. Shepherd, *Silver Magnet*, 17.

9. Alexander Shepherd, as quoted in Pletcher, *Rails, Mines*, 191.

10. For Quintard's background, see George W. Quintard, New York, to Moses Taylor, New York, May 23, 1862, Moses Taylor Papers. On George R. Blanchard and William Frishmuth, see Binczewski, "Point of Monument," 20–25. On Horace Porter, see Mende, *American Soldier*.

11. On Shepherd's trip, the mastiffs, and weaponry, see G. Shepherd, *Silver Magnet*, 13–28, or *Magnate de Plata*, 11–21, and Morgan, *Recollections*, 383–387. The best study of American expansion into Latin America, including its cultural and psychological dynamics, is O'Brien, *Revolutionary Mission*; on expansion into Mexico, see ibid., 251–284. For the description of the Hacienda San Miguel, see Alexander R. Shepherd, folder 2, manuscript 435, Historical Society of Washington, D.C.

12. On the murder of Charlie Mayhew, see G. Shepherd, *Silver Magnet*, 37–49. On the Chihuahua oligarchy, see ibid., 260–265, and Wasserman, *Capitalists, Caciques*. On the land companies and their activities in Mexico, see General Carlos Pacheco, *Memoria de Fomento, 1877–1882*, vol. 1, pp. 292–293. See also Ingeniero Manuel Fernández Leal, *Memoria de Fomento, 1892–1890*, 3, 21–22, and Pacheco, *Memoria de Fomento, 1883–1885*. The land sold for twelve centavos per acre in 1879–80.

13. On the rise of local resentments, see J. Hart, *Empire and Revolution*, 131–304.

14. For a remarkable description of the markets in the provincial mining towns of Mexico, see Fuentes, *Good Conscience*, 46.

15. Sánchez Pareja, "Reseña histórica," 83. On the arrest of Grant Shepherd, see Wasserman, *Capitalists, Caciques*, 87. On Ramón Orozco, see box 5, Sección Presidencia, Batopilas Collection.

16. For more on American mining companies in Mexico, Chihuahua, and neighboring Sonora, see J. Hart, *Empire and Revolution*; Wasserman, *Capitalists, Caciques*; Ruiz, *People of Sonora*; Tinker Salas, *Shadow of Eagles*; and Romero Gil, "Minas, capital."

17. See BMC, Letterbook, 1879–1880. For more on Andros Boynton Stone, see "A. B. Stone" in Joblin, *Cleveland*, pt. 9, available online at http://www.Fullbooks.com.

18. Sánchez Pareja, "Reseña histórica," 62.

19. Morgan, *Recollections*, 388.

20. Sánchez Pareja, "Reseña histórica," 62.

21. Morgan, *Recollections*, 395. For more on the animosity between the batopilenses and Shepherd, see G. Shepherd, *Silver Magnet*, 125, 195–196, 208, and passim; and Sánchez Pareja, "Reseña histórica," 62–81. The information regarding Gondfrey Garner is found in box 2, Sección Justicia, Batopilas Collection.

22. G. Shepherd, *Silver Magnet*, 76–85.

23. For the testimony of police officer Uribe, see "¿Por que?" *El Nacional* (Mexico), November 16, 1897, as cited in Barrera Bassols, *Caso Villavicencio*, 125. See ibid. for a devastating critique of the Díaz regime and its atrocities based on Porfirian-era sources. For more on Chihuahua during the Díaz years, see Wasserman, *Capitalists, Caciques*.

24. For an account of the San Miguel Tunnel imprisonments, see interview of Gil Sandoval, April 12, 2003, HC.

25. On labor debts, see BMC, Letterbook, 1879–1880; BCMC, Letterbooks, 1880–1925, HC; and Sánchez Pareja, "Reseña histórica," 13–15, 82.

26. For a brilliant analysis of mid-nineteenth-century elite beliefs in Maryland and Virginia that describes Shepherd's racial and class outlook in every respect, see Oakes, *Ruling Race*, xi–xii, 5–6, 163–164, 190–191, 203–210.

27. Ibid., 5–6.

28. See the voluminous family correspondence in the Shepherd Papers.

29. G. Shepherd, *Silver Magnet*, 40, 191–201, 215–216.

30. Oakes, *Ruling Race*, 163, 191; and G. Shepherd, *Silver Magnet*, 60–68 and passim.

31. For the quote, see Morgan, *Recollections*, 389. Comisión Industrial, vol. 2, pp. 106–118.

32. For Shepherd's records, see BMC, Letterbook, 1879–1880; and BCMC, Letterbooks, 1880–1925, HC. For Leal's report, see *Memoria de Fomento, 1892–1896*, 81.

33. See L. Hart, "Shepherd's Castle," for the most complete architectural description of the estate. See also G. Shepherd, *Silver Magnet*, 35–36, and Binczewski, "Point of Monument," 20–25.

34. Sánchez Pareja, "Reseña histórica," 13–15, and interview of Gil Sandoval, April 12, 2003, HC.

35. Sánchez Pareja, "Reseña histórica," 15.

36. Ibid., 13–14.

37. For the BCMC's acquisitions of previously overlooked mine properties, see "Contrato celebrado."

Chapter 4. The Patrón Grande, Community, and Corrupt Practices

The first epigraph for chapter 4 is from William Gelenites as quoted in Fred Brock, "On the Retirement Road, 65 Is Still Their Limit," *New York Times*, January 2, 2000. The second epigraph is from Coombes, *These Poor Hands*, 235–236.

1. G. Shepherd, *Silver Magnet*, 218; and Sánchez Pareja, "Reseña histórica," 82.

2. See G. Shepherd, *Silver Magnate*; and Sanchez Pareja, "Resena Historica," 82.

3. On the pursuit of runaway debt peons, see Bailey and Beezley, *Sources in Saltillo*.

4. See G. Shepherd, *Silver Magnet*, 62–64; and Crane, *Gold and Silver*, 496–552. For a description of the cyanide deposits at Batopilillas, see the March 1844 report of Cástulo Chávez in Chávez, *Deposición*, 53–54.

5. G. Shepherd, *Silver Magnet*, 242.

6. Alexander Robey Shepherd Jr., Batopilas, to Crosby Noyes, Washington, D.C., September 12, 1902, folder 1, manuscript 435. Alexander Robey Shepherd Papers, 1869–1942.

7. For the details on the case see Barrera Bassols, *Caso Villavicencio*, 161–287. For the text of Madero's letter, see ibid., 269–271.

8. On customs manipulations in Sonora and Sinaloa, see Tinker Salas, *Shadow of Eagles*, 84–85. For a comprehensive overview of corruption in Chihuahua, see Wasserman, *Capitalists, Caciques*.

9. See Brodie, "Producción total," annex E, and "Minas de plata nativa"; Southworth, *Minas de México*, 78; and González Reyna, *Riqueza minera*, 108–110.

10. See Brodie, "Producción Total de la Batopilas Mining Company," Annex B, "Las Minas de Batopilas," Batopilas File, Centro de Información del Estado de Chihuahua; Southworth, *Las Minas de Mexico*, 78; González Reyna, *Riqueza minera*, 108–110; and Sánchez Pareja, "Reseña histórica," *passim*. See also the BMC and BCMC Letterbooks, 1880–1925, HC.

11. See Brodie, "Producción total," annex E; Southworth, *Las Minas de México*, 78; and the BMC and BCMC Letterbooks, 1884–1902, HC.

12. See Brodie, "Producción total," annex E; and Southworth, *Minas de México*, 34–35.

13. The production and expense data for 1909 are found in Alexander R. Shepherd Jr., "Report of the General Manager," Agency 53, entry 184, Special Claims Commission, Records Group 76, Washington National Records Center-College Park; and HC; and Alberto Robles Gil, *Memoria de Fomento 1911–1912*, xcii. For the arrest, see G. Shepherd, *Silver Magnet*, 214–216.

14. Coombs, *These Poor Hands*. The author discusses the miners' experience, including bell-shaped stones, throughout the work. For Batopilas see G. Shepherd, *Silver Magnet*, 205–206.

15. Alexander Shepherd Jr., Batopilas, to McCall Brothers Planting and Manufacturing Company, McCall, Louisiana, May 14, 1906, BCMC, Letterbooks, vol. 1, p. 20, HC.

16. Coombes, *These Poor Hands*, 235–236.

17. McAteer, *Coal Workers' Pneumoconiosis: Health Information Card*.

18. Stross, "Tarahumara," 1–10. On the Chihuahua Lumber Company, see Holguin Sáenz, *Breve ensayo*, 431.

19. See individual receipts, some titled "Gastos de Hacienda" and others "Hacienda Expense," November 1908, BCMC, Letterbooks, vol. 1, loose pages, HC.

20. For a description of the women, children, and prostitutes in Batopilas, see Sánchez Pareja, "Reseña histórica." For the experience of women in mining towns, see Marks, *Precious Dust*. For the story of a mining-town prostitute and her nurturing role, see Rivera Letelier, *Reina Isabel*.

21. Susan Barger, Santa Fe, New Mexico, to John Mason Hart, Houston, August 5, 1998, HC.

22. See Sánchez Pareja, "Reseña histórica," 13–15; and Marks, *Precious Dust*, 352–362.

23. For the railroad concession, see "Contrato para construcción"; Stillwell, "Concession"; and Shepherd Jr., Batopilas, to Fairbanks, Morse and Company, Saint Louis, July 23, 1906, BCMC, Letterbooks, vol. 1, p. 186, HC.

24. On the lumber to construct a bridge across the river at Batopilas, see Shepherd Jr., Batopilas, to W. R. Kaufman, El Puente, Río Urique, June 26, 1906, BCMC, Letterbooks, vol. 1, pp. 123–125, HC. On the BCMC's shipping sulfur by-products to Monterrey, see Enrique Creel, Chihuahua, to Shepherd Sr., Batopilas, July 21 and 22, 1902, and to Shepherd Jr., January 21, 1903, ibid., loose pages, HC. On the company's importation of dynamite, see Krakauer, Zork and Moye, El Paso, to Shepherd Jr., Batopilas, December 21, 1911, ibid., loose pages; and July 3, 1906, ibid., 144, HC; and Shepherd Jr., Batopilas, to

C. K. Cole, Bocoyna, Chihuahua, July 7, 1906, ibid., 154, HC. On its firearms orders, see Shepherd Jr., Batopilas, to the Shelton Payne Arms Company, El Paso, May 16, 1906, ibid., 40, HC; and Shepherd Jr., Batopilas, to Krakauer, Zork, and Moye, El Paso, May 27, 1906, ibid., 65, HC. On the shortages and recruitment of labor, see Shepherd, Batopilas, to J. M. Thomas, Chicago, July 30, 1906, ibid., 201, HC; Shepherd, Batopilas, to Kaufman, La Puente, July 27 and September 12, 1906, ibid., 194, HC; and Shepherd, Batopilas, to Ramon Fierro, Batopilas, August 2, 1906, ibid., 210, HC.

25. On flour and corn agreements, see T. Robinson Bours Hijo, Álamos, to Shepherd Sr., Batopilas, February 23, 1901, ibid., loose pages, HC. The salt agreement is found in J. Torres, Fuerte, to Shepherd Sr., Batopilas, March 5 and 15, 1901, ibid., loose pages, HC.

26. Shepherd, Batopilas, to Kaufman, La Puente, July 25, 1906, ibid., 191, HC; Shepherd, Batopilas, to Guillermo Schultz, Batopilas, August 5, 1906, ibid., 218, HC. Alexander Shepherd Jr., Batopilas, to A. Leschen & Sons Rope Co., Saint Louis, August 16, 1906, ibid., 262, HC.

27. For the foresters' receipts, see "Gastos de Hacienda," November 8, 1908, ibid., loose pages, HC. The dispute over firewood (leña) is found in Shepherd, Batopilas, to Carlos Bernal, Batopilas, August 10, 1906, ibid., 234, HC. For problems with shipments of equipment and materials, see, for example, Brodie, n.p., to Medart Patent Pulley Company, Saint Louis, October 9, 1906, ibid., 414–416, HC. On the tram between the San Antonio Tunnel and Hacienda San Miguel, see Shepherd, Batopilas, to Carlos Bernal, Batopilas, August 10, 1906, ibid., 234, HC. For freight rates from the San Antonio, Chihuahua, railroad station to Batopilas, see Shepherd, Batopilas, to Thomas, Chicago, July 30, 1906, ibid., 201, HC.

28. See Shepherd, Batopilas, "Report to Manuel Prieto," Manuel Prieto, n.p., ibid., 250–255, HC; and Shepherd, Batopilas, to Enrique Creel, Chihuahua, ibid., 258–259, HC.

29. Shepherd Jr., Batopilas, to Prieto, Chihuahua, August 17, 1906, ibid., 272, HC.

30. E. Kirby Smith, Superintendente, "Resúmen de los gastos erogados en el desagüe," Batopilas, May 6, 1911, and various receipts, ibid., loose pages, HC. For the salaries of mining engineers, see Shepherd, Batopilas, to E. McCormick, Waldo, Oregon, July 28, 1906, ibid., 198, HC; and Shepherd, Batopilas, to Forbes Rickard, Denver, August 9, 1906, ibid., 218, HC.

31. Villaseñor, Rain of Gold, 31.

32. See Shepherd Jr., Testimony and documents, April 1, 1936. For Pascual Orozco and the wider revolutionary conspiracy in the region, see Caraveo Estrada, Mi odisea revolucionaria, 35–37.

33. See J. Hart, Empire and Revolution, esp. 513–530; and Estate of Edward Morris, Agency 185, Entry 184, Deferred Miscellaneous Claims Approved (After 1935) American Mexican Claims Commission, Records Group 76, Washington National Records Center, College Park, and HC.

34. A. Ríos, Mexico City, to Departmento del Estado, April 6, 1916, folder 134, dossier 8, box 49, Ramo Fomento: Minas y Petróleos.

35. Ibid.

36. United States and Mexican Trust Company of Kansas City, La Republica Mine, box 5, CIDECH.

37. Ayuntamiento de Batopilas, September 3, 1919, box 5, CIDECH.

Conclusion

The epigraph for the conclusion is from Wheeler, *Vida ante los ojos*, 47.

1. Holguín Sáenz, *Breve ensayo*, 443–445.

Bibliography

Manuscript Sources

Archivo del Senado, Mexico City.

Archivo General de la Nación (AGN), Mexico City.

Archivo Juárez, Universidad Autonoma de México (formerly housed at Biblioteca Nacional de México), Mexico City.

Bancroft Library (BL), University of California, Berkeley.

Batopilas Collection. Centro de Información del Estado de Chihuahua (CIDECH), Chihuahua City.

Batopilas Consolidated Mining Company (BCMC). Agency 53, entry 184, Special Claims Commission. WNRC.

——. Agency 55, boxes 2–4, American-Mexican Claims Commission, Deferred Miscellaneous Claims Approved after 1935. WNRC.

——. Agency 55, box 8, American-Mexican Claims Commission. WNRC.

——. Letterbooks, 1880–1925. 16 vols. HC.

——. Letterbooks, 1895–1903. Alexander Robey Shepherd. BL.

Batopilas Mining Company (BMC). Letterbook, 1879–1880. Manuel Gil Sandoval Private Collection, Batopilas.

Batopilas Mining Company and Grant Shepherd. Mining Deputation, 1896. University of Texas, El Paso.

Comisión Industrial. Various volumes, 1880–1888. Archivo del Senado, Mexico City.

"Contrato celebrado entre el C. Ingeniero Blas Escontria, Sec. De Estado y del Despacho de Fomento, Colonización e Industria en Rep. Del C. Lic. Justo Prieto, apoderado juricado de Batopilas Mining Company, se celebró el 12 abril 1886 entre el C. General Carolos Pacheco y el Señor Alejandro Shepherd para el desarollo y establecimiento de una explotación especial minera en el Mineral de Batopilas, est. de Chihuahua en los determines siguientes . . . " Folder 5, box 50, Fomento y Obras Publicas, AGN.

"Contrato para la construcción de un ferrocarril, Presidio del Norte a Chihuahua." Folder 5, vol. 27, box 19, 1900, Secretaria de Fomento y Obras Publicas, AGN.

de Loosey, James F. Papers. New York Historical Society, New York City.

Haggin, James Ben Ali, Papers, 1887–1914. Folder 14. Bancroft Library, University of California, Berkeley.

Hart Collection (HC). Houston, Texas.

Herron, Major General Francis Jay. Papers. New York Historical Society, New York City.

Historical Society of Washington, D.C. Kiplinger Library.

Huntington Library, San Marino, California.

Morris, Edward. Estate. Agency 185, entry 184, Deferred Miscellaneous Claims Approved (After 1935), American-Mexican Claims Commission, Records Group 76, WNRC and HC.

New York Public Library, New York City.

Ramo Fomento: Minas y Petróleos. Archivo General de la Nación, Mexico City.

Ramo Inquisición. Archivo General de la Nación, Mexico City.

Ramo Provincias Internas. Archivo General de la Nación, Mexico City.

Ramo Secretaría de Fomento, Colonización e Industria. Archivo General de la Nación, Mexico City.

Read, Ian, and Aldo Musacchio. "Banks, Industrialists and their Cliques: Elite Networks in Mexico and Brazil, 1890–1915." Research Paper, Stanford University, n.d.

Robinson, John Riley. "Diary of John R. Robinson, Feb. 14 to Sept. 15, 1861: His Journey to Batopilas, Mexico to Inspect Silver Mines, with a View to Purchase." HC and Huntington Library, San Marino, California.

———. "Diary of John R. Robinson, Sept. 22–Oct. 23, 1873: Journey from Batopilas, Mexico to New York City." HC and Huntington Library.

Robinson, Juan A. Statement. MSS M-M. BL.

Sánchez Pareja, José. "Reseña histórica de Batopilas." Typescript. Batopilas, 1883. HC.

Sandoval, Manuel Gil. Private Collection, Batopilas.

Shepherd, Alexander R., Jr. "Report of the General Manager." Agency 53, entry 184, Special Claims Commission, Records Group 76, WNRC and HC.

———. Testimony and documents, April 1, 1936, Washington, D.C. Agency 55, entry 184, Deferred Miscellaneous Claims Approved (after 1935), American-Mexican Claims Commission, Records Group 76, WNRC and HC.

Shepherd, Alexander Robey. Collection. Madison Room, Library of Congress, Washington, D.C.

———. Papers, 1869–1942. Historical Society of Washington, D.C., Kiplinger Library.

Stillwell, Arthur E. "Concession for Ports of Call on West Coast of Mexico." VII-16, box 19, 1902, Secretaria de Fomento y Obras Publicas, AGN.

Taylor, Moses. Correspondence. New York Public Library.

Taylor, Moses. Papers. New York Public Library, New York City.

Washington National Records Center (WNRC), College Park, Md.

Published Sources

Acuña, Rodolfo F. "Ignacio Pesqueira: Sonoran Caudillo." *Arizona and the West* 12 (Summer 1970): 139–172.

———. *Sonora Strongman: Ignacio Pesqueira and His Time*. Tucson: University of Arizona Press, 1974.

Aguirre Beltrán, Gonzalo. *Regiones de refugio: El desarrollo de la comunidad y el proceso dominical en Mestizoamérica.* Mexico City: Instituto Indigenista Interamericano, Ediciones Especiales 46, 1967.

Almada, Francisco R. *La intervención francesa y el imperio en el estado de Chihuahua*. Chihuahua City: Ediciones de la Universidad Autónoma de Chihuahua, 1972.

———. *Geografía del estado de Chihuahua*. Chihuahua City, 1945

———. *Diccionario de historia, geografía, y biografía chihuahuenses*. 2nd ed. Chihuahua City: Universidad Autónoma del Estado de Chihuahua: Departmento de Investigaciones Sociales, 1968.

Alvarado, Carlos Mario. *La Tarahumara, una tierra herida: Análisis de la violencia en zonas productoras de estupefacientes en Chihuahua*. Chihuahua City: Talleres Graficos del Gobierno del Estado, 1996.

Bailey, David C., and William H. Beezley. *A Guide to the Historical Sources in Saltillo, Coahuila*. East Lansing: Latin American Studies Center, Michigan State University, 1975.

Bargallo, Ernesto. *La minería y la metalurgia en la América española durante la época colonial*. Mexico City: Fondo de Cultura Económica, 1955.

Barrera Bassols, Jacinto. *El caso Villavicencio: Violencia y poder en el Porfiriato*. Mexico City: Extra Alfaguara, 1997.

Basauri, Carlos. *Monografía de los tarahumaras*. Mexico City: Talleres Gráficos de la Nación, 1929.

Bassols Battala, Angel. *El noroeste de México: Un estudio geografico-económico*. Mexico City: Universidad Nacional Autónoma de México, 1972.

Beauchamp, Tany Edwards. "Adolph Cluss: An Architect in Washington during the Civil War and Reconstruction." In Francis Coleman Rosenberger, ed., *Records of the Columbia Historical Society*, 338–358. Charlottesville: University Press of Virginia, 1973.

Bennett, Wendel C., and Robert M. Zingg. *The Tarahumara: An Indian Tribe of Northern Mexico*. Chicago: University of Chicago Press, 1935.

Bernstein, Marvin. *The Mexican Mining Industry, 1890–1950*. New York: State University of New York Press, 1964.

Binczewski, George J. "The Point of a Monument: A History of the Aluminum Cap on the Washington Monument." *JOM: The Members' Journal of the Minerals, Metals and Materials Society* 47, no. 11 (1995): 20–25.

Brodie, Walter M. "Las minas de plata nativa de la Batopilas Mining Company." N.p., n.d. Batopilas Collection and HC.

———. "Producción total de la Batopilas Mining Company." N.p., n.d. Batopilas Collection and HC.

Cabeza de Vaca, Francisco. *Apuntes sobre la vida de los tarahumaras*. Mexico City: Vargas Rea, 1943.

Calderón, Roberto R. *Mexican Coal Mining Labor in Texas and Coahuila, 1880–1930*. College Station: Texas A&M Press, 2000.

Cancelada Velázquez, Juan. "Breve reseña de Batopilas, vida y costumbres de los tarahumara y paludismo y su tratamiento." Master's thesis, Universidad Nacional Autónoma de México, 1950.

Caraveo Estrada, Baudilio B. *Historias de mi odisea revolucionaria: La Revolución en la*

222   BIBLIOGRAPHY

Sierra de Chihuahua y la Convención de Aguascalientes. Chihuahua City: Doble Helice Ediciones, 1996.

Carmony, Neil B., and David E. Brown, eds. *Mexican Game Trails: Americans Afield in Old Mexico, 1866–1940.* Norman: University of Oklahoma Press, 1991.

Chávez, Cástulo. *Deposición dirigida al Supremo Gobierno por la Junta de Fomento Administrativo de Minería sobre el reconocimiento de criadores de cinabrio en la República, inversión de los fondos destinados al Banco de Azogues, y utilidad de fomentarlo.* Mexico City: Imprenta de Ignacio Cumplido, 1845. AGN.

Clasen, Sophronius. *St. Anthony: Doctor of the Gospel.* Translated by Ignatius Brady. Chicago: Franciscan Herald Press, 1961.

Coombes, B. L. *These Poor Hands: The Autobiography of a Miner Working in South Wales.* London: Gollancz, 1939.

Crane, Walter R. *Gold and Silver.* New York: Wiley and Sons, 1908.

Creel, Enrique C. *El Estado de Chihuahua: Su historia, geografía y riquezas naturales.* Mexico City: Tipografía El Progreso, 1928.

Cross, Ira B. *Financing an Empire: A History of Banking in California.* Vol. 1. Chicago: S. J. Clarke, 1927.

Cullmann, Oscar. *Peter, Disciple, Apostle, Martyr: An Historical and Theological Study.* Translated by Floyd V. Filson. Philadelphia: Westminister Press, 1962.

Dahlgreen, Charles Bunker. *Minas históricas de la República mexicana.* Mexico City: Oficina Tipográfica de la Secretaría de Fomento, 1887.

Doerr, Harriet. *Stones for Ibarra.* New York: Penguin Books, 1984.

Domínguez Soto, Jesús. "Informe general sobre la exploración sanitaria de Batopilas, estado de Chihuahua." Master's thesis, Universidad Nacional Autónoma de México, 1942.

Douglass, David, and Joel Krieger. *A Miner's Life.* London: Routledge and Paul Kegan, 1983.

Dunne, Peter M. *Las antiguas misiones de la Tarahumara.* Mexico City: Editorial Jus, 1958.

Durán Bravo, Bernardo. "Algunos aspectos del problema palúdico en las márgenes del Rió Batopilas y exploración sanitaria del municipio de ese nombre en el estado de Chihuahua." Master's thesis, Universidad Nacional Autónoma de México, 1948.

Eller, Ronald D. *Miners, Millhands, and Mountaineers: Industrialization of the Appalachian South, 1880–1930.* Knoxville: University of Tennessee Press, 1982.

Enciclopedia de los Municipios de Mexico, Estado de Chihuahua. Available online at http://www.e-local.gob.mx/wb2/ELOCAL/EMM—chihuahua (accessed July 22, 2007).

Enríquez Hernández, Jorge. *Análisis geoeconómico del sistema regional de la Sierra Tarahumara.* Mexico City: Universidad Nacional Autónoma de México, 1988

Espinosa Flores, Carlos. "Informe general sobre la exploración sanitaria de Batopilas, Chihuahua." Master's thesis, Universidad Nacional Autónoma de México, 1944.

Evans, James H. *Big Bend Pictures.* Austin: University of Texas Press, 2003.

Fayhee, M. John. *Mexico's Copper Canyon Country: A Hiking and Backpacking Guide.* Boulder, Colo.: Johnson Books, 1994.

Finn, Janet L. *Tracing the Veins: Of Copper, Culture, and Community from Butte to Chuquicamata*. Berkeley: University of California Press, 1998.

French, William E. *A Peaceful and Working People: Manners, Morals, and Class Formation in Northern Mexico*. Albuquerque: University of New Mexico Press, 1996.

Fuentes, Carlos. *The Good Conscience*. Translated by Sam Hileman. New York: Farrar, Straus and Giroux, 1987.

Gómez González, Filiberto. *Rarámuri: Mi diario Tarahumara*. Mexico City: n.p., 1984.

Gómez Izquierdo, Jorge José. *El movimiento antichino en México, 1871–1934*. Mexico City: Instituto Nacional de Antropología e Historia, 1992.

González Reyna, Jenaro. *Riqueza minera y yacimientos minerales de México*, 3rd ed. Congreso Geológico Internacional. Mexico City: Banco de México, 1956.

——. *Los yacimientos agentíferos de Batopilas, Estado de Chihuahua*. Mexico City: Comité Directivo para la Investigación de los Recursos Minerales de México, 1947. Boletín no. 11.

Graham, Martha. *Mobile Farmers: An Ethnoarchaeological Approach to Settlement Organization among the Raramuri of Northwestern Mexico*. Ann Arbor: International Monographs in Prehistory, 1994.

Hale, Charles. *Liberalism in the Age of Mora, 1821–1853*. New Haven: Yale University Press, 1968.

Hart, John Mason. *Anarchism and the Mexican Working Class, 1860–1931*. Austin: University of Texas Press, 1978.

——. *Revolutionary Mexico: The Coming and Process of the Mexican Revolution*. Berkeley: University of California Press, 1987.

——. *Empire and Revolution: The Americans in Mexico since the Civil War*. Berkeley: University of California Press, 2002.

Hart, Lisa June. "Shepherd's Castle: Documentation of a Gothic Revival House in a Mexican Silver Mining Town." Master's thesis, University of Texas, Austin, 1988.

Heyle, Erik. *Early American Steamers*. Buffalo, N.Y.: Privately printed, 1953.

Hittell, John S. *Commerce and Industries of the Pacific Coast of North America*. San Francisco: A. L. Bancroft, 1882.

Holguín Sáenz, Armando A. *Breve ensayo sobre la geografía económica del Estado de Chihuahua*. Mexico City: Ediciones Turistas, 1965.

Hovey, E. O. "A Geological Reconnaissance in the Western Sierra Madre of the State of Chihuahua, Mexico." *American Museum of Natural History Bulletin* 23 (1907): 401–442.

Hu-Dehart, Evelyn. "La comunidad china en el desarrollo de Sonora." In *Historia general de Sonora*, vol. 4: *Sonora moderno, 1880–1929*, 195–211. Hermosillo: Gobierno del Estado de Sonora, 1985.

——. "Immigrants to a Developing Society: The Chinese in Northern Mexico, 1875–1932." *Journal of Arizona History* 21, no. 3 (1980): 49–86.

——. "Racism and Anti-Chinese Persecution in Sonora, Mexico, 1876–1932." *Amerasia Journal* 9, no.2 (1928): 1–28.

Hungerford, Edward. *Wells Fargo: Advancing the American Frontier*. New York: Random House, 1949.

Ingersoll, Ralph McA. *In and under Mexico*. New York: Century, n.d.

Joblin, Maurice. *Cleveland Past and Present*. N.p.: Indypublish, 2004.

Joint Select Committee on the Affairs of the District of Columbia. *Report of the Joint Select Committee of Congress Appointed to Inquire into the Affairs of the Government of the District of Columbia: Together with the Journal of the Committee, Answer of the Governor, Charges, Arguments, and Testimony*. Washington, D.C.: Government Printing Office, 1874. 43d Cong., 1st sess. Library of Congress.

Katz, Friedrich. *The Life and Times of Pancho Villa*. Stanford, Calif.: Stanford University Press, 1998.

Kemble, John H. *The Panama Route, 1848–1869*. Berkeley: University of California Press, 1943.

Kemp, Capt. Donald C. *Quicksilver to Bar Silver: Tales of Mexico's Silver Bonanzas*. Pasadena, Calif.: Socio-Technical, 1972.

Kennedy, John G. *The Tarahumara of the Sierra Madre*. Arlington Heights, Ill.: AHM, 1978.

King, R. E. "Geological Reconnaisance in the Northern Sierra Madre Occidental of Mexico." *Bulletin of the Geological Society of America* (1939): 1625–1722.

Klubock, Thomas Miller. *Contested Communities: Class, Gender, and Politics in Chile's El Teniente Copper Mine, 1904–1951*. Durham, N.C.: Duke University Press, 1998.

Leo García, Ricardo. *Misiones jesuitas en la Tarahumara: Siglo XVIII*. Ciudad Juárez: Universidad Autónoma de Ciudad Juárez, 1992.

Loomis, Noel M. *Wells Fargo*. New York: Clarkson N. Potter, 1968.

Lumholtz, Carl. *Unknown Mexico*. Vol. 1. New York: Scribner's, 1902.

Marks, Paula Mitchell. *Precious Dust: The American Gold Rush Era, 1848–1900*. New York: William Morrow, 1994.

Márquez Montiel, Joaquín. *Hombres célebres de Chihuahua*. Mexico City: Editorial Jus, 1953.

Maury, William M. "Alexander R. Shepherd and the Board of Public Works." In Francis Coleman Rosenberger, ed., *Records of the Columbia Historical Society*, 394–410. Charlottesville: University Press of Virginia, 1973.

McAteer, Assistant Secretary of Labor J. Davitt. *Coal Workers' Pneumoconiosis: Health Information Card*. Mine Safety and Health Administration. U.S. Department of Labor. Washington, D.C.: U.S. Government Printing Office, n.d.

McNamara, Denis R. "One of Our Best and Most Talented Men: Adolf Cluss and German Theory in Nineteenth Century Washington, D.C." Master's thesis, University of Virginia, 1994.

Memorias de Fomento. Mexico City: Oficina Tipográfica de la Secretaría de Fomento, 1856–1857, 1869–1873, 1873, 1877–1882, 1883–1885, 1892–1896, 1908–1909, 1910–1911, and 1911–1912. AGN.

Mende, Elsie Porter. *An American Soldier and Diplomat: Horace Porter*. New York: Frederick A. Stokes, 1927.

Merrill, William L. *Raramuri Souls: Knowledge and Social Process in Northern Mexico*. Washington, D.C.: Smithsonian Institution Press, 1988.

Meyer, Michael. *Mexican Rebel: Pascual Orozco and the Mexican Revolution, 1910–1915*. Lincoln: University of Nebraska Press, 1967.

El Minero Mexicano. Mexico City, 1895.

Montemayor, Carlos. *Los tarahumaras: Pueblo de estrellas y barrancas*. Mexico City: Banobras, 1995.

Mora, Gregorio. "Los comerciantes de Guaymas en el desarrollo económico de Sonora, 1825–1910." In *IX Simposio de Historia de Sonora*. Hermosillo: Instituto de Investigaciones Históricas, 1984.

———. "Entrepreneurs in Nineteenth Century Sonora, Mexico." Ph.D. diss., University of California, Berkeley, 1987.

Morgan, James Morris. *Recollections of a Rebel Reefer*. Boston: Houghton Mifflin, 1917.

Mowry, Sylvester. *Arizona and Sonora: The Geography, History, and Resources of the Silver Region of North America*. New York: Arno Press, 1973.

Muscatine, Doris. *Old San Francisco: The Biography of a City from Early Days to the Earthquake*. New York: Putnam, 1975.

Nabokov, Peter. *Indian Running: Native American History and Tradition*. Santa Fe: Ancient City Press, 1981.

Naranjo, Ascensión Amador. *Los tarahumaras*. Madrid: Agualarga Ediciones, 1995.

Nash, June. *We Eat the Mines and the Mines Eat Us: Dependency and Exploitation in Bolivian Tin Mines*. New York: Columbia University Press, 1979.

Oakes, James. *The Ruling Race: A History of American Slaveholders*. New York: Knopf, 1982.

O'Brien, Thomas F. *The Revolutionary Mission: American Enterprise in Latin America, 1900–1945*. Cambridge: Cambridge University Press, 1996.

Orozco, Victor. *Las guerras indias en la historia de Chihuahua: Primeras fases*. Mexico City: Conaculta, 1992.

Othón de Mendizábal, Miguel. *La evolución del noroeste de México*. Mexico City: Departamento de Estadisticas, 1930.

Pennington, Campbell W. *The Tarahumar of Mexico: Their Environment and Material Culture*. Salt Lake City: University of Utah Press, 1963.

Phelps, Alonzo. *Contemporary Biography of California's Representative Men*. Vol 1. San Francisco: A. L. Bancroft, 1881.

Pletcher, David M. *Rails, Mines and Progress: Seven American Promoters in Mexico, 1867–1911*. Ithaca, N.Y.: Cornell University Press, 1958.

Raat, W. Dirk, and George R. Janecek. *Mexico's Sierra Tarahumara: A Photohistory of the People of the Edge*. Norman: University of Oklahoma Press. 1996.

Randolph, John C. F. *Report on the Pastrana Mine*. New York: E. D. Jenkins, 1881. BL.

———. *The New Mill at Batopilas*. New York, 1882. BL.

Rascón Irigoyen, Fructuoso. *Cerocahui: Una comunidad en la Tarahumara*. Chihuahua City: Centro Librero La Prensa, 1979.

Reyes Heroles, Jesús. *El liberalismo mexicano*. Mexico City: Fondo de Cultura Económica, 1974.

Rivera Letelier, Hernán. *La reina Isabel cantaba rancheras*. Mexico City: Planeta, 1998.

Robinson, Thomas Warren. *Dust and Foam: or, Three Oceans and Two Continents*. New York: Charles Scribner Press, 1858.

Román Alarcón, Rigoberto Arturo. *Comerciantes extranjeros de Mazatlán 1880–1910*. Culiacán: Colegio de Bachilleres del Estado de Sinaloa, 1998.

——. *El comercio en Sinaloa, siglo XIX*. Culiacán: Dirección de Investigaciones y Fomento de Cultura Regional, 1998.

——. "El contrabando de mercancías por Mazatlán (1871–1872)." In *Contribuciones a la Historia del Noroccidente Mexicano: Memoria del VIII Congreso Nacional de Historia Regional*, 145–153. Culiacán: Universidad Autónoma de Sinaloa, 1994.

Romero Gil, Juan Manuel. "Minas, capital, y trabajo en el Noroeste, 1870–1910." Ph.D. diss., Universidad Nacional Autónoma de México, 1999.

Ruiz, Ramon Eduardo. *The People of Sonora and Yankee Capitalists*. Tucson: University of Arizona Press, 1988.

Sánchez Pareja, José. *Reseña histórica de Batopilas: Textos de la Nueva Vizcaya: Documentos para la historia de Chihuahua y Durango, 27 de diciembre de 1883*. Ciudad Juárez: Centro de Estudios Regionales Unidad Chihuahua de la Universidad Autónoma de Ciudad Juárez, 2001.

Sariego Rodríguez, Juan Luis. *El indigenismo en la Tarahumara: Identidad, comunidad, relaciones interétnicas y desarrollo en la Sierra de Chihuahua*. Mexico City: Instituto Indigenista, Conaculta, 2002.

Schmidly, David J. *The Mammals of Trans-Pecos Texas, Including Big Bend National Park and Guadalupe Mountains National Park*. College Station: Texas A&M University Press, 1977.

Schmidt, Robert H. Jr. *A Geographical Survey of Chihuahua*. Southwestern Studies, pamphlet no. 37. El Paso: Texas Western Press, 1973.

Schwatka, Frederick. *In the Land of Cave and Cliff Dwellers*. New York, 1893.

Shepherd, Grant. *Magnate de plata (Batopilas)*. Chihuahua City: Centro Librero La Prensa, 1994.

——. *The Silver Magnet: Fifty Years in a Mexican Silver Mine*. New York: E. P. Dutton, 1938.

Smith, Ralph A. "Mexican and Anglo-Saxon Traffic in Scalps, Slaves, and Livestock, 1835–1841." *West Texas Historical Association Yearbook* 36 (October 1960): 98–115.

——. "The Scalp Hunt in Chihuahua in 1849." *New Mexico Historical Review* 40 (April 1965): 117–140.

——. "The Scalp Hunter in the Borderlands, 1835–1859." *Arizona and the West* 13 (Spring 1964): 5–22.

Southworth, John R. *Las minas de México*. Mexico City: J. R. Southworth, 1905.

——. *The Official Directory of Mines and Haciendas of Mexico*. Mexico City: J. R. Southworth, 1906.

Stagg, Albert. *The Almadas and Alamos, 1783–1867.* Tucson: University of Arizona Press, 1978.

The State of Chihuahua (Mexico), Its Mining Resources. The Mines of Chihuahua by Districts. Chihuahua City: Published by Order of Gobernador Ingeniero Andrés Ortíz, 1920.

Stout, Joseph Allen. *Schemers and Dreamers: Filibustering in Mexico, 1848–1921.* College Station: Texas A&M University Press, 2002.

Stross, Brian. "Tarahumara." Class Notes, Anthropology Department, University of Texas, Austin, 1999.

Terrazas, Joaquín. *Memorias del Señor Coronel Don Joaquín Terrazas.* Ciudad Juárez: Imprenta del Agricultor Mexicano, Escobar Hermanos, 1905.

Terry, T. Philip. *Terry's Mexico: Handbook for Travelers.* Mexico City: Sonora News Company, and Boston: Houghton Mifflin, 1909.

Thompson, E. P. "Time, Work-Discipline, and Industrial Capitalism." *Past and Present* 38 (December 1967): 56–97.

Time-Life Editors. *The Old West: The Miners.* Alexandria, Va.: Time-Life Books, 1976.

Tindall, William, M.D. "A Sketch of Alexander Robey Shepherd." *Records of the Columbia Historical Society* 14: 49–66. Washington, D.C.: Columbia Historical Society, 1911.

Tinker Salas, Miguel. *In the Shadow of the Eagles: Sonora and the Transformation of the Border during the Porfiriato.* Berkeley: University of California Press, 1997.

Traven, B. [Berwick Traven Torsvan]. *The Treasure of the Sierra Madre.* New York: Hill and Wang, 1999.

Van Dyke, John Charles. *The Desert: Further Studies in Natural Appearances.* Circa 1901. Reprint, New York: Scribner, 1925.

Villaseñor, Victor. *Rain of Gold.* Houston: Arte Público Press, 1991.

Voss, Stuart. *On the Periphery of Nineteenth-Century Mexico: Sonora and Sinaloa, 1810–1877.* Tucson: University of Arizona Press, 1982.

Warnock, Barton H. *Wildflowers of the Davis Mountains and the Marathon Basin, Texas.* Alpine, Tex.: Saul Ross State University Press, 1977.

Wasserman, Mark. *Capitalists, Caciques and Revolution: The Native Elite and Foreign Enterprise in Chihuahua, Mexico, 1854–1911.* Chapel Hill: University of North Carolina Press, 1984.

———. *Everyday Life and Politics in Nineteenth Century Mexico: Men, Women, and War.* Albuquerque: University of New Mexico Press, 2000.

———. "La inversión extranjera en México, 1876–1910: Un estudio del caso del papel de las élites regionales." In Enrique Cárdenas, comp., *Historia económica de México,* vol. 3, pp. 267–289. Mexico City: Fondo de Cultura Económica, 1992.

Watson, Sereno. "List of Plants Collected by Dr. Edward Palmer in Southwestern Chihuahua, Mexico in 1885." *Proceedings of the American Academy of Arts and Sciences* 21 (1886): 414–455.

Weed, W. H. "Notes on Certain Mines in the States of Chihuahua, Sinaloa, and Sonora,

Mexico." *Transactions of the American Institution of Mining and Engineers* 63 (1902): 382–407.

Weidner, Frederick. *The Silver Mines of Mexico: Prospectus of the Sinaloa Silver Mining Company of the City of New York. With Documents Relative to its Organization and an Official Plan of the Position of its Mines and Haciendas.* New York: C. S. Westcott, 1866.

West, Steve. *Northern Chihuahuan Desert Wildflowers.* Helena, Mont.: Falcon, 2000.

Wheeler, Romayne. *La vida ante los ojos de un rarámuri.* Guadalajara: Editorial Ágata, 1998.

White, Pamela, comp. "John Riley Robinson: My Family." Available online at http://www.pamsgenealogy.net/SS/p3.htm#i74 (accessed July 22, 2007).

Wilkerson, Gregg. "Geology of the Batopilas Mining District, Chihuahua, Mexico." Ph.D. diss., University of Texas, El Paso, 1983.

Williamson, Bill. *Class, Culture and Community: A Biographical Study of Social Change in Mining.* London: Routledge and Paul Kegan, 1982.

Wilson, Wendell E., and Christopher S. Panczner. "Batopilas Famous Mineral Localities: The Batopilas District, Chihuahua, Mexico." *Mineralogical Record* 17 (January–February 1986): 61–79.

Wyllys, Rufus K. *The French in Sonora.* Berkeley: University of California Press, 1932.

Zarur, Elizabeth Netto Calil, and Charles Muir Lovell. *Art and Faith in Mexico: The Nineteenth-Century Retablo Tradition.* Albuquerque: University of New Mexico Press, 2001.

Zingg, Robert. *Behind the Mexican Mountains.* Edited by Howard Campbell, John Peterson, and David Carmichael. Austin: University of Texas Press, 2001.

Index

About the Author

John Mason Hart is the John and Rebecca Moores Professor of History at the University of Houston. He is the author of *Anarchism and the Mexican Working Class, 1860–1931*, which was fifth on the Mexican nonfiction bestseller list in 1980, and *Revolutionary Mexico: The Coming and Process of the Mexican Revolution* in 1988, which had its tenth anniversary edition in 1998, with a Spanish version that spanned eight editions. A third book, *Empire and Revolution: The Americans in Mexico since the Civil War*, published in 2002, won several national and regional awards. His publications have won prizes from the Pacific Coast Council for Latin American Studies, the Southwestern Council for Latin American Studies, and the Conference of Latin American History of the American Historical Association. Professor Hart has been a Shelby Cullom Davis Research Fellow in the Department of History at Princeton University, a National Endowment for the Humanities Senior Research Fellow, a Postdoctoral Fellow of the American Council of Learned Societies/Social Science Research Council, a Distinguished Visiting Professor at the Escuela Nacional de Antropología e Historia in Mexico City, and a Distinguished Visiting Lecturer at the Instituto Nacional de Antropología e Historia in Mexico City. In recognition of his distinguished research, he was named an honorary lifetime member of the Southwestern Council for Latin American Studies; he has also been the recipient of the Teaching Excellence and Distinguished Research Awards from the College of Liberal Arts and Social Sciences at the University of Houston.